The Boots Book of Home Wine and Beermaking

Ben Turner, author, lecturer and broadcaster, has been making wine since 1945 and beer since 1952. He was President of the National Association of Wine and Beer Makers from 1971 to 1973 and from 1981 to 1983 was the President of the National Guild of Wine and Beer Judges.

The Boots Book of Home Wine and Beermaking

Ben Turner

Published for the Boots Company plc
by Wolfe Publishing Ltd
3 Conway Street, London W1P 6HE

All photography*
by Trevor Haywood ('Real Pictures')
assisted by Yvonne Todd and Tom Wilson

*except for the microscopic yeast picture on page 48, and the
fruit on pages 144, 168, and 172 which are by the author, and
the syphon, heating belt and wine and beer tester on page 31 and the
thermostatic heater, pressure injector and crown corker on
page 179 which are by Richard Prescott.

Design and drawings
by Phil Brown

Printed by
Ebenezer Baylis & Son Ltd, Worcester

In Memory of Mary

Contents

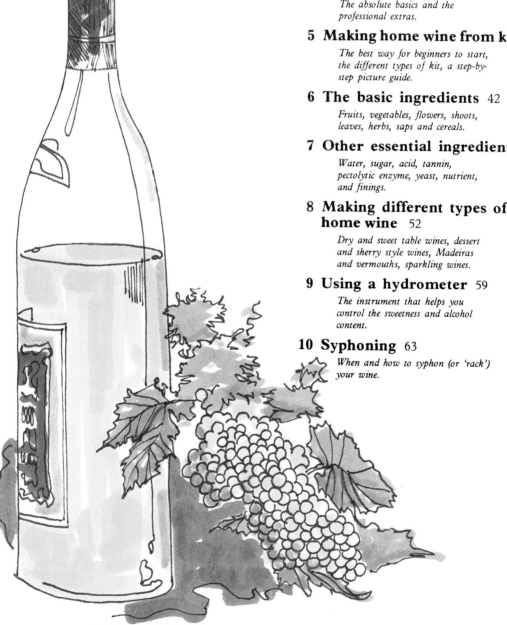

When the word 'wine' occurs in this book, it should be taken to mean 'a beverage which may include fruits or vegetables of a non-vinous nature'.

CHAPTER ONE

The pleasures of home brew

Even if wine and beer were untaxed and cheap to buy many people would still prefer to make their own – for the same reason that they like to make their own jam or bake their own bread. There is the pleasure of a creative hobby, the challenge of taking on the professionals (and perhaps beating them) and the reward of living well, yet saving money.

Not every one who makes wine or beer at home can compete successfully with the commercial manufacturers, but a careful reading of this book, especially the 'technical' chapters, will improve anyone's chances of brewing successfully. It is the constant hope that each brew will turn out a winner that motivates the enthusiast. But even if their brews do not win prizes all home brewers know that they can make a pleasant and palatable drink at a fraction of the cost of buying it.

Kits and country wines

The quality of wine and beer making kits has improved steadily over the past few years and they now produce a very good, value for money, wine or beer. The choice of types has grown wider too: within a few months a busy home brewer could possess a 'cellar' that catered for all tastes.

Jokers say that you can make wine from grass cuttings and old boots. Although this is not true you can make 'country' wines from an extraordinarily wide range of ingredients including flowers, herbs, cereals, leaves, vegetables, spices and all kinds of fruit whether fresh, frozen, dried, canned, juiced, jammed or prepared as a pie filling. Beer, too, can be flavoured with nettles, burdock, yarrow, spruce, honey, fruits or vegetables, even chicken, as well as hops. The area for experiment is enormous. Furthermore, 'home brew' includes the making of ciders, liqueurs, meads, melomels, cyser, pyment, hypocras, methyglin, hot mulls and cool cups – even the growing of vines to make wine from the grapes.

New equipment and simple methods

Home brewing has been made very much easier than it used to be now that cheap and purpose-built equipment is readily available. Gone are the days when odd kitchen utensils had to be pressed into service. Egg crocks, for example, have been replaced by the polythene bin with lid, muslin cloths by the nylon straining bag, an inverted cup by the plastic airlock. Excellent, modern, simple-to-use equipment is now inexpensively and widely available for winemakers and brewers alike. It repays its cost time and time again.

Methods, too, have been changed and streamlined in the light of experience. A kit of beer or wine can be made up in minutes, fermented in from four to fourteen days, cleared and matured and ready for drinking in from five days to five weeks. Kits of all kinds come with step-by-step instructions on how to make them up. Even the once risky area – hygiene – has been eliminated by a substance called sulphite (short for sodium metabisulphite). A solution made from sulphite, reinforced with a little citric acid, will rapidly sterilise every surface with which wine or beer comes into contact. This prevents off-flavours or spoilages caused by infection from invisible airborne moulds and bacteria that have settled on or in the equipment.

Camaraderie and competitions

The pleasures of fellowship from winemaking and brewing must not be overlooked, for they are substantial. There is an extraordinary camaraderie between home brewers that knows no boundary whether of commerce, custom or country. Most towns and villages have an association or club which enables enthusiasts not only to meet and talk about their hobby but to taste and comment on each other's brews. The desire to improve the quality of their wines and beers often takes second place to the sheer enjoyment of a convivial get-together in the company of friends talking about their favourite hobby. Social events are arranged, outings are organised to regional shows, English vineyards and nowadays even to Continental and Californian vineyards.

RICH

Red

Annual dinners are generally very happy occasions, especially if arrangements are made for the drinking of one's own wines with the meal. At regional and national level, the gathering may extend to 1,500 home winemakers and brewers all having a wonderful time, enjoying each other's wines and beers and fellowship. Yet, and this is seemingly incredible, there is never any excessive drinking or drunkenness. It is an atmosphere of warm friendliness and good behaviour that has to be experienced to be believed.

Competitions are held at local, regional and national level for many different styles of wines and beers. The major satisfaction is in winning, or at least in being placed, but there are many silver trophies to be won as well. There is, too, the very real pleasure in drinking a prize winning beer or wine that you have made yourself. Such enthusiasts do not cut costs. They use only the best ingredients and equipment and are meticulously painstaking in their methods – yet even their wines and beers are comparatively cheap.

Gracious living

Perhaps the whole happy atmosphere emanates from another of the pleasures of home brew. Winemaking in particular tends to confer an atmosphere of gracious living on those who enjoy it to the full. There is no point in having a stock of good wines without serving them at meals. This alone improves the look of the table, and imparts an air of graciousness which would otherwise be lacking. Aperitifs can be offered and possibly a dessert wine or liqueur without putting too much strain on the domestic purse. Wine invites comments, conversation flows easily, and the most humble meal gives as much enjoyment as a banquet.

The final pleasure is perhaps the best of all, for the truth is that in moderation wine is good for you. Doctors and scientists have proved from their research that a moderate quantity of wine – about half a bottle of table wine (0.35 litre/13 fl oz) each day – is actually beneficial for the human body. It promotes good health, dilates the blood vessels, relaxes the nerves, assists in digestion, reduces inhibitions, and provides essential trace elements of vitamins and minerals. In short, moderate, daily wine drinkers can look forward to long, healthy and enjoyable lives. On the other hand, it must be said that home brewing is not an appropriate hobby for those who drink too much.

Few hobbies, indeed, have so many good reasons for being popular. Sadly, if you ever stop making your own wine or beer you will eventually lose all the pleasures that go with it. But few who start home brewing ever want to stop.

CHAPTER TWO

A glossary of home brew

Acid   Essential for the fermentation, bouquet and flavour of wines. Citric, tartaric or malic acid may be used. Dry wines need to contain about four to five parts per thousand, sweet wines from six to seven. Acetic acid is the vinegar taste – to be avoided in all fermented beverages by keeping vessels covered at all times.

Adjuncts   Ingredients added to the malt in the preparation of a beer to improve the flavour and to increase the alcohol content, e.g. flaked rice or maize.

Airlock   Also known as a fermentation lock. It is a device used during fermentation to exclude air while permitting carbon dioxide to escape. It maintains anaerobic conditions and prevents airborne infection.

Alcohol   The intoxicating spirit formed during fermentation which gives wine and beer, cider and mead their characteristic satisfaction.

Aldehydes   Chemical compounds formed during the maturation of wine by the interaction of acids with the alcohols. They contribute to the bouquet.

Autolysis   The decomposition of dead yeast cells. Living yeast cells may then use the nitrogenous molecules thus released.

Bentonite   A powdered natural clay used for clearing hazy wines. Also available in a gel and in soluble granules.

Body	The *"fullness"* of wine or beer. The opposite of thin.
Campden tablet	The trade name for a small tablet of sodium metabisulphite one of which releases fifty parts per million of sulphur dioxide when dissolved in one gallon of water or wine. The sulphur dioxide sterilises equipment, prevents oxidation and the growth of moulds, bacteria and spoilage yeasts and improves the flavour of the wine.
Carbon dioxide	The gas formed during fermentation. It can be seen escaping in bubbles and be heard as a hissing sound made by the bursting of the bubbles when they reach the surface. Almost half the sugar is converted into alcohol and half into carbon dioxide thus 2 lb $3\frac{1}{4}$ oz *(1 kg)* of sugar will produce 1 lb $\frac{1}{2}$ oz *(approx 470 g)* of carbon dioxide gas and 1 lb 1 oz *(480 g)* of alcohol. The remaining sugar is used by the yeast.
Decant	To pour clear wine or beer from a bottle in which a sediment has been formed into a glass vessel suitable for use at the table. The bottle is held to the light and tipped carefully so that clear wine or beer slides slowly into the vessel. As the sediment nears the neck of the bottle pouring is stopped.
D.M.S.	Abbreviation for Diastatic Malt Syrup; i.e. one containing some diastase enzymes capable of converting starch to sugar. See Mashing.
Dry	A term used to describe a wine or beer in which there is no taste of sweetness.
Dry hopping	The addition of some dry hops, hop pellets or hop oil during the fermentation of a wort to improve the hoppy tang of the finished beer.
Enzyme	Molecules of protein joined to an organic compound which acts as a catalyst in specific circumstances. Many different enzymes are necessary in winemaking and brewing. They are secreted by the yeast cells and cause changes in the substances around them. They are not changed themselves. Each different enzyme is effective in only one change. For example invertase causes sucrose to separate into glucose and fructose. It cannot cause any further changes. A different enzyme is responsible for each of the many complicated changes in the long process of the conversion of sugar into alcohol and carbon dioxide.
Fermentation	The process of converting sugar in a must or wort into alcohol and carbon dioxide. It is caused by enzymes secreted in the yeast cells.

Macerating flower petals with the back of a wooden spoon.

Filtration	The removal of minute solid particles suspended in a wine, by passing it through a filter kit.
Fining	The removal of minute solid particles suspended in a wine or beer by the addition of finings such as gelatine, isinglass or Bentonite. As the finings sink to the bottom they attract to themselves the solid particles and carry them down to form a sediment from which the clear beverage can be racked.
Fortification	The adding of alcohol to a wine so as to increase its strength. Usually only Vodka or Polish spirit are used since they do not affect the flavour of the wine.
Hardening salts	Mineral salts including carbonates and sulphates, added to water lacking them i.e. soft water. It improves the quality of the bitter style beers.
Heading agent	A compound that can be added to a beer before bottling to improve the retention of froth on the surface after it has been poured into a glass.
Hops	Bitter tasting flowers of the bine *Humulus lupulus* used for flavouring beer.
Hydrometer	An instrument for measuring the specific gravity of a liquid. This indicates the approximate quantity of sugar in a given liquid.
Invert sugar	A mixture of fructose and glucose produced from sucrose. Ordinary white sugar is sucrose. Invert sugar is sometimes used in brewing to ensure a speedy fermentation.
Lactose	An unfermentable sugar used to sweeten brown ales and stouts.
Lees	The dross or sediment consisting of dead yeast cells, dust, fruit pulp, etc, which falls to the bottom in fermentation and storage vessels as wines and beers fall bright.
Maceration	The bruising of flower petals, as shown on page 15.
Malt	Barley grains that have been stimulated by moisture and warmth to start growing and are then roasted. Malt is the basic ingredient of beer. It is available in the form of cracked grains, malt flour and malt extract – a toffee-like syrup.
Mashing	The infusing for several hours in hot water of brewing ingredients containing starch. The unfermentable starch in the

ingredients is converted by the action of the diastase enzymes in the malted barley grains or syrup into a fermentable sugar called maltose.

Maturation The ageing of a wine or beer to the point at which it is most pleasant to drink.

Must The name given to liquid before it is fermented into wine.

Nutrient Nitrogenous matter essential for yeast growth. Usually bought in the form of a tablet or crystals containing di-ammonium phosphate and/or ammonium sulphate.

Original gravity The specific gravity of a wine or beer before fermentation begins. The *'total original gravity'* includes the addition of sugar during fermentation.

Pectolytic enzyme A compound which breaks down the pectin in fruit, thus increasing the extraction of the juice and clarity of the wine.

Potassium sorbate A salt used in conjunction with sulphite to terminate fermentation.

Priming The addition of a small quantity of sugar to a beer or wine to cause a secondary fermentation during maturation. Essential for giving life and vitality to beer and to sparkling wines.

Proof A liquid that is *"Proof"* contains 57.1% alcohol by volume. 70° Proof means that the liquid contains 70% of 57.1% i.e. 40% alcohol.

Racking A process of transferring clear or clearing wine or beers from jars containing lees or sediment into clean vessels. Usually performed with the aid of a syphon.

Sediment Another name for lees.

Sparging The rinsing of brewing ingredients with warm water after they have been mashed. This washes off the remaining maltose adhering to the grains.

Specific gravity The weight of a given volume of liquid compared with the same volume of water at 15°C *(59°F)*, or the temperature specified on the hydrometer. Used in winemaking and brewing to measure the approximate amount of sugar in a liquid.

Starter bottle A sterilised bottle, partly filled with water in which a small

An 'airlock', containing a sterilising solution, allows the fermentation gas to escape from this apple wine.

The 'lees' in the same apple wine a few weeks later. The wine will soon be ready for its first 'racking'.

quantity of fruit juice (or malt extract), citric acid and nutrient salts have been dissolved. When dried yeast granules are added and the bottle is stood in a warm position – 35–40°C *(95–104°F)* – the yeast cells are re-hydrated. Usually within a couple of hours the yeast is ready to start the fermentation of a must or wort.

Sugar Syrup *A Definition of sugar in water.*

Any quantity of sugar may be dissolved in any quantity of water to make a syrup. The sugar dissolves more quickly in hot water and should be left covered until it is cool enough to add to the must. In making up a recipe the quantity of sugar suggested may be dissolved in about 1 pint of the quantity of water suggested. Do not use more water in addition to the quantity suggested. Mix the syrup into the must instead of the dry sugar.

Sulphite The short name for potassium or sodium metabisulphite from which sulphur dioxide is released in solution. See also Campden tablet.

Sweet A wine or beer which contains some residual sweetness after fermentation. The opposite of dry.

Syphon In its simplest form no more than a plastic or rubber tube through which a clear wine or beer can be conveyed from a jar containing sediment into a clean jar or bottle.

Tannin A bitter substance which gives *"bite"* and slight astringency to wine. Essential in a well balanced red wine, and an aid to preserving it.

Thin The term used to describe a wine or beer that lacks substance and has a watery consistency. The opposite of a wine or beer with plenty of body.

Wort A liquid containing a solution of malt and hop essence before fermentation into beer.

Yeast Microscopic botanical cells which secrete enzymes that cause fermentation by the reduction of sugar to alcohol and carbon dioxide. Wine and beer yeasts are called *Saccharomyces*, which means sugar fungi. Yeast is essential to the making of a wine or beer.

A note on yeasts recommended in this book.

G.P. Yeast Means a General Purpose Yeast such as Boots' Wine Yeast Compound, Unican *'Super Yeast'* and C.W.E. *'Formula 67'*. They are suitable for most table wines. G.P. Yeast may be used instead of the named varieties if you so wish.

CHAPTER THREE

The importance of hygiene

Moulds, fungi and bacteria

More wines and beers are spoiled by careless attention to hygiene than by anything else. Fermented beverages attract a number of moulds, fungi and bacteria, which float invisibly in the air and settle on the equipment, the ingredients and on uncovered musts and worts during fermentation.

Mycoderma aceti, a fungus, attacks the alcohol while it is still in a dilute solution and turns it into a vinegary acetic acid. *Mycoderma vini* grows on the surface of a fermented beverage which is exposed to the air and which is unprotected by a high alcohol content or by sulphur dioxide. A creamy skin is formed, which we call flowers of wine. The fungus converts the alcohol into carbon dioxide and water.

A whole range of bacteria (lacto-bacilli) cause ailments that produce unpleasant smells and tastes, and moulds, too, cause distinctive smells and tastes. They settle in crevices and corners of equipment, especially if it is put away wet or damp into a dark place.

Many ingredients are smothered in millions of tiny spoilage organisms. They mix with the bloom on grapes and plums for example. These can be seen by the naked eye, but they are on all other fruit whether we can see them or not. Dried fruit, too, is prone to surface infection especially if it has not been properly protected.

Sterilisation

All these enemies of the home winemaker and brewer can be easily overcome with a little care. An old method was to scald wine-making vessels or burn sulphur in them. Sulphur has long been known as an efficient sterilising agent. Only in this century, however, has it been available in a simple-to-use form that is completely effective and free from side effects. It is called metabisulphite and is a salt of either of the elements potassium or sodium. Sulphite, as it is commonly called, has been wisely called the winemaker's best friend. It is available as a fine white crystalline powder or as a small tablet called a Campden tablet. One tablet contains sufficient sodium metabisulphite to release fifty parts per million of the gas sulphur dioxide into one gallon of a liquid.

The loose powder can be made up into a solution *(100 g dissolved in tepid water and made up to 1 litre)* 5 ml of which has the same effect as one tablet. The effect of a metabisulphite solution can be reinforced by mixing it with a solution of citric acid at the moment of use.

After cleaning and washing a piece of equipment, it must be sterilised before use. Two crushed Campden tablets or two teaspoonsful *(10 ml)* of a 10% solution *(100 g sulphite dissolved in 1 litre water)* mixed with half a teaspoonful *(2.5 ml)* of citric acid in 500 ml *(18 fl oz)* of cold water makes a very powerful sterilising agent. Pour the solution into a bottle or jar, hold your hand over its mouth and swirl the solution over every part of the inner surface several times. Pour the solution into the next vessel to be sterilised and repeat the process. The sterilised vessel need only be drained of any loose moisture before being used. The traces of sulphur dioxide gas will have no harmful effects on the contents.

Every piece of equipment and most natural ingredients must be so sterilised before use: funnels, syphons, spoons, trial jar, hydrometer, thermometer, straining bag, press. All fruit should be washed in a weak sulphite solution – 1 Campden tablet per gallon – before use. Bruised, damaged or very ripe fruits need a doubly strong solution and ideally should not be used – certainly all bad parts must be cut away.

There are alternatives to sulphur for sterilising equipment, for example, the chlorine based agent Chempro. This is very effective but must not be used in the presence of an acid since it would produce the poisonous gas chlorine. The vessels and equipment must also be rinsed in clean running water after sterilisation. The Silana pine-free disinfectant may also be used but like Chempro or ordinary household bleach the sterilised equipment must be thoroughly rinsed in running cold water. *None of these alternatives to sulphur may be used on ingredients.*

Protecting musts and worts

Having sterilised equipment and ingredients it is important to protect the must and wort from subsequent airborne infection. All vessels should be covered with a close fitting lid or thick cloth. A sheet of polythene secured with a rubber band or piece of wool is also effective, but any fermenting gas must be permitted to escape.

At the pressing stage the must should be protected as much as possible. Use narrow necked jars such as demijohns and funnels rather than widenecked vessels. An airlock filled with a sulphite solution will protect the wine during the remainder of the fermentation.

For beers, the fermenting wort should also be kept covered, although it is to some extent protected by the substantial quantity of carbon dioxide that lies heavier than air on the surface of the

Make up a sterilising solution as described on page 21. Avoid inhaling the fumes as sulphur dioxide can cause irritation to the eyes, nose and throat.

Wash the equipment thoroughly, and rinse any detergent away, before sterilising. Drain the equipment after sterilisation but do not rinse it.

Pass the same solution from one piece of equipment to another for the maximum economy.

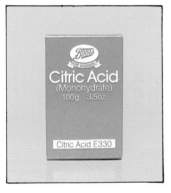

To produce a strong sterilising solution dissolve 21g ($\frac{3}{4}$ oz) of sodium metabisulphite in 284ml ($\frac{1}{2}$ pint) of water and separately dissolve 7g ($\frac{1}{4}$ oz) of citric acid in 284ml ($\frac{1}{2}$ pint) of water. Then mix the two solutions together.

wort. For this reason it is best to ferment worts in vessels with a capacity larger than the quantity being brewed. For example, brew 22.5 litres *(5 gallons)* in a 25 litre *(5$\frac{1}{2}$ gallon)* fermenting bin.

The ingredients of beer do not have to be sterilised because some boiling process is usually involved. This is in itself a sterilising process. But at the bottling or casking stage the same care and protection is required as for wine. The bottles, the wine corks and the beer crown corks should be sterilised.

Storage

Sulphur dioxide too is an anti-oxidant. When wine is being syphoned from its sediment into a storage jar, and when it is being filtered, one Campden tablet per gallon should be added to the receiving vessel to protect the wine, mead or cider. The priming of beer and the creation of carbon dioxide in solution protects beer during its period of maturation.

During this period of storage all vessels should be airtight except when making sherry style wine. Here a plug of cotton wool acts as a filter for micro organisms and the pure air admitted helps create the right bouquet and flavour.

Safety corks and bungs which are not expelled by the expansion of the wine during a warm period are available.

Low alcohol wines are especially vulnerable to infection. Alcohol in sufficient quantity is a bactericide, so too is carbon dioxide. But never take a chance. Sterilise all equipment and ingredients with sulphite, keep musts and worts covered at all times, sulphite wines after racking and, whatever else, your beverages will, at least, always be clean and wholesome.

CHAPTER FOUR

The equipment needed

Happily, the days of making wine in a glazed earthenware breadcrock covered with a piece of butter muslin are now long gone. The home winemaker of today is very well supplied with excellent equipment made specially for the purpose.

A **fermenting bin** is the first requirement. Do not use coloured plastic – the best ones are made from natural polythene that is safe for use with food. They are light to carry, easy to clean and to sterilise, inert to acid and available in suitable sizes. The Boots Fermenting Bins hold 15 litres (about $3\frac{1}{4}$ gallons) and 25 litres ($5\frac{1}{2}$ gallons) respectively. They have graduated markings on their sides so that the contents can be easily measured. A superior version of their 25 litres bin is fitted with a draw off tap at the bottom. All the bins have good fitting lids that protect the contents from airborne infection during pulp fermentation.

Fermenting bins have many uses including the mixing of liquids, fermenting on the pulp, and the receiving of must into which sugar must be stirred. The bin should always be considerably larger than the contents to prevent splashing and spillage. Once you become interested in making wine at home you will find that it is a great help to have several bins and occasions will arise when they are all in use. A long handled **plastic paddle** or **spoon** is needed for stirring, especially when dissolving sugar in a must.

Straining bags come next. Fine or coarse mesh nylon bags are easy to sterilise, effective in use and available in standard and large sizes. The standard size is suitable for smaller volumes of pulp, soft fruits, dried fruits, canned fruits etc. The large size has been especially designed by Boots to fit their fermenting bins and is ideal for larger quantities of pulp.

A **wine press** takes the hard work out of extracting the juice from crushed fruit or fermented pulp. It is particularly useful when pressing apples and any large quantity of pulp. In designing the press, attention has been given not only to its effectiveness in use, but also to good hygiene. It can be easily cleaned and sterilised and used without making a mess.

Glass demijohns with a nominal capacity of 4.5 litres (one gallon) are the most suitable fermentation jars for liquid musts. Glass is a perfectly safe material and can be easily cleaned and sterilised. The activity of the fermentation, and subsequently the clarification, of the wine can be clearly observed. A **bored bung** made from cork or rubber is needed to fit into the neck of the jar and the bore hole must be fitted with a **fermentation lock**. These are available in a variety of shapes and sizes and are made from glass or plastic. All are equally effective when filled with a sulphite solution. They allow the gas from the fermentation to escape but prevent air and airborne contamination from entering the jar.

A **label** should always be attached to the jar so that there is no mistake in recognising the type of wine in it, or the date it was made. Boots demijohn labels are designed to slip on to one of the carrying handles and can be washed and re-used. They are available in a range of colours for easier reference and solve the problem of identification in a very satisfactory manner.

Ideally, fermentation should be conducted in an evenly warm place. If you lack such a place, a **heating belt** can be fitted to the jar to provide sufficient and constant warmth. An alternative to this is an **electric heating tray** on which two demijohns can be stood at a time. For one gallon or larger quantities a **thermostatic immersion type heater** can be used in the must to maintain a warm, even temperature.

Few instruments are needed to control the quality of home made wine but they are very well worthwhile having to obtain the best results. The first is a 12″ long **wine thermometer** to check the temperature of the must at different times. If, for example, yeast is added when the temperature is too high it will be killed. Much safer to check it and be sure. The second is a **hydrometer** to measure the sugar content of a liquid. Glass or plastic hydrometers are equally effective when used in conjunction with a tall narrow **hydrometer jar** containing a sample of the must or

Glass and plastic wine hydrometers, a wine press, a 15 litre fermenting bin and a heating tray big enough for two demijohns, as described in the text.

A lever corking machine, a selection of brightly coloured capsules, some bottle labels, the tag labels that clip onto a demijohn's 'ears', the essential record book, and (below) a wine filter kit (the kind that uses filter pads).

wine. For convenience there is the **Wine and Beer Tester** that combines a hydrometer inside a large 'pipette' which serves as a hydrometer jar. The tube attachment allows a sample of the liquid to be drawn up without disturbing any sediment. Finally you should have, and use, a roll of specially impregnated acid indicator paper, a portion of which can be torn off and dipped into the must or wine. The change in its colour indicates the degree of acidity of the liquid. **Boots Acid Indicator Paper** comes in a neat holder with the colour markings for comparison to indicate whether the acidity is low, normal or high. Although the result is an approximate one, it is quite sufficient for most purposes.

A selection of **polythene funnels** will often be required and the Boots range includes funnels to fit standard wine bottles and demijohns for problem free use. It is important to use the right size for the different purposes to avoid overflow and spillage.

A **syphon** is used for removing a clear or clearing wine from its sediment without disturbing the latter. A length of plastic or rubber tubing may be used, but a more effective version has **glass or plastic J shaped tubing** attached to one end and a **syphon tap** to the other. The J shape of the tubing causes the wine to be sucked down into the tube and thus there is less likelihood of disturbing the sediment. A straight end sucks the wine up from the sediment and so can cause difficulty unless great care is exercised. The tap at the other end regulates the flow of the wine and is especially useful when filling bottles. These can be bought separately or ready assembled as a syphon kit.

Demijohns are just as useful as storage containers as they are for fermentation. For this purpose, however, they must be sealed with a new solid cork or a re-usable rubber bung. Both should be sterilised before use. When a larger volume of wine has been made fermentation and storage can be effected in a 25 litre polythene vessel that can be fitted with a bored bung and upright air-lock and later with a solid bung. Specially **long handled brushes** are available for cleaning this as well as glass demijohns. Both fermentation and storage vessels need to be scrubbed with such a brush after use to ensure an adequate standard of cleanliness before sterilisation.

Most wines clear naturally and many do not even need fining, but sometimes both fining and filtering is necessary to ensure a star bright finish to a wine. **Filter kits** using filter pads are very effective when necessary, but there is an alternative form using a filter bag plus crystals and powders. Both types come with detailed instructions.

Standard and half size glass **wine bottles** are needed next: green for red wines, colourless for rosé, white and golden wines. They should be cleaned with a bottle brush before sterilising them. Orange squash, vinegar, screw top and plastic bottles are not suitable and should not be used. Straight sided cylindrical **corks** are needed for those bottles that are to be stored on their sides while the wine in them matures. T shaped or flange stoppers may be used for those bottles of wine that are to be stood upright and consumed without long storage.

A **corking machine** will be needed to insert the straight corks after they have been softened and sterilised. A wooden hand corking machine, consisting of a cylinder in which the cork is placed and a piston that pushes the cork into the neck of the bottle, is effective and inexpensive. Firm pressure from the heel of the hand, or the gentle use of a light hammer or mallet will be required to drive the piston downwards. Another easy-to-operate model has two hand levers which compress the cork and a second mechanism to push it into the neck of the bottle in a single movement.

For bottles of sparkling wine, hollow domed plastic, **champagne-type stoppers** are necessary. They are designed to be fitted with a **wire cage** that can be fastened on to the champagne bottle. Only heavy champagne bottles may be used for sparkling wine. No other kind is strong enough.

Presenting your finished wine is a satisfying moment and foil or plastic **capsules** are available in a variety of colours to complete the neat appearance of the bottle. A splendid range of ready gummed and attractively decorated wine bottle **labels** and neck bands are also available for you to identify the name, type and vintage of your wines.

The finished appearance of your star bright wine in its proper bottle, suitably corked, capsuled and labelled should be as professional as you can manage. This brings credit not only to your own wines but also to the hobby as a whole.

A **wine rack** is desirable for storing your finished wines. There is the sturdy wood and metal rack as used commercially, as well as the all-wood or all-plastic self assembly styles. The great advantage of these is that you can easily add to them as your stock increases.

Finally, yet really something with which you should begin, is a **record book**. Boots Winemakers Record Book and Record Cards are ideal for this purpose. The loose leaf holder contains a supply of printed, punched cards. Simply fill in the details on the card as you progress each wine so that you have a permanent record of the names and quantities of the different ingredients used, the method followed, dates started, racked and bottled. Re-reading the cards will sometimes help you to identify a mistake or, better still, repeat a success.

One of the range of polythene funnels, a wooden hand corking machine, and some essential chemicals and ingredients.

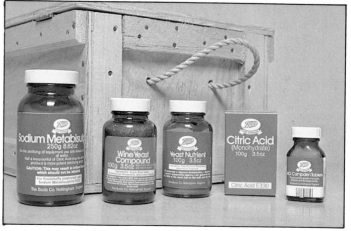

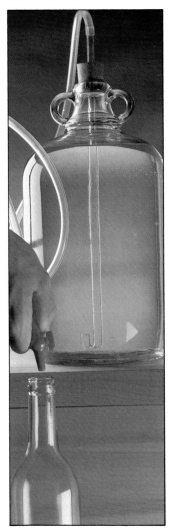

Syphoning with a glass J tube and tap, a heating belt and the 'wine and beer tester' (a hydrometer inside a pipette).

CHAPTER FIVE

Making home wine from kits

If you have never made wine before you will need certain basic equipment and ingredients. Boots Winemaker Beginner's Kit contains all that you need, except water, to make your first gallon of wine. Apart from the corks, all the equipment is re-usable and can be employed to make many more gallons of wine. The Kit includes a standard glass demijohn for fermentation, bored demijohn corks, fermentation lock, syphon tubing, a funnel, six standard wine bottles and corks, Campden tablets, yeast, sterilising solution ingredients and, the heart of the kit, a can of concentrated grape juice – red, white or rosé – of your choice.

The easiest and best way for a newcomer to learn something about winemaking at home is to make a few wines from cans of concentrate. There is an extremely wide choice of home wine concentrates available – some two dozen producing different grape wines and another half a dozen or so producing fruit wines. There is also a wide price range. As a general rule, the higher the price the more concentrated is the grape juice. In turn, this produces wine of higher quality. But there are some excellent concentrates of Standard and Budget quality that produce good wines every time for less than one-fifth of the cost of their commercial counterpart. Read the small print on the labels and choose those that contain the most grape and require the least additional sugar. By experimenting you will find those that best suit your palate.

Most kits consist of a 1 kg can of concentrated grape juice with added flavourings and balanced acidity and make one gallon (six

A beginner's kit provides the basic equipment and ingredients for making a gallon of wine. When you make the second gallon you only need to buy the ingredients, as the equipment (apart from the corks) can be used over and over again.

standard bottles) of wine. Since 1972 when the kits first appeared, the quality of the concentrate has improved considerably. Indeed, many hundreds of thousands of people now make their wines only from kits. The end product is entirely satisfactory to them and they can make these wines with the very minimum of effort and trouble. Wines from the standard kits mature in three or four months and will keep for several years. But there are now fast fermenting and maturing concentrates available that produce wine ready for drinking in just three or four *weeks* from the start.

Four categories of kits can now be identified:

High quality. The most expensive, consisting of concentrated pure grape juice from good vineyards. They require no additional sugar.

Standard. Kits consisting of pure grape juice but requiring a small quantity of additional sugar.

Budget. Kits that have been skilfully prepared from a mixture of ingredients to produce a sound wine as inexpensively as possible.

Fast ferment kits. These are designed to produce an acceptable wine in the shortest possible time. They are ideal for those just starting who have no stock of wines.

Make your choice and an early start, for the sooner you begin the sooner will your wine be ready for drinking. Instructions for making wine from high quality, standard or budget kits are given on pages 35 to 36 and a simple step-by-step picture guide is on pages 40 to 41. Look at both accounts before making any wine, as the text account is more detailed. Also remember that this is a generalised version of the process, and that any particular kit will come with its own instructions, and that it would be wise to follow those wherever they differ. General instructions for fast fermenter kits are given on pages 38 to 39.

Making home wine with high quality, standard or budget kits

1. Activate the yeast

A sachet of yeast granules is usually supplied with each kit. The yeast cells are dormant, however, and must be re-activated before they can begin to ferment the grape sugar and convert it into alcohol. They can be sprinkled direct on to the diluted concentrate, but it is better to activate them beforehand so that the fermentation begins with the minimum of delay. First sterilise a bottle, pour in 140 ml *(5 fl oz)* of tepid boiled water, add one teaspoonful of the grape concentrate for preference, or the strained juice of half an orange and a level teaspoonful of castor sugar. Shake well to mix the contents and dissolve the sugar, then add the yeast. Plug the neck of the bottle with a piece of clean cotton wool or screwed up paper tissue to keep out airborne infection, then stand the bottle in a warm place, 40°C *(104°F)*. Give the bottle a shake from time to time to mix air into the liquid and after a few hours you will see thousands of tiny bubbles rising to the surface. This is called a starter bottle and the activated yeast is ready to begin the fermentation.

2. Sterilise the equipment, and begin

As the starter reaches a state of readiness, usually between six and twelve hours, wash and sterilise the fermentation jar, funnel, the bored cork or bung and the airlock. If you have not already done so, open the can of concentrate, pour the contents into the jar, rinse out the can with a pint of tepid water and add this together with five more pints of cold water and the yeast starter. Swirl the contents around the jar to distribute the concentrate and yeast, then fill the airlock with a sulphite solution, gently slide it into the bored bung and press this into the neck of the jar. Leave the jar in an even temperature, 21–27°C *(70–77°F)*, for about ten days. The precise period may vary from one kit to another and is not critical to the precise hour and day.

3. Adding the sugar

At the recommended time on the instructions, sterilise a large jug or bowl, remove the bung and airlock from the fermentation jar and pour about one pint of the fermenting must into it. Add the recommended amount of sugar, usually 140 g *(5 oz)*, and with a sterilised plastic spoon stir the must until the sugar is dissolved. Return the must to the jar slowly to avoid frothing, refit the airlock and continue the fermentation for a further five days.

The process is then repeated, the jar topped up with cold boiled water and the must left to ferment out. This may take several weeks or finish in a few more days, depending on a number of different factors, including amongst others the strength of the yeast colony and the evenness of the fermentation temperature.

4. The first racking

When the wine begins to clear and the bubbles have stopped rising in the jar and passing through the airlock, syphon the clearing wine into a clean and sterilised jar. Top up with cold boiled water, add one Campden tablet and seal the jar with a softened and sterilised bung. Attach a label showing the name of the wine and the date it was started, then store it in as cool a place as you can find for a few weeks until the wine is crystal clear, then repeat the process for a few more weeks storage, or bottle it.

5. Bottling

Wash and sterilise six standard wine bottles and submerge six new corks in a sulphite solution for several hours. Syphon the clear wine into the bottles leaving a gap of about one inch (25 mm) between the top of the wine and where the bottom of the cork will be. Shake any surplus moisture from the softened corks and push them into the neck of the bottles. The top of the cork should fit flush with the neck of the bottle. A corking machine makes this much easier.

Label the bottles with the name of the wine and the date it was started, then lay them on their sides in a cool place for a month or two at least, and longer if you can. Your white wines will be more enjoyable if the bottles are stood in the refrigerator for one hour before serving. Your red wines are best after an hour in a comfortably warm room.

The wide range of grape juice concentrates and compounds: high quality, standard, budget and the fast fermenting 'express'.

Fast ferment kits

The contents of these kits include not only the concentrate but also a sachet of pectolytic enzyme to promote clarity, a clearing agent to ensure trouble free fining, a mixture of potassium sorbate and sulphite to stabilise the wine and, of course, a fast fermenting yeast and nutrient. All that the home winemaker has to provide – apart from the basic equipment – is sugar and water.

Each kit is supplied with detailed step-by-step instructions that must be faithfully followed to achieve good results. This is most important and failure to comply may create a wine with an off flavour, or one that is not clear, or even still fermenting. The kits are available in both one gallon and five gallon packs. Whilst the instructions vary slightly from kit to kit, the following is a summary of the process.

1. Clean and sterilise a fermentation vessel suitable for the quantity of wine to be made. Detergents should be avoided in the cleaning process since even a small trace can adversely affect the finished wine.

2. Empty the concentrate into the vessel, and rinse out the container to make sure that none is wasted.

3. Dissolve the specified amount of sugar in the specified amount of water and add it to the must.

4. Make up some fining agent as prescribed and add this to the must.

5. Add the pectolytic enzyme and shake or stir the must to ensure that the mixture is thoroughly dispersed.

6. Add the yeast and top up with cold water.

7. Fit an airlock and leave the vessel in a warm situation where the temperature is not less than 21°C nor more than 27°C *(70° to 77°F)*. The airing cupboard is a popular location. This rather high temperature is critical to ensure a fast fermentation which should be complete in 14 days. If you haven't a suitable warm location in the house, invest in a wine heating belt, heating tray or thermostatic heater.

8. The fermentation vessel should now be moved to a cooler situation around 13°C *(55°F)*. A tiled or cement floor helps.

9. More finings are now prepared and added, together with the stabilising agent. The vessel must be thoroughly shaken to ensure not only complete dispersion of these additives but also the release of carbon dioxide in the wine. This is an important factor in the process of producing a drinkable wine quickly.

10. The airlock should be left in place and the vessel shaken three times a day for three days to ensure the release of as much more of the dissolved carbon dioxide as possible.

11. The fermentation vessel is then left undisturbed in a rackable but cool position for four days while the sediment settles.

12. Next, the wine is carefully racked from its lees into a sterilised jar. A further vigorous shake up is given to release yet more carbon dioxide and the neck of the jar is plugged with cotton wool. The wine is then left undisturbed for one week to mature and clear to brilliance.

13. The new wine is now ready for sampling and bottling. If it is too dry for your palate, the dryness may be reduced with sugar at the rate of 45 g *(1½ oz)* per gallon (10 g per litre) or with saccharin tablets at the rate of one tablet per standard wine bottle (700 ml).

14. The general impression of the wine improves if stored in bottles for two to three months at a temperature of 13°C *(55°F)*. Both the red and the white wines are at their best when drunk young and just below room temperature.

The advantages of kits

For those with little time to spare and limited facilities and storage space, kits produce very acceptable wines. They require the minimum of equipment and take very little time to make and mature. To provide just one bottle of wine each day a one gallon kit needs to be started every week. But a five gallon pack is no more trouble and would produce enough wine to last a month.

Another advantage of kit wines, particularly for the enthusiast, is that they provide wine to drink while fruit and other wines are maturing. It has been a constant complaint of would-be wine-makers that they haven't the patience to wait for a year or longer while their hedgerow wines mature. By making up kit wines the strain on their patience is considerably reduced.

So, making wine from a Beginner's Kit is an excellent way to learn about the hobby. And making wine from kits in general is ideal not only for the busy person with limited time and facilities but also for the enthusiast waiting impatiently for country wines to mature.

A step-by-step picture guide to making wine from a kit is given overleaf.

1. Prepare a yeast starter bottle as described on page 35. This should be done several hours before anything else, as it may take that long to reach a state of readiness.

2. Wash and sterilise the demijohn, the funnel, and the fermentation lock. The bored cork should be softened in a sterilising solution for a few hours.

3. Pour the concentrate into the demijohn, rinse out the can with a pint of tepid water and add this together with five more pints of cold water and the yeast starter.

4. Swirl the contents around to mix them thoroughly, then fill the airlock with a sulphite solution and gently fit it in the neck of the demijohn.

5. A heating belt will help to maintain the correct temperature for about ten days while the wine ferments. The exact period varies from kit to kit.

6. At the recommended time add some sugar syrup, mixed in a sterilised bowl using about a pint of the must. When the sugar is dissolved, return the must to the jar slowly to avoid frothing. Ferment for five more days then repeat the process.

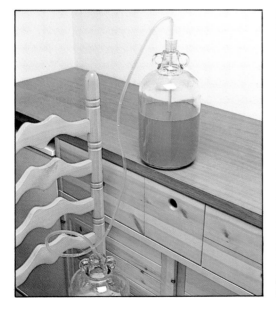

7. Rack the clearing wine from its sediment into a clean sterilised jar, top up with cold boiled water, add a Campden tablet and seal the jar with a softened and sterilised bung. Label and store in the cool till clear.

8. Soften and sterilise six corks. Syphon the wine into clean, sterilised bottles, cork and label them, then store on their sides in a cool place for at least a month or two.

CHAPTER SIX

The basic ingredients

The best wine is made from grapes. Experience has shown this over the centuries. Grapes contain a better balance of sugar, acid, tannin and juice than any other fruit. But not all varieties of grape are equally suitable and many other fruits make a better wine than some grapes. Other ingredients, too, can be used to make attractive and 'different' wines.

Fruits

All kinds of fruits can be used as a base ingredient from which to make wine. They may be used alone, but quite often, better results are obtained by mixing them. This gives a better balance of flavour, sugar, acid and tannin. Some fruits with a light flavour, such as the apple, must be used in much larger quantities than those with a strong flavour like the raspberry, so these would mix well. All fruits contain sugar in different degrees, dates being notably high, with cooking cherries and lemons at the low end of the scale. Again, all fruits contain acid – mostly citric or malic acid, but in some the acid content is very high, for example, the blackcurrant, and in some it is very low, as in the pear. The black grape is very high in tannin, a substance that gives character and firmness to red wines. A few other fruits also contain some tannin in their skins, notably apricots, damsons, elderberries, pears and sloes, but in most fruits the quantity is negligible and so mixing is again indicated.

Sugar, acid and tannin can all be added artificially, of course, and will be dealt with separately, but an awareness of differences in the nature of fruits will help you to understand the possibilities for blending.

Pectin is another component in all fruits. It is highest in those fruits that make the best jam since it is the gelling factor. When making wine from fruits we get rid of the pectin by adding a pectin destroying enzyme, such as Boots pectolytic enzyme, at the very outset.

A further factor that needs to be taken into account when mixing fruits together is the style of wine being made. Table wines need rather less fruit than dessert wines with their fuller body and stronger flavour. Mixing fruit diminishes individual flavours and produces more complex and interesting flavours.

Frozen fruit, dried fruit, fruit juices and fruit syrups can be used as successfully as fresh, ripe fruit. So can tinned fruit in sugar syrup, and fruit in jams, jellies and even pie fillings. Check the labels carefully and avoid those that have been artificially sweetened or that contain added pectin, preservative or starch.

Vegetables

The advantage of using vegetables is the contribution they make to the body or fullness of a wine. Unfortunately they all lack acid, tannin and sugar, and frequently flavour too. Beetroot, carrot and parsnip seem to be the best of the root vegetables, while pea pods, broad beans and runner beans are the best of the rest. Marrow is unworthily popular and spinach has been used. The salads are best avoided. Lettuce wine is anaemic, tomatoes make a tasteless white wine – the colouring remains in the skin. Onion wine has a disastrous effect on the palate and radishes and cucumber are best forgotten.

Flowers

The one asset of a flower as a base for wine is its perfume. It contributes enormously to bouquet and flavour, but acid, sugar, tannin and water have all to be added in the maximum quantity. Dandelion, elderflower and rose petal are among the best, but broom, coltsfoot, garden pinks, golden rod, hawthorn blossom, lime bracts, and primroses have also been used. Some flowers such as laburnum have toxic tendencies and must be avoided – as well as those grown from bulbs. A list of poisonous plants is given in the appendix.

Shoots, leaves, herbs and saps

Bramble shoots and the summer prunings from vines have been used successfully and oak and walnut leaves can be tried. Birch and sycamore tree saps make a basis for wine but need some flavouring.

Herbs are not widely used, although parsley makes a distinctive wine. They contribute some flavour, vitamins and minerals, but everything else has to be added. Tea leaves contain tannin as well as flavour, but coffee beans and ginger root contribute nothing but flavour.

Cereals

Grains are sometimes used in conjunction with raisins – notably rice and wheat. Grains contribute body and some flavour, as well as nitrogen for the yeast. They should be fermented with the yeast *Saccharomyces diastaticus* – known as the cereal yeast. Some fungal amylase is required to reduce the starch to a fermentable sugar and additional nutrient must be added to prevent the formation of fusel oils.

Vegetables make excellent dessert wines and the parsnip is particularly popular. Fruits are ideal for table wines, as well as for aperitifs and dessert wines. They also blend well together to improve the balance of acid sugar and body in a wine. Recipes using all these fruits and vegetables will be found in the 'Country wine' chapter.

CHAPTER SEVEN

Other essential ingredients

Water

British tap water is pure and safe for winemaking – at least, most of the time. Heavily chlorinated water should be boiled to drive off the chlorine, which doesn't mix happily with acids and which taints the wine. Boiling also precipitates the calcium carbonate *(chalk)* of hard water which the wine can happily do without. But there seems to be no special advantage in very soft water.

Spring water is usually excellent for winemaking unless it is heavily carbonated with calcium. Well water is also suitable, as long as it is safe for drinking. Rain water is best avoided unless it is first filtered and then boiled to remove the sulphur and micro-organisms that contaminate it.

Sugar

White granulated sugar *(sucrose)* is best for most wines. It can be readily split by an enzyme secreted in the yeast cells into its component sugars – fructose and glucose. So, too, of course, can caster sugar, icing sugar and cube sugar but these are more expensive and have no advantages over the granulated form. The different brown sugars are also easily split but they confer a caramel flavour on the wine and are only recommended to be used in the making of Madeira type wines.

Sucrose can be split into fructose and glucose by boiling it in water with a little citric acid for twenty minutes. Some wine-makers prepare a litre of syrup by boiling 1 kg *(2¼ lbs)* of sugar with 5 g *(5 ml spoonful)* citric acid in 620 ml *(22 fl oz)* of water. This mixes more readily with the must than dry sugar granules but less water is then needed in the recipe.

Invert sugar may be bought but this mixture of fructose and glucose and water is more expensive than the syrup and no different. Fructose and glucose powders may be bought and used separately or in a fifty/fifty mixture but are more expensive than granulated sugar.

Golden syrup may be used, especially in Madeira type wines or in strongly flavoured dessert wines. This syrup includes some flavouring. Darker treacles are not recommended since they convey an overwhelming flavour to a wine.

Honey may be used in moderation; it also conveys a flavour that can be distinctive and noticeable. Use only light and bland honeys and remember that 4 lb *(1.81 kg)* honey is the equivalent of 3 lb *(1.36 kg)* sugar.

Lactose *(milk sugar)* is not fermentable by wine yeasts and so may be used only for sweetening wines. However, it is more expensive than saccharin pellets, which are equally effective and unfermentable.

Acid

Most musts need the addition of some acid. Citric is commonly used because it produces a good fermentation and is cheap. Malic is sometimes used because it promotes a fruity flavour in the finished wine. There seems to be no great advantage in using the more expensive tartaric acid – at least as far as flavour is concerned. Malic acid, especially in red wines, is sometimes partially converted into the less sharp-tasting lactic acid and carbon dioxide, by lactic acid bacteria, particularly if the wine has not been sulphited at the time of racking. Tartaric acid is sometimes precipitated during cold weather in the form of crystals of potassium tartrate *(cream of tartar)*. They can be seen as tiny glass-like crystals adhering to the cork, sides of the jar or bottle or in the deposit. They do no harm and their presence indicates that the wine will taste smoother and softer than before.

As a rule of thumb, one level 5 ml spoonful of citric acid in one gallon *(4.5 litres)* of must is the equivalent of one part acid in one thousand parts of wine. Table wines need to contain four to five parts per thousand and dessert wines six to seven parts. Remember that some acid will be present in most fruit ingredients, so test for acidity.

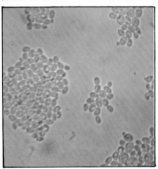

Yeast in sachets, in a starter bottle, and active under a microscope. Dried yeast keeps for several months in a cool, dry atmosphere.

Brown sugars give a caramel flavour and should only be used for Madeira wines. Honeys should be light and bland and used in moderation, or they also give too strong a flavour to the wine.

The degree of acidity or pH is more important for the taste of the wine than the precise quantity. This degree of acidity can be easily and quickly measured with a Boots Wine Indicator Paper, especially when testing white wines. The colour of red wine makes it marginally more difficult to test but it can still be done with a reasonable degree of accuracy. A reading of around pH 3.4 is desired, this falls into the 'normal' range on the wine indicator scale.

Tannin

This is the substance that gives 'bite', firmness and character to a wine. Use grape tannin prepared from the skins, seeds and stalk of grapes. The reddish-brown powder seems to be more effective than the liquid. If a wine needs it, a half to one level 5 ml spoonful per gallon is enough. Cold tea which contains tannin is not recommended since the amount of tannin in tea varies.

Pectolytic enzyme

Since all fruits contain some pectin, a pectolytic enzyme should be added to all fruit musts whatever the kind of crushed fruit, fruit juice or jam used. Jam in fact needs a double dose to dissolve the extra pectin which helped it to set. One rounded 5 ml spoonful per gallon is usually added right at the outset – before the sugar. Allow it to work for twenty-four hours before the addition of the yeast. Fungal amylase should be used in the same way when added to musts containing pie filling or cereals.

Yeast

All the various ingredients are important in the making of a balanced and successful wine, but none more so than yeast, for you cannot make wine without it. A true wine yeast should be used and the best results are obtained with a yeast sympathetic to the particular must. Each of the different yeast strains conveys something of its own characteristics to the wine. Some are tolerant of more alcohol than others, e.g. Madeira and Tokay. Sherry yeast produces more acetaldehyde than other yeasts. Sauternes yeast has difficulty in fermenting fructose and so often leaves a residue of sugar that sweetens the wine. It also produces a little more glycerine and tends to give a smoother finish to the wine. Champagne yeast ferments well under pressure and should, therefore, always be used for sparkling wines.

An all purpose yeast is marketed for those wines not requiring subtle distinctions and is best used when making flower wines or social wines of no particular style or flavour.

Most yeasts are sold in granulated form and need to be activated before use. Every sachet or spoonful of yeast granules contains millions of dead cells as well as the seeds of living cells. It is important to ensure that these are viable before adding them to the must. Yeast tablets and liquid yeasts should be treated similarly. Instructions for revitalising the yeast are usually given on the label and it often takes no more than six hours. Yeast multiplies itself every three hours in favourable conditions of temperature and environment but dies after twenty-five to thirty reproductions.

The simplest and most effective solution for re-vitalising dormant yeast cells can be made by rinsing out a can of concentrated grape juice that has just been added to a must, with 250 ml *(9 fl oz)* of tepid boiled water. Pour this into a sterilised standard wine bottle, add the yeast, plug the neck loosely with cotton wool and stand the bottle in a very warm position – 35–40°C *(95–104°F)* for 1–2 hours. The diluted concentrated grape juice contains all the elements needed by the yeast to re-awaken it and make it viable. As an alternative the strained juice of half an orange and one level teaspoonful of sugar dissolved in 250 ml *(9 fl oz)* of tepid boiled water is equally effective.

One level 5 ml spoonful of dried yeast granules, or one sachet or phial of yeast activated as described above, is sufficient to ferment from one to five gallons of must. For larger quantities of must a larger yeast starter should be prepared.

The shelf life of both dried and liquid yeast is limited. Keep it in a cool dry place, preferably in a sealed container.

It is not easy to package absolutely pure yeast and there is a danger that wild yeasts and other organisms may have crept in. So buy the best and purest yeast available. Baker's yeast and brewer's yeast are the most likely to be affected and should be avoided. They also impart a doughy or a hoppy smell to the wine.

Nutrient

To ferment efficiently yeast cells need nitrogen. Many foods contain nitrogenous matter, including bread. This was, no doubt, why it was the old practice to spread yeast on a slice of toast and float this on the must. But many wine ingredients contain insufficient nitrogen to enable the yeast cells to ferment out all the sugar in a must before they die from lack of nitrogen. Some nutrient salts should always, therefore, be added to a must at the same time as the yeast. The salts consist of ammonium phosphate or ammonium sulphate or a mixture of both, and are available in packets as fine white crystals or compressed into tablets. One tablet, or half a level 5 ml spoonful of the crystals, per gallon is adequate. If you wish to ferment the must on to a high alcohol content add one 3 mg tablet of vitamin B_1 also.

If insufficient nutrient is added, the living yeast cells extract nitrogen and vitamins from the dead cells, causing them to decompose more quickly. Bacteria then feed on the amino acids released by this process, called autolysis, and impart very unpleasant smells and flavours to the wine.

Finings

Most wines clear naturally when fermentation is finished. Racking the wine from its sediment into a clean container, adding sulphite, and moving the wine to a cooler place all help the clearing process and soon the wine is star bright.

Occasionally, however, a wine is slow to clear and needs the addition of a fining agent. A number of proprietary brands are available and should be used in accordance with the manufacturer's instructions. Bentonite gel, gelatine and isinglass are the most popular, but the white of an egg beaten into some wine can be effective for a ten gallon quantity, while a tablespoonful or two of fresh milk is sometimes effective for a single gallon.

CHAPTER EIGHT

Making different types of home wine

Dry table wines

Unless you have a large juicing machine, the best way to extract the flavour, acid, sugar, juice and trace elements in fruit is by a short period of pulp fermentation followed by straining through a nylon bag and pressing the pulp as dry as possible. Hot or cold water can be used, but red fruits generally need to have hot water poured on them to help extract the colour. Leave them to cool before adding pectic enzyme. Hard fruits that are difficult to crush can be softened in hot water. Hot water does not imply boiling water, but rather water at a temperature of around 80°C (175°F), as this does not give a stewed flavour.

White fruits, apples, peaches, rhubarb, etc should be added as soon as they are cut or crushed to cold water in which sulphite, acid and pectic enzyme have already been dissolved. All fruit oxidises when bruised, crushed or cut, and it is important to prevent spoilage by protecting it with sulphite as quickly as possible.

Cover the vessel and leave it for twenty-four hours in a warm room while the pectic enzyme reduces the pectin. Pectic enzyme is less efficient in the presence of too much sugar, so do not add sugar at this stage.

After twenty-four hours a sample of the must should be withdrawn, strained through meshed nylon, and poured into a trial jar. Measure its specific gravity with a hydrometer and calculate the additional sugar required to produce a wine containing the quantity of alcohol appropriate for the particular wine. A dry white table wine can be about 10% alcohol and a dry red wine up to 13%.

By this time the effectiveness of the sulphite will have diminished and it will be safe to add an activated yeast. If the yeast is added too soon, it will be inhibited by the sulphite and may even be killed. **Always leave twenty-four hours between the addition of sulphite and the addition of yeast.**

During fermentation on the pulp, the floating fruit must be kept submerged so that the sugar, acid, colour, etc can be leached out. Traditionally, this was done by pressing down and stirring the fruit at least twice a day. This practice is now rare in commercial wineries where machines do the work. In the home a china plate may be sterilised and used, if necessary weighed down with a sterilised bottle containing water. An oaken platen with holes drilled in it is even better. Uncoloured plastic will also do, but avoid anything metallic, unless it is high quality stainless steel. Remember that the vessel must be kept covered as closely as possible whilst still allowing the fermentation gas to escape.

Use the hydrometer, before adding the yeast, to find out the natural sugar content of the must. Add just enough sugar to increase that reading to achieve the alcohol content that's right for the particular wine. Use the hydrometer again at the end of fermentation. A table wine made from fruit juice and sugar should have a starting specific gravity of around 1.080, and at the end of fermentation it should have fallen to below 1.000, as seen here. A sweet wine should have sugar added during fermentation and finish at around 1.016.

After a period, usually of from three to six days of actual fermentation, the must should be strained through a fine meshed nylon bag and squeezed or pressed dry. Open the bag from time to time and stir up the pulp, otherwise the outside becomes dry while the inside remains wet with juice.

Sugar is now stirred in and care taken to ensure that it is all dissolved. Some winemakers dissolve their sugar in hot water, leave the syrup to cool and add this to the must. The standard solution is 2 lb *(1 kg)* sugar in 1 pint *(620 ml)* of water with one level teaspoonful *(5 ml)* of citric acid which is boiled for twenty minutes. This produces 2 pints *(1.25 litres)* of syrup with a specific gravity of 1.300. Allowance must be made in the recipe for the water and acid in the syrup.

Fermentation should now be continued in a glass fermentation jar fitted with an airlock and the must fermented out to dryness – S.G. 0.990 to 0.996.

Sweet table wine

A sweet table wine to accompany the dessert course of a meal needs to be full bodied, about 12% alcohol and distinctly sweet – S.G. 1.016 to 1.024. The fermentation is stopped at the level of sweetness required by racking, and adding potassium sorbate, or a proprietary brand such as Sorbistat, and sulphite. The normal dose is one gram potassium sorbate and one crushed Campden tablet per gallon. Alternatively, the wine can be fermented to dryness and sweetened just prior to serving.

Dessert wine *(Port/Tokay)*

These wines require much more body and flavour than table wines. Up to a total of 6 lb fruit of various kinds would not be out of place per gallon. In addition to the main base ingredient it helps to add others such as very ripe bananas, dried apricots, prunes, raisins, etc to improve the body and flavour. Root vegetables such as beetroot, carrots and parsnips are best made into dessert wines.

To get the high alcohol content more sugar is needed than for table wines. It should be added in stages at intervals of seven or eight days. In this way the yeast develops a tolerance to the alcohol and keeps on fermenting up to its limit. Use a Tokay or Port yeast, together with additional nutrient and acid. Make frequent checks on the specific gravity, allowing it to fall to around 1.006 before adding any more sugar. Keep the fermentation going for as long as possible, to produce the maximum amount of alcohol. By adding together the total number of specific gravity units that have been fermented, it is possible to get a fair idea of the quantity of alcohol in the wine by reference to the tables in the appendix.

Sherry style wines

These are started in the same way as table wines, and are fermented in the same way as dessert wines, by the addition of sugar in small doses. Dry sherry style is achieved by watching the attenuation of the sugar even more closely. Keep the specific gravity reading between 1.002 and 1.006 and as fermentation becomes slower let the figures fall to, say, 0.998 and 1.002 respectively. It is a matter of judgment when to stop adding sugar and leave the wine to ferment right out. A sweet sherry is fermented in the same way as a dessert wine.

Sherries must be fermented and matured, however, in the presence of air to achieve the distinctive flavour. Do this in a jar not quite full and plugged with cotton wool instead of an airlock. The quality of sherry is much improved by blending and with age. Blend together as many different 'sherries' as you can, even of different years and leave them under cotton wool for as long as possible – three or four years at least. Plastic polypins or ex sherry plastic containers are ideal for this purpose.

A sherry flor yeast should be used for dry sherries and a plain sherry yeast for others.

Madeiras

These are also full bodied wines fermented on to the maximum alcohol content. A brown sugar should be used and maturation should be in a very warm place for six months or so once the wine is bright. This helps to develop the caramel flavour of this attractive wine. Vegetables make a good base provided other ingredients like rose hips, figs, prunes, raisins etc are included. Keep the acid level high and finish the wine sweet.

Vermouths

These are best made with a vermouth style concentrated grape juice. Sachets of herbal flavourings should be used in accordance with the manufacturer's instructions. A nondescript base wine that has been fermented on to about 17% alcohol and matured for at least one year is used. White wines are normally used for dry vermouths and red wines for sweet. They may be drunk cold and neat or with ice and tonic, lemonade etc.

Making sparkling wine. Re-ferment the wine, and as soon as the fermentation starts syphon it into sterilised champagne bottles, fit sterilised hollow-domed plastic stoppers and wire cages. Later, when the sediment is ready for disgorging from the stopper, chill the bottle (still, as it's been stored, upside down) in the fridge (not the freezer). Then place the stopper and neck of the bottle in a mixture of ice and salt. After 10 minutes the wine inside the stopper should be frozen and it can be removed with the bottle upright. A clean softened stopper and a cage, which were standing by, can now be popped on after one or two saccharin tablets have been added.

Sparkling wines

Grapes, early gooseberries, rhubarb, pears or white currants make the best sparkling wines, but other white fruits may be used. A champagne yeast is essential. The body should be light, but not thin, as should the flavour. An original total specific gravity of around 1.076 is adequate. Ferment the wine out to dryness, rack, fine and store until bright then rack again. It is essential for the wine to be crystal clear and bone dry (S.G. 0.096 or lower) before starting the second stage when the wine should be some six months old.

When you come to the second stage first check if there is any sediment in the jar. If there is the wine must be racked into a clean jar before proceeding. Then stir in precisely 17 g sugar per litre. *(2½ oz per gallon)* and when this is dissolved add a freshly activated champagne yeast for the second time. Fit an airlock and as soon as the wine is fermenting pour it into sterilised champagne bottles that are free from scratches and chips. Leave a space of about 5 cm *(2 in)* in the neck, fit a sterilised, hollow domed plastic stopper and wire it on with a cage. Lay the bottles on their sides in a warm room for a week then move them to a cool store, still on their sides, for at least another six months, preferably longer. But do keep them on their sides.

To disgorge the sediment, place the bottles head first in a bottle carton, prop this up at an angle of 45° and each day give the bottles a little shake and a twist to encourage the sediment to detach itself from the side of the bottle and slide down into the hollow dome of the stopper. After about one month the carton may be stood upright with the bottles on their heads.

Make up a basinful of a dozen crushed ice cubes and two tablespoonsful of cooking salt. Place the stopper and neck of the bottle in the mixture and leave it there for about ten minutes. By this time the wine in the stopper will be frozen, encapsulating the sediment within it. Remove the bottle, stand it upright, undo the wire, remove the stopper, pop into the bottle one or two saccharin pellets to suit your taste and promptly push home another stopper that has already been softened in hot water. Replace the cage and the wine is ready to be served whenever you fancy. Provided the wine was quite dry, that no more sugar than indicated was added, that an *active* champagne yeast was used and that the process described was followed, there are no problems at all in disgorging the sediment. The removal of one stopper and the replacement with the other takes only a second or two if you organise yourself beforehand.

Before serving sparkling wine, chill it for several hours in the refrigerator. Have available your champagne glasses and a clean glass water jug. Remove the cage, extract the stopper and promptly pour the erupting foam into the jug. The foaming subsides within seconds and the wine in the jug may be returned to the bottle. The wine may now be slowly and gently poured into the glasses from the bottle. Always remove the stoppers from sparkling wine carefully as they can fly off with enough power to cause injury. Never point the bottle towards anyone when removing the stopper.

CHAPTER NINE

Using a hydrometer

A wine must basically consists of water and sugar – with a relatively tiny quantity of acid and traces of mineral salts, colouring and flavouring. When a base ingredient contains no sugar at all, for example, flowers, it is easy to work out how much sugar to add. When the must contains an unknown quantity of sugar, as it would if prepared from fruit, it is important to find out how much sugar is already present so that the additional sugar needed can be calculated with a reasonable degree of accuracy.

The sugar naturally present in such a must is measured with a hydrometer. This instrument measures the gravity or weight of a sample of liquid compared with the same volume of water at a given temperature. The warmer a liquid gets the lighter it becomes relative to water of a lower temperature. The temperature of the sample liquid must therefore be the same as that of the water against which the hydrometer has been graduated. If the temperature of the sample varies from that of the water then due allowance must be made.

The weight of any liquid is called its specific gravity, i.e. its gravity or weight is specific to the same volume of water at the given temperature. The weight of water at 20°C *(68°F)* is recorded as 1.000. If a liquid contains some sugar, it will weigh more than the same volume of water. The hydrometer measures this difference.

It is a simple instrument. The basic shape varies but one of the most popular ones consists of a glass tube enlarged and weighted at the bottom end. A printed scale is fixed inside the thinner, top end. On the scale, figures are printed to indicate the temperature of the water at which the hydrometer was graduated. The usual figure is 20°C or 68°F. The graduated scale commonly runs from 0.990 at the top in units of 2 through 1.000 to 1.150 at the bottom.

The hydrometer is used with a hydrometer jar or trial jar, which is just big enough to contain the hydrometer and a sample of the liquid to be tested. To check the accuracy of the hydro-meter scale first wash the jar and the hydrometer clean, sterilise them in a sulphite solution, and shake off the surplus drops. Place the hydrometer carefully in the trial jar *(to merely drop it in might break it)*. Fill the jar with water at the temperature marked on the scale and note the position where the hydrometer floats in the

Give the hydrometer a little twist after you have lowered it into the liquid to remove any air bubbles (which could falsify the reading) and take the reading when the hydrometer is completely still, and not touching the sides of the jar, with your eye just at the level of the liquid. The red zone on these glass beer hydrometers indicates starting gravities and the green zone shows the bottling specific gravity below 1.010.

Reading before fermentation

mild & brown ales 1.030
sweet stouts 1.034

bitter beers 1.040
lager 1.044
export ales 1.046
Irish stout 1.048
strong ale 1.054

sparkling wine 1.076

white table wine 1.080

red table wine 1.090
barley wine 1.090

aperitifs and
dessert wines 1.130

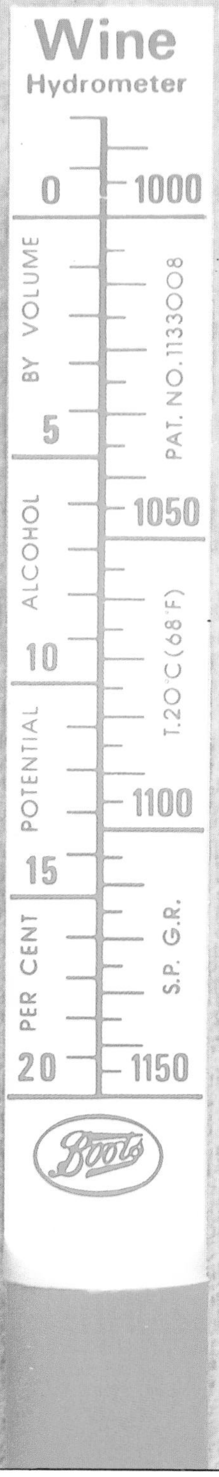

Wine
Hydrometer

0 — 1000

BY VOLUME

PAT. NO. 1133008

5

1050

ALCOHOL

T.20 C (68°F)

10

POTENTIAL

1100

15

S.P. G.R.

PER CENT

20 — 1150

Boots

Reading after fermentation

dry wine 1.000 or less
WATER at 20°C 1.000

light beers 1.000
full bodied beers 1.008

medium sweet
wine 1.000 to 1.010

sweet wine 1.010 to 1.030

water. The 1.000 line should be at the bottom of the 'saucer' *(meniscus)* of water between the hydrometer and the jar. The edges of the water creep slightly higher up the side of the glass. If the reading is not 1.000, it should be regarded as the base figure and an appropriate allowance made when using that instrument. It might, for example, be two points too high or too low.

The hydrometer should first be used just prior to the addition of yeast. The must should be stirred and any pulp in it well squeezed. Remove a sample and strain it through fine nylon to remove particles of pulp. Then pour it into the trial jar, check the temperature and insert the hydrometer. Twist it, then leave it to settle and become still before recording the reading. Now refer to the table in the appendix. Look down the specific gravity column until you reach the figure you have recorded and then into the next column to see the weight that this figure represents. Look further to the right and you will see the approximate quantity of alcohol likely to be produced if that quantity of sugar is completely fermented. The readings for example might be:

S.G. 1.025   318 g/11 oz sugar   2.8% alcohol.

Now decide how much alcohol you want in your finished wine. Look down the alcohol content column on the extreme right of the tables and when you have found your figure look at the adjacent sugar content figure. Your choice might be as follows:

12% alcohol   1.094 kg/38½ oz.

The quantity of sugar to add to your must is the difference between the two sugar readings i.e.

1.094 kg—318 g = 776 g.   38½ oz—11 oz = 27½ oz.

Allow for any other sugar-containing ingredients still to be added, for example, concentrated grape juice. As a rule of thumb two-thirds of the weight of sultanas, raisins or concentrated grape juice is sugar. The sugar in the concentrate can always be calculated by taking a reading immediately before adding it and again after it has been well stirred in. Sultanas or raisins are best added with the base ingredient so that the sugar has been leached out in the twenty-four hours steeping in the presence of pectolytic enzyme. If for any reason this is not done, the two-thirds calculation is a fair estimate.

The hydrometer can also be used at other times; when the fermentation ends, for example. This indicates the residual sugar content. A reading below 1.000 shows that virtually all the sugar has been fermented and that the wine is dry. Alcohol is lighter than water and so dilutes it, hence the reading below 1.000.

CHAPTER TEN

Syphoning

The syphon is just a length of plastic tubing, but without it, and without proper respect for the handling of wine during racking, you will never make a drinkable wine.

Some experts are able to work with a plain piece of tubing, others prefer to fit a glass or plastic 'J' tube to the end in the jar, to make sure no sediment is sucked into the tube. Others go all the way and fit a syphon tap to the outlet end, which makes it easier to turn off and on. Whatever apparatus you use, the process is the same.

Stand the jar of wine on a work surface, table or stool and place the receiving vessel, whether jar or bottle on the floor beneath it. Take care not to handle the jar of wine carelessly for this may disturb the sediment and cloud the wine.

Sterilise the syphon inside and out, then remove the airlock and bored bung and insert the J tube, or end of a syphon into the wine. Place the tap end of the syphon in your mouth (with the tap open if you are using one) and suck steadily until the tube is full of wine. Then turn off the tap or pinch the open end between your finger and thumb, and place it into the mouth of the jar to be filled. Now turn on the tap and the wine will flow from the full jar into the empty jar. It is important in syphoning to keep the outlet always nearer to the ground than the inlet. Indeed a drop of about an arm's length is preferred.

Always keep the inlet end of the syphon above the sediment,

(this is why a J tube is useful) and hold it steady so as not to disturb the sediment. Threading a bored bung on to the top end of the J tube before it is fitted into the plastic tube is helpful. Soften the bung first and make sure that it has a vent hole or a small channel cut into the side. This is to let air into the jar as the wine is sucked out. If you use a bung without a vent hole the wine will cease to flow. A bored bung cut in half lengthwise through the bore may be fitted round the tube in the neck of the jar as an alternative to threading the bung on to the J tube. In both methods the tube is kept firmly in position.

As the level of wine in the jar falls nearer to the sediment, carefully tilt the jar so that the depth of wine beneath the inlet of the syphon is kept at an effective level. In this way, nearly all the clear wine can be removed and only the sediment is left to be discarded. If for any reason there is a worthwhile quantity of wine left in the jar, pour this into a sterilised narrow bottle, fit a cork and stand the bottle in a cold place for a few days until the wine is again clear. Carefully syphon or pour this into the bulk of the wine, so that no more than necessary is wasted.

The wine to be racked must always be at a higher level than the empty jar. The greater the drop the faster the flow. The syphon tube can be prevented from moving and disturbing the sediment by passing it through a bung fitted with a vent hole (inset picture). Store red wine in amber jars to prevent the wine from fading or keep clear jars in the dark.

CHAPTER ELEVEN

Testing for acidity

As well as checking the sugar content of a must before adding more sugar, the experienced winemaker also checks the acidity before adding more acid.

The acidity can be expressed in two ways:

"fixed" acidity – the quantity of the combined acids in the must which can be measured by titration as a percentage of the volume of must;

"real" acidity – the degree or intensity of acidity as expressed by pH, the hydrogen ion concentration.

The real acidity is that tasted on the palate and is often thought to be more important than the fixed acidity. To be measured accurately, real acidity should be checked with a pH meter – a fairly expensive piece of laboratory equipment. A measurement that is sufficiently accurate for most winemakers can be obtained by the use of pH paper and a colour code. A treated absorbent paper is dipped into the liquid, left for a few moments to dry and the colour then compared with the code supplied. This can be in the broad bands of High, Normal or Low as shown by Boots Acid Indicator Paper or in finer gradations as shown by BDH indicator papers. A pH of 3.4 is regarded as ideal for most musts and wines.

Titration can be carried out in the home with a simple acidi-metric outfit consisting of a small pipette and flask together with a solution of 1% phenolphthalein in methyl alcohol in a bottle

Dip the indicator paper into the must. When it is dry compare it to the colour code on the packet to see if the acidity is high, normal or low.

fitted with a dropper and a bottle of a decinormal solution of sodium hydroxide. The kit is quite small and comes with detailed instructions. In general, 10 ml of the must is placed in the flask with approximately 25 ml distilled water *(as used for topping up car batteries)* and two drops of phenolphthalein. Sodium hydroxide is then run in to the flask which must be constantly agitated to mix the contents. As soon as a permanent faint pink tint is observed, the quantity of sodium hydroxide added is noted. Half that quantity multiplied by 1.4 gives the number of parts per thousand of mixed fruit acids in the must. For example, if 8 ml sodium hydroxide is added, half that figure is 4 and when multiplied by 1.4 equals 5.6. This would be an adequate fixed acid content for most wines. Dry light wines could be a little less, say, 4 ppt, sweet strong wines rather more, say, 7 ppt.

Carbon dioxide affects the reading and if the must is fermenting the sample should first be boiled to drive off the gas.

Red wine musts are more difficult to assess, and it helps to filter the sample first. A greyish colour indicates that the end point has been reached. A sheet of white paper under the flask, or a clear light behind it, makes it easier to see the colour change.

One level 5 ml spoonful of citric acid added to one gallon of must increases the fixed acidity by approximately 1 ppt.

CHAPTER TWELVE

Fermentation

It wasn't until the middle of the 19th century that Pasteur discovered that the fermentation of sugar into alcohol was caused by yeast. Since then scientists have discovered that it is actually caused by enzymes secreted in the yeast cell. The cell is so tiny it is invisible unless magnified some five hundred times. The enzymes act as catalysts and cause the changes in the molecular structure of the sugar without being changed themselves. The yeast cell contains a whole complex of enzymes, each one separately responsible for one of the different steps in the complicated chain of the reduction of the sugar.

In addition to ethyl alcohol, a number of different substances are produced including traces of other alcohols such as amyl, butyl and methyl, also glycerine, proprionic, succinic and valerianic acids, as well as large quantities of carbon dioxide. The molecules of sugar pass through the cell wall of the yeast, are converted, and the resulting substances then pass out of the cell. The alcohols and acids remain in the wine and the carbon dioxide comes off as gas, rising to the surface in tiny bubbles that burst with a low, hissing sound.

Whilst fairly tolerant, experience and experiment show that yeast functions best in certain conditions. The yeast needs:

1. An acid solution.

2. Access to nitrogen. *(Access to oxygen is needed for reproduction but not for fermentation.)*

A yeast starter is necessary when making country wines, in particular, to ensure a quick-starting fermentation and to prevent spoilage of the must (see p. 35). Wines are cloudy during fermentation due to the presence of solid particles in suspension and the activity of the yeast. As fermentation nears its end some yeast cells die and fall to the bottom, forming the 'lees'. Move the wine to a cool place to reduce movement caused by thermal currents. The removal of the lees and the addition of one Campden tablet per gallon stimulates the clearing process.

3. A fairly steady temperature in the range of 10°C to 30°C *(50°F to 86°F)*.

   At both ends, fermentation is slow and at much below or above these figures, it stops altogether. For white wines 15°C *(59°F)* is recommended and for red wines 20°C *(68°F)*. Reactivation of dormant yeast is best at 40°C *(104°F)*.

4. A modest sugar content.

   If the specific gravity of the must is too high, i.e. much above 1.100, the weight of the sugar kills the yeast by osmosis. The yeast fluid, weighing less than the heavy syrup, is squeezed out through the cell wall to create an equilibrium. The cell then collapses in on itself and dies. For this reason it makes good sense to start a fermentation with a modest sugar content, around 1.080 or less. When you know how much extra sugar is required, it can be added in portions at weekly intervals. The alcohol tolerance of the yeast is slowly built up and the yeast is kept well and active.

   This method of adding sugar in small portions each week is especially important in the making of high alcohol wines such as aperitifs and dessert wines. In this way the yeast can ferment up to 17% or 18% of alcohol.

5. A slow fermentation.

   This is preferred to a fast one as it frequently produces a wine of much better bouquet and flavour than one which is over in a week or so. During a fast fermentation at a high temperature, many esters and aldehydes, formed by the interaction of acids with alcohols and the reduction of alcohol by oxygen, are driven off with the carbon dioxide.

Too high a fermentation temperature can also cause the formation of acetic acid, and encourage the growth of spoilage bacteria.

A cooler fermentation on the other hand gives all the interactions and reactions a better chance of completion. In a very warm atmosphere, Australia for example, the musts are refrigerated to obtain a cool fermentation temperature. In the United Kingdom atmospheric temperatures are rarely high enough to worry the home winemaker. With the spread of central heating and double glazing, however, homes are now much warmer. Serious consideration should, therefore, be given to finding the most suitable place for fermentation, especially of white wines. Remember that the fermentation itself generates a few degrees of warmth. It is worth checking the actual temperature of the must from time to time.

Stuck Ferments

Most fermentations are trouble free. Occasionally, however, a must will stop fermenting prematurely or for no apparent reason. First check that the fermentation has not been completed. A hydrometer reading will soon tell you whether the fermentation is stuck or complete. If it is stuck, then pour the must through a sterilised funnel into a sterilised jar or bin. Pour it so the must splashes and thereby absorbs some oxygen. This not only stimulates the yeast to reproduce itself and increase the size of the viable colony but also disperses dissolved carbon dioxide which can inhibit yeast activity. At the same time check that the temperature of the must is neither too high nor too low. If it is, move it to a warmer or cooler position. Check also from your records whether sufficient acid and nutrient was included in the must. A lack of either can cause the yeast to stop fermenting. It may not be too late to add some more diammonium phosphate and vitamin B, dissolved in a little tepid water with half a teaspoonful of citric acid.

If all this fails, make up a fresh yeast starter and when it is working well, add to it an equal quantity of stuck must. When this is working, add another equal quantity. Continue adding equal quantities of stuck must to the fermenting must until all is mixed and working. It is difficult to re-start a stuck must just by adding a fresh yeast to it, but this way is easy. Happily the problem doesn't often arise, especially if you ensure at the outset that there is sufficient acid and nutrient in the must, that a pure wine yeast has been activated before adding it to the must and that a correct temperature has been maintained.

CHAPTER THIRTEEN

Maturation and storage

When fermentation is complete, the dross of pulp and dead yeast cells, no longer supported by the ever rising bubbles of carbon dioxide, begins to settle on the bottom of the fermentation vessel. At first the wine in the neck of the jar becomes clear and there is an obvious shading in clarity from the top to the bottom. This process can be encouraged by stirring in wine finings and moving the vessel to the coolest place that can be found. Thermal currents that support the minute particles of dross are reduced in the cooler position.

After a few days in the cool, whether finings have been added or not, the wine will be clear enough for its first racking. **Removing the wine from the sediment as soon as possible is most important.** Failure to do so will cause an unpleasant smell and taste in the wine as decomposing pulp and dead yeast cells smell like rotting cabbage!

Keep the outlet of the syphon tube beneath the surface of the racked wine to prevent splashing and minimise the absorption of air. As soon as the racking is finished, crush one Campden tablet and add it to the clearing wine. This will prevent oxidation of the wine due to the absorption of air during the racking, as well as protecting the wine from infection during its storage.

If the receiving jar is no longer full and there is no wine of a similar style with which to top it up, cold boiled water may be used. Alternatively, you can add some sterilised glass marbles or beach pebbles. These take up space, raise the level of the wine and push out the air. A good softened cork or moistened rubber bung should be fitted into the neck of the jar leaving only about 2.5 cm *(1 in)* air gap between the bottom of the bung and the surface of the wine in the neck of the jar.

A larger air gap than this is, however, essential in the storage and maturation of sherry style wines. The surface are of the wine should be the full diameter of the jar and about 10 cm *(4 in)* from the bottom of the plug of cotton wool used instead of a bung. The wool permits the passage of air during the expansion and contraction of the wine due to changes in atmospheric temperature, but filters out any micro-organisms that may be in the air.

The jar should now be labelled with its name, the date started and the date racked. Place it in a cool dark store, free from vibrations. The coolness encourages further clarification and the deposit of sediment, discourages the development of any spoilage organisms that may be present and ensures an orderly development of the chemical reactions which so improve the bouquet and flavour of a wine during maturation. The darkness prevents oxidation and fading. If a dark store is not available, keep your jars covered with thick cloth, brown paper or anything that excludes the light. A place free from vibrations is desirable as movement in the wine would inhibit the maturing processes. A cellar or garage is ideal.

Within six or eight weeks the wine should be crystal clear and ready for its second racking. Then return the new full jar (not quite full if sherry style) to the cool dark store until it is ready for bottling. The one exception to this is Madeira style wine, which now benefits from a period of six months or so in a very warm store – close to a hot water tank for example. A wine temperature of about 50°C *(122°F)* helps to give the characteristic caramel flavour of Madeira wine.

Wine should be stored at a constant, cool temperature of 10°C (50°F), in the dark if possible, and should not be disturbed. Bottles with driven corks should be stored on their sides in suitable racks to keep the corks moist. If stored in bulk (in a demijohn) the wine should come to within one inch of the bung. Wine that is almost fermented out can be placed in the cold store to speed up the clearing process. Everything should be fully labelled and recorded.

Some wines mature much more quickly than others. Light, white wines are often best matured in bottles as soon as they are bright. Wines made from concentrates, canned fruit, jams and fruit juices usually mature much more quickly than wines made from fresh, frozen or dried fruits, or from vegetables, which need the longest period of storage. Strong dessert wines and aperitifs also need longer storage. Each wine is different, even fruits vary from year to year according to the quality of the crop. There is no firm rule and each wine must be judged on its individual merits. A little experience soon indicates those wines that taste young and in need of longer storage.

Bottling

When the time for bottling comes, select some half size wine bottles as well as some of standard size, especially if you are new to winemaking and have only a limited stock. Sterilise each bottle, drain it, then place the bottles in a suitable position beneath the jar. Repeat the syphoning process described and fill each bottle to within 2.5 cm *(1 in)* or less of where the bottom of the cork will be. The corks should be well softened by thoroughly soaking them in a sulphite solution. For this use a small basin and weight the corks down with a saucer to keep them submerged within the sulphite solution.

Shake the surplus solution from each cork, place it in the corking tool and fit it flush into the neck of the bottle. Wipe the moisture off the surface of the cork and fit a plastic or foil cap over it. Label the bottle with the name and date of the wine and store it on its side in the same cool dark store where it was matured. A few weeks or months in bottle does wonders for a wine. Proper wine racks should be used for preference, but empty bottle cartons laid on their sides will do.

Casks

Some winemakers like to store their red wines for a while in an oak cask. Experts disagree about the value of this for small quantities of wine, and some have tried adding oak shavings to a wine to get that attractive oaky flavour.

Size is important. No cask with a capacity of less than 25 litres *(5½ gallons)* is suitable for storing wine. In smaller casks the surface area of the wine touching the inside of the cask is too great compared with the volume, and the wine rapidly oxidises.

Make sure the cask is new, or has never been used for vinegar and was cleaned and sterilised after last being used. Remove the bung, put your nose to the hole and inhale deeply. If the cask does not smell clean, have nothing to do with it.

If the cask is clean enough and the right size, a third factor must then be taken into account – where to put it. Casks of wine should be stored in a cool dry atmosphere. In a humid or damp place there will be a tendency for the alcohol rather than the water to evaporate from the wine. This soon causes deterioration. Furthermore, when full the cask will be very heavy. It must, therefore, be somewhere where it can be filled and emptied without being moved.

If the cask is still suitable soak it in clean cold water to swell the staves and stop seepage between the joints.

Next pour into the cask a gallon of boiling water in which a handful of washing soda has been dissolved. Fit the bung and roll the cask around for as long as you can ensuring that every part of the inner surface is washed time and time again.

Remove the bung, drain the cask and rinse it with clean cold water. Make up a strong sulphite solution of, say, ten Campden tablets and 10 ml *(2 tsp)* citric acid in one gallon of cold water and again roll the cask around and around until the staves are thoroughly soaked in the sulphite solution. A Chempro solution would also be very effective. If the latter is used, the cask must be rinsed several times in clean cold water after the Chempro has been drained out.

Then sweeten the cask with a bottle of sound wine, rolling it around and around as before. When this has been drained out, the cask may be put into position on supporting chocks or a cradle so that the belly staves are standing clear.

Fill the cask to the bung with wine, press home the bung, and label the cask, noting especially the date. As wine evaporates slightly in the cask, although not in the bottle, remove the bung every week and top up the cask with the same or a similar wine. It is important not to allow an airspace beneath the bung or the wine will become over oxidised and taste flat and dull. Six months in such a cask is long enough for even the most robust wine. The wine should now be bottled and stored for a few more months.

The cask should be washed out, sterilised and immediately refilled to prevent it drying out and becoming leaky or infected. If you have no wine ready to put into it, fill it with a sulphite solution and replace this every month.

Apart from the maturation of a single wine, a cask can be very useful for blended wines.

Blending

As in the commercial world, not every wine turns out perfectly. These can be greatly improved by blending them together. Select only wines that are sound but uninspiring. Wines with off-flavours of any kind must not be used. Syphon the sound wines into a suitable container, endeavouring to mix opposites, e.g. a wine that is too sharp with one that is too bland; one that is too dry with one that is too sweet. Mix them all together, fit an airlock for a few days, then if no refermentation occurs add one Campden tablet per gallon and leave the blend to homogenise for about one month. It may then be bottled, stored for a while longer and then served.

Soak corks thoroughly in a sulphite solution so they are softened as well as sterilised. Those with a flange can be easily removed and replaced by hand. Such 'stopper' corks are used for strong sherry-type wines, those to be stored upright and drunk young, and for wines entered in competitions. Straight driven corks, fitted with one of the tools illustrated, are for wines matured on their sides. They should be fully driven home with no part visible above the neck of the bottle.

Any wine may be used in the blend as long as it is clean and sound. Colours and styles may be mixed. A further fermentation often occurs, but the blend usually clears extremely well and the resultant wine is very much better than the sum of its parts. Too many poor wines are drunk unblended when they could have been improved.

Winemaids

A Winemaid is a polythene bag laminated with nylon 66, Sarinex or other strong and suitable material and fitted with a tap. The bag when filled is supported inside a carton. Present Winemaids hold five litres and are relatively expensive, but they do save on bottling time. When a wine has been fully matured in bulk, it can be syphoned into a Winemaid, and then dispensed as needed. The bag collapses as the wine is withdrawn so there is never any air space inside. The wine does not, therefore, oxidise and deteriorate as it would in a half empty bottle. The storage life of wine in a Winemaid is up to six months.

One Winemaid with white wine can be kept in the refrigerator and another with red in the kitchen. A glass or a decanter of either wine is then always ready for serving. These containers are useful for everyday table wines, but higher quality dessert wines are best bottled and stored in the traditional manner.

When a Winemaid is empty the tap can be removed, and the bag washed out with a sulphite solution and refilled. They are a great boon to the busy winemaker, with a fair stock of wine, who serves wine every day at the family meal.

CHAPTER FOURTEEN

Problems in wine making

Even in a well-run commercial winery there are sometimes problems, and there can also be a few at home, although most can be avoided by good hygiene, the choice of good ingredients and a proper understanding of the methods.

The most common cause of complaint is no bouquet and poor flavour – or worse – an unpleasant smell and taste.

Bouquet

Acid is the very cornerstone of bouquet and flavour. If you failed to include sufficient acid in the must, the wine will have little bouquet. If you are using a fairly bland ingredient then you must also include something to help create bouquet. Grape in one form or another is ideal, a few scented rose petals, or dried orange blossom or elderflowers may also be used, but use them meanly. An overpowering bouquet can also fail to please. Once the wine is finished it is too late to doctor it, but blending it with a wine with a pleasanter bouquet is the best remedy.

Poor flavour or a medicinal taste

This is also caused by lack of acid in the must during fermentation. Blending is the remedy.

Unpleasant smell and taste

This can be caused by poor ingredients; for example, using

bruised or damaged apples already affected by the vinegar bacteria carried by wasps, flies and other insects, without cutting out the bad portions and sterilising the rest in a sulphite solution. Bruised peaches, plums, grapes, indeed any fruit that has brown patches from bruising is likely to impart a dull flat taste to the wine. The fruit will have become partly oxidised.

Leaving fruit, must or wine partly exposed to the air can also cause acetification – a vinegar taint – or oxidation. If the taint is only slight you may be able to sweeten it sufficiently to mask it, or the wine may be used in cooking. A wine badly tainted with vinegar taste could be turned into vinegar – see chapter 30. A slightly oxidised wine might be saved by refermentation. Make up a starter bottle with a fresh Tokay yeast and add the poor wine, sweetened if necessary with 250 g *(9oz)* sugar, to the starter in ever increasing quantities; half a pint at first, then when that is working add a pint and when that is working add a quart and so on until the whole gallon is fermenting. When fermentation is finished, rack, top up, add one Campden tablet and seal.

The importance of keeping jars and bottles full and securely sealed cannot be over-emphasised in the prevention of oxidation and airborne infection *(with the exception of sherry style wines).*

Putrefaction

Some wines offered to the author for an opinion have tasted of rotten cabbage! The wine was left on its sediment after fermentation had finished. Particles of fruit pulp and vegetable debris, as well as dead yeast cells, decompose and impart this foul smell and taste to the wine. There is no known remedy and the wine should be discarded. Prevention is simple: rack the wine as soon as fermentation finishes and as soon as a further deposit appears. Keep the wine clean. Some winemakers always add finings after the first racking to assist in clearing the wine quickly. While this is a safe precaution, it is not always necessary since most wines clear quickly by themselves. Finings nearly always remove some of the tannin in the wine as well as the unwanted suspended solids. There is a fear, too, that they may also remove some of the other flavour ingredients.

Other winemakers carry this process a step further and always filter their wines. The same objection applies, but with the added risk of oxidation as the wine drips into a container full of air.

Fining and filtering may be looked upon as a last resort when the wine fails to clear or show signs of clearing within six or eight weeks of the first racking. If you must filter, place a crushed

Campden tablet in the empty jar before you commence. In most wines, racking, the addition of one Campden tablet per gallon and storage in a cold place, is enough to make the wine clear and to sink the suspended particles which can then be removed by a further racking.

Bad egg smell

This rare complaint is caused by lack of vitamin B_1 in the must during fermentation. The inclusion of concentrated grape juice, sultanas or raisins prevents it; so does one 3 mg tablet per gallon of vitamin B_1 *(Benerva tablets)*. There is no later remedy for this problem. Discard the wine.

Pear-drop smell

This is caused by a lack of nitrogen in the must. The yeast needs it during fermentation, so always add some nutrient. One tablet or half a teaspoonful of ammonium phosphate or sulphate per gallon is usually enough. Concentrated grape juice, sultanas or raisins also help. No known remedy; discard the wine.

Bitter almond smell

If fruit stones are left in a must, especially if one or two are damaged, this pungent smell develops. It is caused by the production of prussic acid from the kernels of large stones and from broken pips of smaller fruit. Be very careful not to crush or cut pips and always exclude the stones from the large family of plums, peaches, apricots, etc. No known remedy, so discard the wine.

Geranium smell

Fairly rare, this smell is caused by the breakdown of potassium sorbate when it is used on its own to stop fermentation in the production of sweet, low alcohol wines. Potassium sorbate or any tablet containing this substance e.g. Sorbistat or Stabiliser, must be used in conjunction with one Campden tablet per gallon.

Sulphur

Too much sulphur in a wine can cause an unpleasant smell. One or two Campden tablets per gallon is perfectly safe but more than this may result in an off smell. This will eventually disappear especially when the wine is aerated.

Hazes

These can be caused not only by suspended solids in the wine

Fining always comes before filtering. Leave the jar overnight in a cool place before adding the fining agent. If the wine still doesn't clear filtering can save a lot of waiting. The top picture shows a filter kit in which the wine is treated with crystals and powder in a mixing bucket, then strained through a bag in a second bucket which stands on top of a demijohn. The bottom picture shows an exploded view of a filter kit in which the wine is syphoned through an enclosed funnel containing a filter pad.

but also by pectin, starch and **metal**. To check if pectin is the cause pour two tablespoonsful of methylated spirits into a small bottle, add one 5 ml spoonful of wine and shake the bottle vigorously. Leave it for up to an hour and if strings, clots or dots appear in the mixture the haze is caused by pectin. The cure is to add a pectolytic enzyme.

Starch can be produced during the making of grain wines. It can be proved by the addition of two or three drops of household iodine to two tablespoonsful of wine. If the wine turns blue or darkens then there is starch in the wine. The remedy is to add fungal amylase in the quantity recommended by the manufacturer.

Metal haze can be recognised by a metallic taste in the wine. It is caused by allowing the must or wine to come into contact with iron, lead, copper, brass or zinc. The remedy is too dangerous for use in the home and the wine should be poured down the drain.

Ropiness

Very occasionally a wine will develop a shiny, oily appearance. It is caused by ropes of lactic acid bacteria. The remedy is to add two crushed Campden tablets per gallon and to break up the ropes with a wooden spoon. Move the wine to a cool place and within two days the wine will look normal and there will be a deposit of dead bacteria on the bottom of the jar. Rack the wine into a clean jar; the wine can be drunk when it is mature.

Malo-lactic ferment

Other members of the family of lactic acid bacteria can change malic acid into lactic acid and carbon dioxide. The gas may blow the cork or simply make the wine petillant. The wine will be found smoother and less sharp than previously.

CHAPTER FIFTEEN

Serving wine well

On the Continent wine is served at table much as water is served in Britain. The care of wine is taken for granted. White wines are served cool, red wines at room temperature and sparkling wines well chilled. Carafes are commonplace, appropriate glasses are used and a suitable wine chosen to go with a particular food. The proper serving of wine is a natural phenomenon.

Not so in Britain, where there is no tradition of serving wines in such a way as to complement the food. This is a great pity. The pleasure of wines can be greatly enhanced if they are served more thoughtfully, and this is especially true of homemade wines.

Selecting the wine

The old dictum of red wine with red meats and game, and white wine with fish, pork and poultry, is based on centuries of experience. Not the experience alone of connoisseurs, but also that of peasants and the people at large, both in town and country. It is not some law that cannot be broken, but it is a habit of life of millions of people, generation after generation.

Aperitifs

Many wines may be served as an aperitif before a meal. A dryish white table wine, a sparkling wine, a herb flavoured wine, an oxidised wine with a sherry flavour: all these may be served as long as they are cold.

Table wines

The white table wine is sometimes carried on into the fish course of the meal if one is served. For roast meats, meat pies and puddings, casseroles, kebabs and fondues, stews, sausages and liver a dry red wine will be found best. Select your best red wines for roast beef and lamb joints and serve them unchilled. Red table wines need to be dry to offset the fattiness of the meat – however lean that may be. The dessert course calls for a really sweet and full white wine to match the sweetness and richness of the food. But this wine, too, should be served cold.

Dessert wines

After the meal or with cheese, a full, rich, sweet red or white wine may be served. These are the port and Madeira style wines and they should be served unchilled.

Parties and picnics

No wine seems quite so good at a party or picnic as a nicely chilled rosé that is not quite dry. The colour enhances the gaiety of the occasion, the balance and texture of the wine is just right for sandwiches, sausage rolls, quiche, cheese dips and similar savoury morsels. For picnics you will need to carry it in a refrigerated container.

Temperatures

White wines, aperitifs, sparkling and rosé wines may be cooled by standing them in the refrigerator for an hour or two. Red wines are best left on a table in a warm kitchen for four or five hours. Preferably draw the cork beforehand. Indeed, it is worth decanting the wine and leaving it in the decanter with the stopper in place.

Decanters

All wines look best when served from a plain, glass decanter. The clarity and colour of the wine can be easily seen and so gladden the eye. This is much to be preferred to a green bottle with a large label stuck on the side, so hiding the wine from view. Furthermore, red wine is better able to absorb both air and warmth while in a decanter. As a result it reaches the glass in a much more matured manner than when poured from a recently opened bottle.

Glasses

Glasses for red table wine are usually spherical in shape and are called goblets, while those for white wine are somewhat taller and thinner and usually called tulips. Sparkling wines are best served from an even longer and thinner glass called a flute. This encourages the bubbles of gas to sparkle all the way up the glass. Aperitif wines are served in a smaller version of the flute called a copita. Glasses made of colourless, plain glass, free from embellishment set off the wine to its best advantage. They should be filled to between one half and two thirds of their capacity. This looks aesthetically pleasing, the wine is not spilled when carried and room is left in the glass for the bouquet to develop on the surface of the wine and be retained there. Glasses of wine, whether red or white, look best when served from a silver salver or from a white cloth. The appearance of the wine is diminished when placed on dark wood or a coloured tray. Keep your decanters fresh and clean by washing them in warm soapy water immediately after use, then rinsing them in plenty of cold water. Drain them well before drying and store upright in a cupboard. Polish them with a clean dry glass cloth before use, so that the wine can be shown off to its best advantage.

Company

Good wine needs not only good food to complement it, but also good company. There is no merit in serving your best wine to those who prefer beer or spirits, or a fruit squash. Save your wine for someone who will appreciate it to the full. Indeed, there is an added art in serving the wine appropriate to the company as well as to the food.

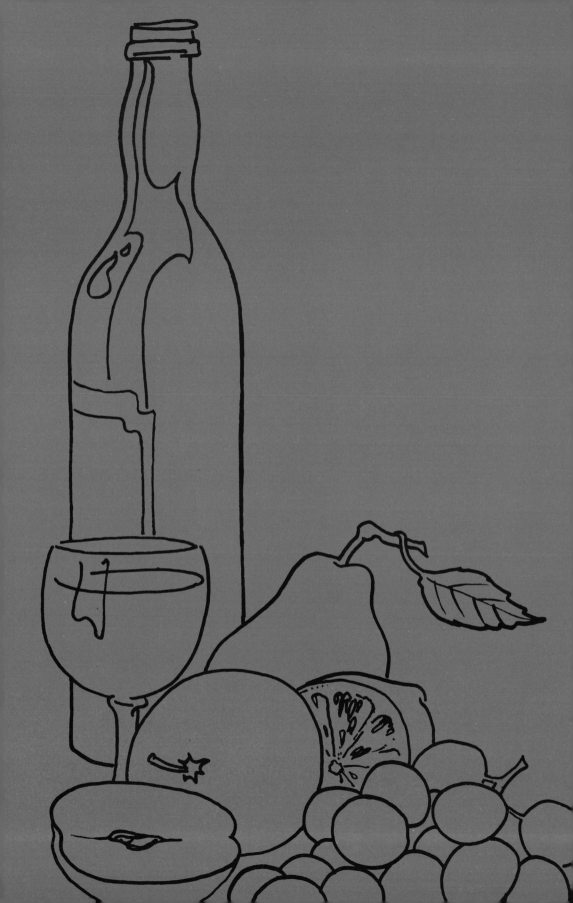

CHAPTER SIXTEEN

Making country wines

The range

A wide variety of ingredients have been mentioned in the recipes in an endeavour to meet the needs of as many wine-makers as possible. Those people living in town houses and flats may have limited facilities and access only to supermarkets. They will find recipes that use fruit juices, canned and dried fruits, jams and pie fillings. But people with large gardens who grow their own fruit and vegetables will want to use the recipes using fresh ingredients – the fresher the better. Still others have access to hedgerow fruits and flowers from the countryside and there are recipes especially for them, too.

The quantities

Although the recipes necessarily give the quantities to use for each ingredient, these figures are not sacred. A little more or less of most of the ingredients is not likely to affect the result significantly.

Larger quantities of wine from any recipe can be made by increasing the quantity of each ingredient, *except yeast*, in the same proportion. A sachet of yeast is usually sufficient to ferment five or six gallons of must.

Metrication

Reasonably accurate comparisons with Imperial measurements

Grapes, apples, pears, oranges, pineapple, parsnips, parsley, carrots, potatoes and turnips are only some of the fruits and vegetables which can be turned into superb wines following the recipes on these pages.

have been made. It does not matter very much whether you use metric or Imperial or a mixture of both. The precise differences are usually minimal, e.g. 1 lb 10 oz sugar *(750 g)* a difference of less than ½ oz, or, to put it another way, just under 2%.

Concentrated grape juice

Because the recipes are based on one gallon units, the quantity of concentrated grape juice recommended is the Boots miniature can containing *approx.* 250 g *(9 oz)*. For either a four or five gallon batch you can use the entire contents of a 1 kg can.

Whenever possible, use a concentrated grape juice similar in style to the wine being made and the yeast being used. Under E.E.C. laws it is not legal to use proper wine names to describe concentrated grape juice. The descriptions now given on labels, however, may be translated into wine types as follows:

Crisp dry red	— Beaujolais type
Full dry red	— Burgundy type
Light dry red	— Claret type
Dry red	— Bordeaux type (red)
Crisp dry white	— Chablis type
Dry white	— Bordeaux type (white)
Full dry white	— Graves type
Sweet white	— Sauternes type
Delicate dry white	— Moselle type
Med-dry full white	— Hock type
Med-dry smooth white	— Liebfraumilch type
Dry rosé	— Rosé type

Concentrated grape juice alternatives

Concentrated grape juice is not an essential ingredient in itself, although it is easier to use than the alternatives and therefore recommended in the recipes. But grape in some form or another does ensure a good fermentation and a vinous finish to the wine. It is, therefore, very strongly recommended that to obtain the best results you always include some grapes in one form or another.

Fresh grapes may be used 1 kg *(2 lb)* to the gallon or washed and chopped sultanas or raisins at the rate of 225 g *(8 oz)* to the gallon. In general, use sultanas for white wines, raisins for red wines and muscatels for dessert wines. Dried currants may be used for rosés, but on the whole they are less satisfactory than sultanas or raisins.

Pectic enzyme

The quantity to use is given on the label of both the powder and liquid forms. It varies from one manufacturer to another but one level 5 ml spoonful is usually enough when making one gallon of wine.

Nutrient

Many yeasts are sold in sachets containing a sufficient quantity of nutrient. Where this is not so, a single nutrient tablet or 2.5 ml of ammonium phosphate or ammonium sulphate or a mixture of both is usually adequate for one gallon. When making wines of a high alcohol content, it is wise to add one 3 mg tablet of vitamin B to help the yeast.

Apples

Apples are the most abundant of English fruits. In autumn there is often a glut. They make a splendid white wine on their own and blend well with all other fruits to make many different flavoured wines. They can be stored in a freezer – sliced and sulphited for later use. People who do not want to use the fresh fruit can substitute 2 litres of pure, unsweetened apple juice for the 9 lb of apples in any of the recipes that follow. If possible buy the cartons of juice from different sources and mix them so that the must contains the juice of a number of different kinds of apples.

Fruit in syrup

These are, of course, canned and bottled fruits. The total approximate weight given in the recipes represents the total weight of whatever cans and/or bottles you are able to use. If you have, say, four cans of varying weights, provided the total weight is approximately the quantity given in the recipe, you will have sufficient.

1. Wash the apples in plenty of cold water to remove mud, dust, leaves, grass, slugs and insects.

2. Cut away any bruised or damaged parts and crush the rest as finely as possible.

3. Pour 3 pints of cold water into a fermenting bin, add a crushed Campden tablet, pectic enzyme and citric acid.

4. As each bag of apples is crushed empty them at once into the bin to avoid browning.

5. Put a plate on top of the apples and cover the bin for 24 hours while the pectic enzyme reduces the fruit pectin. Check the specific gravity and acidity.

6. Add the concentrated grape juice, tannin, nutrient and contents of the yeast starter bottle. Cover and ferment on the pulp for 7 days with the fruit submerged or pressed down twice a day.

7. Pour the apple pulp into a sterilised nylon straining bag set in a sterilised press.

8. Apply steady pressure. When the flow of juice slows down, stir up the apple pulp and press again. Do this several times.

9. When all the juice has been extracted the 'cake' should look dry and firm. If it isn't, press again, then discard the fruit.

10. Stir in the required amount of sugar (in syrup form) and top up with cold water.

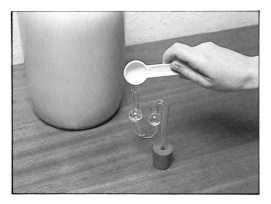

11. Fit an airlock filled with a sulphite solution and make sure the seal is effective.

12. Leave the jar in a warm place to ferment. This heating tray will hold two demijohns. Then rack and mature as usual.

Apple 1

A dry wine, good as an aperitif

eating and cooking apples	4kg	*9lb*
concentrated white grape juice	*approx.* 250g	*9oz*
sugar	740g	*1lb 10oz*
water	1.7 litres	*3 pints*
citric acid	10ml	*2 tsp*
tannin	2.5ml	*½ tsp*
pectic enzyme		
Campden tablets		
nutrient		
Champagne yeast		
finings		

1. Pour the water into a mashing bin containing the acid, pectic enzyme and one crushed Campden tablet.

2. Wash the apples, remove any bad parts, cut them into small pieces including skins and cores, or crush them into a coarse mash. Drop them into the bin without delay to avoid browning. If they are available, a few quince, crab apples or cydonia japonica may be added to improve the bouquet and flavour.

3. Cover the bin and leave it in a warm place for twenty-four hours.

4. Stir in the concentrated grape juice, tannin, nutrient and activated yeast. Replace the cover and ferment on the pulp for seven days, pressing down the floating fruit twice daily if you cannot keep it submerged the whole time.

5. Strain out, press dry and discard the fruit, stir in the sugar, pour the must into a jar, top up with cold boiled water if necessary, fit an airlock and ferment out to dryness.

6. Rack into a clean jar, top up, add one Campden tablet, bung tight, label and store for two months.

7. If the wine is still hazy, add some proprietary brand of wine finings or two tablespoonsful of fresh milk. Shake the jar well to disperse the finings through the wine and leave it in a cold place for about one week, by which time a further deposit will be seen and the wine should be bright.

9. Rack again, add a half Campden tablet, and store for six or eight months before bottling.

9. Keep for a further three months. If the wine is too dry for your palate add one saccharin pellet per bottle.

Apple 2

A dry wine made with apple juice

unsweetened apple juice	2 litres	*3½ pints*
concentrated white grape juice	*approx.* 250g	*9oz*
water	2 litres	*3½ pints*
sugar	900g	*2lb*
citric acid	10ml	*2 tsp*
tannin	2.5ml	*½ tsp*
pectic enzyme		
nutrient		
G.P. yeast		
Campden tablet		

1. Mix the apple and grape juice, water, citric acid, tannin and pectic enzyme together in a fermentation jar. Seal and leave for twenty-four hours.

2. Add the nutrient and active yeast, fit an airlock and ferment for two days.

3. Remove some of the must, dissolve the sugar in it, return it to the jar, top up with cold boiled water, replace the airlock and ferment out to dryness.

4. Leave the wine in a cold place for two days then rack it into a clean jar. Top up, add one Campden tablet, bung tight, then label and store in a cool place.

5. As soon as the wine is bright syphon it into bottles and store until it is six months old. Serve it cold as a light dry table wine or aperitif.

A mixture of apples, including a few crab apples if you can get them, makes the best apple wine.

Apple & Banana

A sweet dessert wine

mixed eating and cooking apples	4.5kg	*10lb*
very ripe bananas		4
concentrated white grape juice	*approx.* 250g	*9oz*
sugar	900g	*2lb*
water	1.7 litres	*3 pints*
citric acid	10ml	*2 tsp*
tannin	2.5ml	*½ tsp*
pectic enzyme		
Campden tablets		
nutrient		
Sauternes yeast		
wine finings		
potassium sorbate		

1. Wash, crush or cut the apples into small pieces including the skin and core but excluding damaged parts. Drop them at once into a bin containing the water, acid, pectic enzyme and one crushed Campden tablet.

2. Peel and mash the bananas and add to the apples. Cover and leave for twenty-four hours.

3. Stir in the concentrated grape juice (sweet style for preference), tannin, activated yeast and nutrient, and ferment on the pulp for five days keeping the fruit submerged.

4. Strain out, press dry and discard the pulp, stir in the sugar, pour the must into a jar, fit an airlock and ferment down to S.G. 1.016.

5. Rack into a clean jar containing 1g potassium sorbate, one Campden tablet and some wine finings. Top up, bung tight, label and store in a cold place.

6. As soon as the wine is bright, rack again. Mature this wine in bulk for one year before bottling. Serve it cool as a sweet dessert wine.

Apple & Bilberry 1

A dry wine, fresh or frozen bilberries

mixed eating and cooking apples	4kg	*9lb*
fresh or frozen bilberries	225g	*½lb*
concentrated grape juice		
(red or white)	*approx.* 250g	*9oz*
sugar	680g	*1½lb*
water	1.7 litres	*3 pints*
citric acid	5ml	*1 tsp*
tannin	2.5ml	*½ tsp*
pectic enzyme		
Campden tablets		
nutrient		
Burgundy yeast		

1. Wash, crush or cut the apples into small pieces including the skin and core, but excluding the damaged parts. Drop them at once into a bin containing the water, acid, pectic enzyme and one crushed Campden tablet.

2. Stalk, wash and crush the bilberries and add them to the apples. Cover and leave for twenty-four hours.

3. Stir in the concentrated grape juice, tannin, activated yeast and nutrient. Ferment on the pulp for five days keeping the fruit submerged.

4. Strain out, press dry and discard the pulp, stir in the sugar, pour the must into a jar, top up, fit an airlock and ferment out to dryness.

5. Move the jar to a cold place for two days, then rack the wine into a clean jar, top up and add one Campden tablet. Bung tight, label and store until the wine is bright.

6. Rack again and store for one year. Serve as a dry table wine.

NOTE:
2 lb fresh Cypriot or Almeria grapes may be used instead of the concentrate. Wash, crush and add the grapes to the apples at the outset.

Apple & Bilberry 2

A dry wine made with bottled bilberries

mixed eating and cooking apples	4kg	*9lb*
bilberries in sugar syrup	450g	*1lb*
concentrated grape juice		
(red or white)	*approx.* 250g	*9oz*
sugar	680g	*1½lb*
water	1.7 litres	*3 pints*
citric acid	5ml	*1 tsp*
tannin	2.5ml	*½ tsp*
pectic enzyme		
Campden tablets		
nutrient		
Burgundy yeast		

1. Wash, crush or cut the apples into small pieces including the skin and core, but excluding damaged parts. Drop them at once into a bin containing the water, acid, pectic enzyme and one crushed Campden tablet.

2. Strain out and crush the bilberries, then add them and the syrup to the apples. Cover and leave for twenty-four hours.

3. Stir in the concentrated grape juice, tannin, activated yeast and nutrient. Ferment on the pulp for five days keeping the fruit submerged.

4. Strain out, press dry and discard the pulp, stir in the sugar, pour the must into a jar, top up, fit an airlock and ferment out to dryness.

5. Move the jar to a cold place for two days, then rack the wine into a clean jar, top up and add one Campden tablet. Bung tight, label and store until the wine is bright.

6. Rack again and store for one year. Serve as a dry table wine.

Apple & Blackberry 1

A dry wine, fresh or frozen blackberries

mixed eating and cooking apples	4kg	*9lb*
fresh or frozen blackberries	450g	*1lb*
concentrated grape juice		
(red or white)	*approx.* 250g	*9oz*
sugar	680g	*1½lb*
water	1.7 litres	*3 pints*
citric acid	5ml	*1 tsp*
tannin	2.5ml	*½ tsp*
pectic enzyme		
Campden tablets		
nutrient		
Burgundy yeast		

1. Wash, crush or cut the apples into small pieces including the skin and core, but excluding damaged parts. Drop them at once into a bin containing the water, pectic enzyme, citric acid and one crushed Campden tablet.

2. Wash and crush the blackberries and add to the apples. Cover and leave for twenty-four hours.

3. Stir in the concentrated grape juice, tannin, activated yeast and nutrient. Ferment on the pulp for five days keeping the fruit submerged.

4. Strain out, press dry and discard the pulp, and stir in the sugar. Pour the must into a jar, top up, fit an airlock and ferment out to dryness.

5. Move the jar to a cold place for two days, then rack the wine into a clean jar, top up and add one Campden tablet. Bung tight, label and store until the wine is bright.

6. Rack again and store for one year. Serve as a dry table wine.

A dry wine made with bramble jelly

mixed eating and cooking apples	4kg	*9lb*
bramble jelly	450g	*1lb*
concentrated grape juice (red or white)	*approx.* 250g	*9oz*
sugar	450g	*1lb*
water	1.7 litres	*3 pints*
citric acid	5ml	*1 tsp*
tannin	2.5ml	*½ tsp*
pectic enzyme (double dose)		
Campden tablets		
nutrient		
Burgundy yeast		

1. Dissolve the jelly in half a pint of hot water and pour it into a polythene bin. Add the rest of the water (cold), the acid, pectic enzyme and one crushed Campden tablet.

2. Wash, crush or cut up the apples into small pieces including the skin and core but excluding damaged parts. Drop them at once into the bin. Cover and leave for twenty-four hours.

3. Stir in the concentrated grape juice, tannin, activated yeast and nutrient. Cover and ferment on the pulp for five days keeping the fruit submerged.

4. Strain out, press dry and discard the pulp, and stir in the sugar. Pour the must into a jar, top up, fit an airlock and ferment out to dryness.

5. Move the jar to a cold place for two days, then rack the wine into a clean jar, top up and add one Campden tablet. Bung tight, label and store until the wine is bright.

6. Rack again and store for six months. Serve as a dry table wine.

A dry wine made with pie filling

apple and blackberry pie filling	1.35kg	*3lb*
concentrated red grape juice	*approx.* 250g	*9oz*
sugar	680g	*1½lb*
water	3.4 litres	*6 pints*
citric acid	10ml	*2 tsp*
tannin	5ml	*1 tsp*
pectic enzyme		
amylase		
Campden tablets		
nutrient		
Bordeaux yeast		

1. Empty the pie filling into a polythene bin containing hot water and stir until the pulp is well dispersed. Cover and leave to cool.

2. If the label indicates that the pie filling includes 'edible starch', add the quantity of amylase recommended by the manufacturer – it varies. The amylase converts the starch to sugar. If it is omitted the wine may contain a starch haze. An alternative is to use a cereal yeast (*Saccharomyces diastaticus*) which is able to ferment a small amount of starch.

3. Stir in the concentrated grape juice, citric acid, tannin, pectic enzyme and one crushed Campden tablet. Cover and leave for twenty-four hours.

4. Add the activated yeast and nutrient and ferment on the pulp for three days.

5. Strain the must through a fine meshed nylon straining bag to remove the solid particles. Stir in the sugar and, when it is dissolved, pour the must into a fermentation jar, top up if necessary, fit an airlock and ferment out to dryness.

6. Move the jar to a cold place for a few days, then rack the wine into a clean jar, top up, add one Campden tablet, bung tight and store until the wine is bright.

7. Syphon into bottles, cork and label them and keep the wine until it is four months old. Serve as a light table wine.

NOTE:
Blackberry flavoured gelatine for making into party jellies is NOT suitable. Use only the jelly or conserve prepared from blackberries and sugar.

Fermentation on the pulp. Press down the floating fruit twice daily or keep it submerged with a china plate.

Apple & Blackcurrant 1

A dry wine made with fresh blackcurrants

mixed eating and cooking apples	4kg	*9lb*
fresh or frozen blackcurrants	450g	*1lb*
concentrated grape juice		
(red or white)	*approx.* 250g	*9oz*
sugar	680g	*1½lb*
water	1.7 litres	*3 pints*
tannin	2.5ml	*½ tsp*
no acid		
pectic enzyme		
Campden tablets		
nutrient		
Burgundy yeast		

1. Wash, crush or cut the apples into small pieces including the skin and core, but excluding damaged parts. Drop them at once into a bin containing the water, pectic enzyme and one crushed Campden tablet.

2. Stalk, wash and crush the blackcurrants and add them to the apples. Cover and leave for twenty-four hours.

3. Stir in the concentrated grape juice, tannin, activated yeast and nutrient and ferment on the pulp for five days keeping the fruit submerged.

4. Strain out, press dry and discard the pulp, and stir in the sugar. Pour the must into a jar, fit an airlock and ferment out to dryness.

5. Move the jar to a cold place for two days, then rack the wine into a clean jar, top up and add one Campden tablet. Bung tight, label and store until the wine is bright.

6. Rack again and store for one year. Serve as a table wine.

Apple & Blackcurrant 2

A dry wine made with tinned blackcurrants

mixed eating and cooking apples	4kg	*9lb*
blackcurrants in sugar syrup	450g	*1lb*
concentrated grape juice		
(red or white)	*approx.* 250g	*9oz*
sugar	680g	*1½lb*
water	1.7 litres	*3 pints*
citric acid	5ml	*1 tsp*
tannin	2.5ml	*½ tsp*
pectic enzyme		
Campden tablets		
nutrient		
Burgundy yeast		

1. Wash, crush or cut the apples into small pieces including the skin and core, but excluding damaged parts. Drop them at once into a bin containing the water, acid, pectic enzyme and one crushed Campden tablet.

2. Strain out and crush the blackcurrants, then add them and the syrup to the apples. Cover and leave for twenty-four hours.

3. Stir in the concentrated grape juice, tannin, activated yeast and nutrient. Ferment on the pulp for five days keeping the fruit submerged and the bin covered.

4. Strain out, press dry and discard the pulp, and stir in the sugar. Pour the must into a jar, top up, fit an airlock and ferment out to dryness.

5. Move the jar to a cold place for two days, then rack the wine into a clean jar, top up and add one Campden tablet. Bung tight, label and store until the wine is bright.

6. Rack again and store for one year.

Apple & Blackcurrant 3

A dry wine made with blackcurrant jam

mixed eating and cooking apples	4kg	*9lb*
blackcurrant jam	450g	*1lb*
concentrated grape juice		
(red or white)	approx. 250g	*9oz*
sugar	450g	*1lb*
water	1.7 litres	*3 pints*
citric acid	5ml	*1 tsp*
tannin	2.5ml	*½ tsp*
pectic enzyme (double dose)		
Campden tablets		
nutrient		
Burgundy yeast		

1. Dissolve the jam in half a pint of hot water and pour it into a polythene bin. Add the rest of the water (cold), the acid, pectic enzyme and one crushed Campden tablet.

2. Wash, crush or cut up the apples into small pieces including the skin and core but excluding damaged parts. Drop them at once into the bin. Cover and leave for forty-eight hours.

3. Stir in the concentrated grape juice, tannin, activated yeast and nutrient. Cover and ferment on the pulp for five days keeping the fruit submerged.

4. Strain out, press dry and discard the pulp, and stir in the sugar. Pour the must into a jar, top up, fit an airlock and ferment out to dryness.

5. Move the jar to a cold place for two days, then rack the wine into a clean jar, top up and add one Campden tablet. Bung tight, label and store until the wine is bright

6. Rack again and store for one year.

Apple & Blackcurrant 4

A dry table wine made with pie filling

apple and blackcurrant		
pie filling	1.35kg	*3lb*
concentrated red grape juice	approx. 250g	*9oz*
sugar	680g	*1½lb*
water	3.4 litres	*6 pints*
citric acid	10ml	*2 tsp*
tannin	5ml	*1 tsp*
pectic enzyme		
amylase		
Campden tablets		
nutrient		
Bordeaux yeast		

1. Empty the pie filling into a polythene bin containing hot water and stir until the pulp is well dispersed. Cover and leave to cool.

2. If the label indicates that the pie filling includes 'edible starch', add the quantity of amylase recommended by the manufacturer – it varies. The amylase converts the starch to sugar. If it is omitted the wine may contain a starch haze. An alternative is to use a cereal yeast (*Saccharomyces diastaticus*) which is able to ferment a small amount of starch.

3. Stir in the concentrated grape juice, citric acid, tannin, pectic enzyme and one crushed Campden tablet. Cover and leave for twenty-four hours.

4. Add the activated yeast and nutrient, cover and ferment on the pulp for three days.

5. Strain the must through a fine meshed nylon straining bag to remove the solid particles. Stir in the sugar and when it is dissolved pour the must into a fermentation jar, top up if necessary, fit an airlock and ferment out to dryness.

6. Move the jar to a cold place for a few days, then rack the wine into a clean jar. Add one Campden tablet and store until the wine is bright.

7. Syphon into bottles, cork and label them and keep the wine until it is four months old. Serve as a light table wine.

Apple & Damson 1

A dry wine made with fresh damsons

mixed eating and cooking apples	4kg *9lb*
fresh or frozen damsons	450g *1lb*
concentrated grape juice (red or white)	approx. 250g *9oz*
sugar	680g *1½lb*
water	1.7 litres *3 pints*
citric acid	5ml *1 tsp*
tannin	2.5ml *½ tsp*
pectic enzyme	
Campden tablets	
nutrient	
Burgundy yeast	

1. Wash, crush or cut the apples into small pieces including the skin and core, but excluding any damaged parts. Drop them at once into a bin containing the water, acid, pectic enzyme and one crushed Campden tablet.

2. Stalk, wash and stone the damsons and add them to the apples. Cover and leave for twenty-four hours.

3. Stir in the concentrated grape juice, tannin, activated yeast and nutrient. Cover and ferment on the pulp for five days, keeping the fruit submerged.

4. Strain out, press dry and discard the pulp, and stir in the sugar. Pour the must into a jar, top up, fit an airlock and ferment out to dryness.

5. Move the jar to a cold place for two days, then rack the wine into a clean jar, top up and add one Campden tablet. Bung tight, label and store until the wine is bright.

6. Rack again and store for one year. Serve as a dry table wine.

Apple & Damson 2

A dry wine made with damson jam

mixed eating and cooking apples	4kg *9lb*
damson jam	450g *1lb*
concentrated grape juice (red or white)	approx. 250g *9oz*
sugar	450g *1lb*
water	1.7 litres *3 pints*
citric acid	5ml *1 tsp*
tannin	2.5ml *½ tsp*
pectic enzyme (double dose)	
Campden tablets	
nutrient	
Burgundy yeast	

1. Dissolve the jam in half a pint of hot water and pour it into a polythene bin. Add the rest of the water (cold), the acid, pectic enzyme and one crushed Campden tablet.

2. Wash, crush or cut up the apples into small pieces including the skin and core but excluding any damaged parts. Drop them at once into the bin. Cover and leave for forty-eight hours.

3. Stir in the concentrated grape juice, tannin, activated yeast and nutrient. Cover and ferment on the pulp for five days, keeping the fruit submerged.

4. Strain out, press dry and discard the pulp, and stir in the sugar. Pour the must into a jar, top up, fit an airlock and ferment out to dryness.

5. Move the jar to a cold place for two days, then rack the wine into a clean jar, top up and add one Campden tablet. Bung tight, label and store until the wine is bright.

6. Rack again and store for six months. Serve as a dry table wine.

Apple & Elderberry

A dry red table wine

mixed eating and cooking apples	4kg *9lb*
elderberries	450g *1lb*
concentrated red grape juice	*approx.* 250g *9oz*
sugar	680g *1½lb*
water	1.7 litres *3 pints*
citric acid	10ml *2 tsp*
tannin	2.5ml *½ tsp*
pectic enzyme	
Campden tablets	
nutrient	
Burgundy yeast	

1. Wash, crush or cut the apples into small pieces including the skin and core, but excluding any damaged parts. Drop them at once into a bin containing the water, acid, pectic enzyme and one crushed Campden tablet.

2. Prepare, wash and crush the elderberries and add them to the apples. Cover and leave for twenty-four hours.

3. Stir in the concentrated grape juice, tannin, activated yeast and nutrient. Cover and ferment on the pulp for five days keeping the fruit submerged.

4. Strain out, press dry and discard the pulp, and stir in the sugar. Pour the must into a jar, top up, fit an airlock and ferment out to dryness.

5. Move the jar to a cold place for two days, then rack the wine into a clean jar, top up and add one Campden tablet. Bung tight, label and store until the wine is bright.

6. Rack again and store for one year. Serve as a red table wine.

Apple & Gooseberry

A dry white table wine

mixed eating and cooking apples	4kg *9lb*
fresh or frozen gooseberries	450g *1lb*
concentrated white grape juice	*approx.* 250g *9oz*
sugar	680g *1½lb*
water	1.7 litres *3 pints*
citric acid	5ml *1 tsp*
tannin	2.5ml *½ tsp*
pectic enzyme	
Campden tablets	
nutrient	
Burgundy yeast	

1. Wash, crush or cut the apples into small pieces including the skin and core, but excluding any damaged parts. Drop them at once into a bin containing the water, acid, pectic enzyme and one crushed Campden tablet.

2. Top and tail, wash and crush the gooseberries, then add them to the apples. Cover and leave for twenty-four hours.

3. Stir in the concentrated grape juice, tannin, activated yeast and nutrient. Cover and ferment on the pulp for five days, keeping the fruit submerged.

4. Strain out, press dry and discard the pulp, and stir in the sugar. Pour the must into a jar, top up, fit an airlock and ferment out to dryness.

5. Move the jar to a cold place for two days, then rack the wine into a clean jar. Top up, add one Campden tablet, bung tight, label and store until the wine is bright.

6. Rack again and store for one year. Serve cold as a white table wine.

Apple & Loganberry

A dry wine made with tinned loganberries

mixed eating and cooking apples	4kg *9lb*
loganberries in sugar syrup	450g *1lb*
concentrated grape juice	
(red or white)	*approx.* 250g *9oz*
sugar	680g *1¼lb*
water	1.7 litres *3 pints*
citric acid	5ml *1 tsp*
tannin	2.5ml *½ tsp*
pectic enzyme	
Campden tablets	
nutrient	
Burgundy yeast	

1. Wash, crush or cut the apples into small pieces including the skin and core, but excluding any damaged parts. Drop them at once into a bin containing the water, acid, pectic enzyme and one crushed Campden tablet.

2. Strain out and crush the loganberries, then add them and the syrup to the apples. Cover and leave for twenty-four hours.

3. Stir in the concentrated grape juice, tannin, activated yeast and nutrient. Cover and ferment on the pulp for five days, keeping the fruit submerged.

4. Strain out, press dry and discard the pulp, and stir in the sugar. Pour the must into a jar, top up, fit an airlock and ferment out to dryness.

5. Move the jar to a cold place for two days, then rack the wine into a clean jar. Top up, add one Campden tablet, bung tight, label and store until the wine is bright.

6. Rack again and store for one year. Serve as a table wine.

NOTE:
1 lb fresh or frozen loganberries may be used if available.

Apple & Raspberry 1

A dry rosé made with fresh raspberries

mixed eating and cooking apples	4kg *9lb*
fresh or frozen raspberries	450g *1lb*
concentrated grape juice	
(rosé for preference)	*approx.* 250g *9oz*
sugar	680g *1¼lb*
water	1.7 litres *3 pints*
citric acid	5ml *1 tsp*
tannin	2.5ml *½ tsp*
pectic enzyme	
Campden tablets	
nutrient	
Burgundy yeast	

1. Wash, crush or cut the apples into small pieces including the skin and core, but excluding any damaged parts. Drop them at once into a bin containing the water, acid, pectic enzyme and one crushed Campden tablet.

2. Wash and crush the raspberries and add them to the apples. Cover and leave for twenty-four hours.

3. Stir in the concentrated grape juice, tannin, activated yeast and nutrient. Cover and ferment on the pulp for five days keeping the fruit submerged.

4. Strain out, press dry and discard the pulp, and stir in the sugar. Pour the must into a jar, top up, fit an airlock and ferment out to dryness.

5. Move the jar to a cold place for two days, then rack the wine into a clean jar. Top up, add one Campden tablet, bung tight, label and store until the wine is bright.

6. Rack again and store for one year. Add one saccharin pellet per bottle and serve chilled as a rosé wine.

Apple & Raspberry 2

A dry rosé made with raspberry jam

mixed eating and cooking apples	4kg	*9lb*
raspberry jam	450g	*1lb*
concentrated rosé grape juice *approx.* 250g		*9oz*
sugar	450g	*1lb*
water	1.7 litres	*3 pints*
citric acid	5ml	*1 tsp*
tannin	2.5ml	*½ tsp*
pectic enzyme (double dose)		
Campden tablets		
nutrient		
Burgundy yeast		

1. Dissolve the jam in half a pint of hot water and pour it into a polythene bin. Add the rest of the water (cold), the acid, pectic enzyme and one crushed Campden tablet.

2. Wash, crush or cut the apples into small pieces, including the skin and core but excluding damaged parts. Drop them at once into the bin. Cover and leave for forty-eight hours.

3. Stir in the concentrated grape juice, tannin, activated yeast and nutrient. Cover and ferment on the pulp for five days, keeping the fruit submerged.

4. Strain out, press dry and discard the pulp, and stir in the sugar. Pour the must into a jar, top up, fit an airlock and ferment out to dryness.

5. Move the jar to a cold place for two days, then rack the wine into a clean jar, top up and add one Campden tablet. Bung tight, label and store until the wine is bright.

6. Rack again and store for one year.

Apple & Redcurrant 1

A dry rosé made with fresh redcurrants

eating and cooking apples	4kg	*9lb*
fresh or frozen redcurrants	450g	*1lb*
concentrated red grape juice *approx.* 250g		*9oz*
sugar	800g	*1¼lb*
water	1.7 litres	*3 pints*
citric acid	5ml	*1 tsp*
tannin	2.5ml	*½ tsp*
pectic enzyme		
Campden tablets		
nutrient		
Bordeaux yeast		

1. Pour cold water into a bin containing the acid, pectic enzyme and one crushed Campden tablet.

2. Wash the apples, remove any bad parts, cut them into small pieces including skins and cores, or crush them into a coarse mash. Drop them into the bin without delay to avoid browning.

3. Wash, stalk and crush the redcurrants and add these to the bin. Cover and leave for twenty-four hours.

4. Next day add the grape juice, tannin, nutrient and an activated yeast. Cover the bin and ferment on the pulp for five days, keeping the fruit submerged.

5. Strain out, press dry and discard the pulp, and stir in the sugar. Pour the must into a sterilised jar, top up, fit an airlock and ferment out.

6. Rack the wine into a clean jar, top up, add one Campden tablet, bung tight and store the wine until it is bright.

7. Rack again, store in bulk for one year then bottle, add one saccharin pellet to each and keep a few months longer. Serve this wine cold as a luncheon or picnic rosé.

Apple & Redcurrant 2

A dry rosé made with redcurrant jelly

mixed eating and cooking apples	4kg *9lb*
redcurrant jelly	450g *1lb*
concentrated rosé grape juice	*approx.* 250g *9oz*
sugar	450g *1lb*
water	1.7 litres *3 pints*
citric acid	5ml *1 tsp*
tannin	2.5ml *½ tsp*
pectic enzyme (double dose)	
Campden tablets	
nutrient	
Burgundy yeast	

1. Dissolve the jelly in half a pint of hot water and pour it into a polythene bin. Add the rest of the water (cold), the acid, pectic enzyme and one crushed Campden tablet.

2. Wash, crush or cut up the apples into small pieces including the skin and core but excluding any damaged parts. Drop them at once into the bin. Cover and leave for forty-eight hours.

3. Stir in the concentrated grape juice, tannin, activated yeast and nutrient. Cover and ferment on the pulp for five days, keeping the fruit submerged.

4. Strain out, press dry and discard the pulp, and stir in the sugar. Pour the must into a jar, top up, fit an airlock and ferment out to dryness.

5. Move the jar to a cold place for two days, then rack the wine into a clean jar. Top up, add one Campden tablet, bung tight, label and store until the wine is bright.

6. Rack again and store for six months before sweetening with one saccharin tablet per bottle and serving cold as a rosé wine.

Apple & Strawberry 1

A dry rosé made with fresh strawberries

mixed eating and cooking apples	4kg *9lb*
fresh or frozen strawberries	450g *1lb*
concentrated rosé grape juice	*approx.* 250g *9oz*
sugar	680g *1½lb*
cold water	1.7 litres *3 pints*
citric acid	5ml *1 tsp*
tannin	2.5ml *½ tsp*
pectic enzyme	
Campden tablets	
nutrient	
Bordeaux yeast	

1. Wash, crush or cut the apples into small pieces including the skin and core, but excluding any damaged parts. Drop them at once into a bin containing the water, acid, pectic enzyme and one crushed Campden tablet.

2. Stalk, wash and crush the strawberries and add them to the bin. Cover and leave for twenty-four hours.

3. Stir in the concentrated grape juice, tannin, nutrient and activated yeast. Cover and ferment on the pulp for five days, keeping the fruit submerged.

4. Strain out, press dry and discard the pulp, and stir in the sugar. Pour the must into a sterilised jar, top up, fit an airlock and ferment out to dryness.

5. Rack the wine into a clean jar, top up, add one Campden tablet, bung tight and store until the wine is bright.

6. Rack again, store in bulk for one year, then bottle and add one saccharin pellet to each. Serve cold as a luncheon or picnic rosé.

The home freezer helps us to make country wines all year round. Clean and sulphite the fruit before sealing it in containers. The freezing process breaks the cell walls of the fruit, making for easier crushing and better juice extraction.

NOTE:
Redcurrant flavoured gelatine for making into party jellies is NOT suitable. Use only the jelly or conserve prepared from redcurrants and sugar.

NOTE:
Small or mis-shaped strawberries from the garden can be set aside and frozen for use in making this wine.

Apple & Strawberry 2

A dry rosé made with strawberry jam

mixed eating and cooking apples	4kg	*9lb*
strawberry jam	450g	*1lb*
concentrated grape juice		
(red or white)	*approx.* 250g	*9oz*
sugar	450g	*1lb*
water	1.7 litres	*3 pints*
citric acid	5ml	*1 tsp*
tannin	2.5ml	*½ tsp*
pectic enzyme (double dose)		
Campden tablets		
nutrient		
Burgundy yeast		

1. Dissolve the jam in half a pint of hot water and pour it into a polythene bin. Add the rest of the water (cold), the acid, pectic enzyme and one crushed Campden tablet.

2. Wash, crush or cut the apples into small pieces including the skin and core but excluding any damaged parts. Drop them at once into the bin. Cover and leave for forty-eight hours.

3. Stir in the concentrated grape juice, tannin, activated yeast and nutrient. Cover and ferment on the pulp for five days, keeping the fruit submerged.

4. Strain out, press dry and discard the pulp, and stir in the sugar. Pour the must into a jar, top up, fit an airlock and ferment out to dryness.

5. Move the jar to a cold place for two days, then rack the wine into a clean jar. Top up, add one Campden tablet, bung tight, label and store until the wine is bright.

6. Rack again and store for six months. Sweeten each bottle with one saccharin pellet and serve the wine cold as a rosé party or picnic wine.

Apricot 1

A light dry wine made with fresh apricots

fresh apricots	2kg	*4½lb*
concentrated white grape juice	*approx.* 250g	*9oz*
sugar	900g	*2lb*
water	2.5 litres	*4½ pints*
citric acid	10ml	*2 tsp*
tannin	2.5ml	*½ tsp*
pectic enzyme		
Campden tablets		
nutrient		
Hock yeast		

1. Wash the apricots, remove and discard the stones. Cut up or crush the fruit, pour hot water over it and fit a cover.

2. When cool, add the acid, pectic enzyme, one crushed Campden tablet. Replace the cover and leave for twenty-four hours.

3. Stir in the concentrated grape juice, tannin, nutrient and active yeast. Ferment on the pulp for three days, keeping the fruit submerged and the bin loosely covered.

4. Strain out, gently press and discard the fruit, and stir in the sugar. Pour the must into a sterilised jar, top up with cold boiled water if necessary, fit an airlock and ferment out to dryness.

5. Move the jar to a cool place for a few days then rack the wine into a clean jar. Top up, add one Campden tablet, bung tight, label and store until the wine is bright.

6. Syphon into bottles and store the wine for six months. Serve it cool as a light dry table wine.

Apricot 2

A sweet wine made with fresh apricots

fresh apricots	2.5kg *5½lb*
concentrated white grape juice	*approx.* 250g *9oz*
sugar	1.13kg *2½lb*
water	2.5 litres *4½ pints*
citric acid	10ml *2 tsp*
tannin	2.5ml *½ tsp*
pectic enzyme	
Campden tablets	
nutrient	
Sauternes yeast	
potassium sorbate	

1. Wash the apricots, remove and discard the stones. Cut up or crush the fruit and pour hot water over them.

2. When cool, add the acid, pectic enzyme and one crushed Campden tablet, cover and leave for twenty-four hours.

3. Stir in the concentrated grape juice, tannin, nutrient and active yeast. Ferment on the pulp for three days, keeping the fruit submerged and the bin loosely covered.

4. Strain out, gently press and discard the fruit, and stir in the sugar. Pour the must into a sterilised jar, top up with cold boiled water if necessary, fit an airlock and ferment down to S.G. 1.010.

5. Rack into a clean jar containing 1g potassium sorbate and one crushed Campden tablet and leave in a cool place.

6. When the wine is bright, rack again and store in bulk for six months before bottling.

Apricot 3

A dry wine made with dried apricots

dried apricots	340g *12oz*
concentrated white grape juice	*approx.* 250g *9oz*
sugar	900g *2lb*
water	3.7 litres *6½ pints*
citric acid	15ml *3 tsp*
tannin	2.5ml *½ tsp*
pectic enzyme	
Campden tablets	
nutrient	
Hock yeast	

1. Wash and cut up the apricots, and pour hot water over them. Cover and leave them to soak overnight.

2. Add the acid, pectic enzyme and one crushed Campden tablet. Cover and leave for twenty-four hours.

3. Stir in the concentrated grape juice, tannin, nutrient and active yeast. Cover and ferment on the pulp for three days, keeping the fruit submerged.

4. Strain out and gently press the fruit, and stir in the sugar. Pour the must into a sterilised jar, top up with cold boiled water if necessary, fit an airlock and ferment out to dryness.

5. Move the jar to a cool place for a few days then rack the wine into a clean jar. Top up, add one Campden tablet, bung tight, label and store until the wine is bright.

6. Syphon into bottles and store the wine for six months before serving it cool as a light dry table wine.

Apricot 4

A dry wine made with tinned apricots

apricot pulp or pieces	1.35kg *3lb*
concentrated white grape juice	*approx.* 250g *9oz*
sugar	800g *1¾lb*
water	2.8 litres *5 pints*
citric acid	15ml *3 tsp*
tannin	2.5ml *½ tsp*
pectic enzyme	
Campden tablets	
nutrient	
Hock yeast	

1. Separate the fruit from the syrup, and set the syrup aside for later use.

2. Mash the fruit, place in a bin with 3½ pints water, the acid, pectic enzyme and one crushed Campden tablet. Cover and leave for twenty-four hours.

3. Add the fruit syrup, concentrated grape juice, tannin, nutrient and yeast and ferment for three days, keeping the fruit submerged.

4. Strain out the pulp, and stir in the sugar. Pour into a fermentation jar, top up, fit an airlock and ferment to dryness.

5. Rack, add one Campden tablet and as soon as the wine is bright, syphon it into bottles and store for three months.

Apricot 5

A medium sweet wine made with apricot jam

apricot jam	1.35 kg *3lb*
concentrated white grape juice	*approx.* 250g *9oz*
sugar	450g *1lb*
water	3.4 litres *6 pints*
citric acid	15ml *3 tsp*
tannin	2.5ml *½ tsp*
pectic enzyme (double dose)	
Campden tablets	
nutrient	
Sauternes yeast	
potassium sorbate	

1. Dissolve the jam in hot water and when cool add the acid, pectic enzyme and one crushed Campden tablet. Cover and leave for two days.

2. Stir in the concentrated grape juice, tannin, nutrient and active yeast and ferment for two days.

3. Strain through a fine mesh nylon bag, stir in the sugar and pour the must into a sterilised jar. Top up with cold boiled water if necessary and fit an airlock.

4. Ferment down to S.G. 1.006, then rack into a sterilised jar containing 1g potassium sorbate and one crushed Campden tablet.

5. Bung tight, label and store in a cold place until the wine is bright, then syphon into bottles. This is a light, golden, pleasant flavoured, social wine. Serve it cold with sweet biscuits.

Apricot 6

A sweet wine made with apricot nectar

apricot nectar	900ml *32fl oz*
concentrated white grape juice *approx.*	500g *18oz*
sugar	680g *1½ lb*
water	2.8 litres *5 pints*
citric acid	10ml *2 tsp*
tannin	2.5ml *½ tsp*
pectic enzyme	
nutrient	
Campden tablets	
Sauternes yeast	
potassium sorbate	

1. Empty the apricot nectar into a fermentation jar, add 3½ pints cold water, the acid, pectic enzyme and one crushed Campden tablet. Shake the jar to mix the ingredients, then seal and leave in a warm place for twenty-four hours.

2. Dissolve the sugar, concentrated grape juice and tannin in the rest of the water and pour this into the jar. If need be, top up with cold water.

3. Add the nutrient and active yeast, then fit an airlock.

4. Ferment down to S.G. 1.010, then rack the wine into a clean jar containing 1g potassium sorbate and one Campden tablet.

5. Bung tight, label and store in a cold place until the wine is bright.

6. Syphon the clear wine into bottles and keep it until it is six months old. Serve it cold as a social wine.

Apricot & Banana

A sweet wine made with fresh fruit

fresh apricots	1.8kg *4lb*
ripe bananas	450g *1lb*
concentrated white grape juice *approx.*	250g *9oz*
sugar	900g *2lb*
water	2.5 litres *4½ pints*
citric acid	10ml *2 tsp*
tannin	2.5ml *½ tsp*
pectic enzyme	
Campden tablets	
nutrient	
Sauternes yeast	
potassium sorbate	

1. Wash and stalk the apricots and place them in a bin with the peeled and thinly sliced bananas. Pour hot water over them and, when cool, remove and discard the apricot stones.

2. Add the pectic enzyme, acid and one crushed Campden tablet. Cover and leave for twenty-four hours.

3. Stir in the concentrated grape juice, tannin, nutrient and activated yeast. Replace the cover and ferment on the pulp for four days, keeping the fruit submerged.

4. Strain out, press dry and discard the fruit pulp, stir in the sugar and when it is dissolved pour the must into a sterilised jar. Top up with cold boiled water if necessary, fit an airlock and ferment down to S.G. 1.016.

5. Rack the wine into a clean jar containing 1g potassium sorbate and one crushed Campden tablet to terminate fermentation. Top up, bung tight and store in a cold place until the wine is bright.

6. Rack again and store until the wine is one year old. Serve cold with the sweet course of a meal or as a social wine with sweet cake or biscuits.

Banana

A sweet wine made with ripe fruit

very ripe bananas	2.25kg *5lb*
concentrated white grape juice *approx.*	250g *9oz*
sugar	1kg *2¼lb*
water	3.7 litres *6½ pints*
citric acid	20ml *4 tsp*
tannin	2.5ml *½ tsp*
pectic enzyme	
Campden tablets	
nutrient	
G.P. yeast	
potassium sorbate	

1. Use bananas with almost black skins. Peel off and discard the skins, slice the bananas, place them in a pan, add one teaspoonful of acid and as much of the water as you can, bring to the boil, cover and simmer gently for thirty minutes, then leave to cool.

2. Strain out, drain well and discard the pulp, stir in the rest of the water and acid, the pectic enzyme and one crushed Campden tablet. Cover and leave for twenty-four hours.

3. Stir in the concentrated grape juice, the tannin, nutrient and an activated yeast, pour the must into a jar, leaving room for the sugar. Fit an airlock and ferment for four days.

4. Remove some of the must, dissolve half the sugar in it and when it is completely dissolved, return it to the jar. Replace the airlock and continue the fermentation for another seven days.

5. Repeat this process with the rest of the sugar and ferment down to S.G. 1.016.

6. Rack into a clean jar containing 1g potassium sorbate and one crushed Campden tablet, bung tight and store in a cold place until the wine is bright.

7. Rack again and store for one year before bottling. Serve this wine cold with sweet cakes.

Banana & Lemon

A dry or slightly sweetened wine

ripe bananas	1.35kg *3lb*
fresh lemons	3
concentrated white grape juice *approx.*	250g *9oz*
sugar	900g *2lb*
water	3.7 litres *6½ pin*
tannin	2.5ml *½ tsp*
no acid	
pectic enzyme	
Campden tablets	
nutrient	
G.P. yeast	

1. Peel the bananas, discard the skins, slice the fruit and place it in a pan with the thinly pared rind of the lemons. Add three pints of water, bring to the boil, cover, simmer for thirty minutes, then leave to cool.

2. Strain out, drain and discard the fruit, add the rest of the water, the strained expressed juice of the lemons, the pectic enzyme and one crushed Campden tablet. Cover and leave for twenty-four hours.

3. Stir in the sugar, concentrated grape juice, tannin, nutrient and activated yeast. Pour the must into a jar, top up with cold boiled water, fit an airlock and ferment out to dryness.

4. Rack into a clean jar, add one Campden tablet, top up, bung tight, label and store in a cold place until the wine is bright.

5. Rack again and store for one year. If needs be, sweeten slightly with saccharin and serve cold as a social wine.

Banana & Orange

A dry or slightly sweetened wine

ripe bananas	1.35kg *3lb*
bitter oranges	2
sweet oranges	2
concentrated white grape juice	*approx.* 250g *9oz*
sugar	900g *2lb*
water	3.7 litres *6½ pints*
pectic enzyme	
Campden tablets	
nutrient	
G.P. yeast	
no acid or tannin	

1. Peel the bananas, discard the skins, slice the fruit and place it in a pan with the thinly pared rind of the oranges. Add three pints of water, bring to the boil, cover, simmer for thirty minutes then leave to cool.

2. Strain out, drain and discard the fruit. Add the rest of the water, the strained expressed juice of the oranges, the pectic enzyme and one crushed Campden tablet. Cover and leave for twenty-four hours.

3. Stir in the sugar, concentrated grape juice, nutrient and activated yeast. Pour the must into a sterilised jar, top up with cold boiled water, fit an airlock and ferment out to dryness.

4. Rack into a clean jar, add one Campden tablet, top up, bung tight, label and store in a cold place until the wine is bright.

5. Rack again and store for one year. If needs be, sweeten slightly with saccharin and serve cold as a social wine.

Beetroot

A strong, sweet dessert wine

fresh beetroot	2kg *4¼lb*
concentrated red grape juice	*approx.* 500g *18oz*
brown sugar	1.25kg *2¾lb*
water	3.5 litres *6 pints*
citric acid	20ml *4 tsp*
tannin	5ml *1 tsp*
whole ginger	15g *½oz*
cloves	12
nutrient	
Madeira yeast	

1. Select tender, freshly dug beetroots, and scrub them carefully to remove every trace of soil. Top and tail them, cut into small cubes, place them in a pan together with the well bruised ginger, the cloves and as much of the water as you can. Bring to the boil, cover and simmer until the beetroot is quite tender, but not mushy, then leave to cool.

2. Strain out, drain well and discard the beetroot and spices. Stir in the concentrated grape juice, acid, tannin, nutrient and an activated yeast. Pour the must into a jar, leaving room for the sugar. Fit an airlock and ferment for seven days in a warm place, 75°F *(24°C)*.

3. Remove half the must, stir in one third of the sugar and when it is completely dissolved, return the must to the jar. Replace the airlock and continue the fermentation.

4. After a further seven days, repeat the process with half the remaining sugar and seven days later add the remaining portion.

5. When fermentation is finished, move the wine to a cold place for a few days to help it to clear, then rack it into a clean jar, top up, if possible with vodka (but not too much), if not with another red wine or cold boiled water.

6. Store this strong, sweet, dessert wine for at least one year and preferably two before bottling it.

NOTE:
If a dark brown sugar is not available use white sugar and a Port yeast.

Bilberry 1

A dry red made with fresh bilberries

fresh bilberries	1.35kg	*3lb*
concentrated red grape juice	*approx.* 250g	*9oz*
sugar	900g	*2lb*
water	3.7 litres	*6½ pints*
citric acid	10ml	*2 tsp*
tannin	5ml	*1 tsp*
pectic enzyme		
Campden tablets		
nutrient		
Burgundy yeast		

1. Stalk, wash and crush the bilberries, pour hot water over them, cover and leave to cool.

2. Add the pectic enzyme, acid and one crushed Campden tablet. Cover and leave for twenty-four hours.

3. Stir in the concentrated grape juice, tannin, nutrient and activated yeast. Cover and ferment on the pulp for three days, keeping the fruit submerged.

4. Strain out, press dry and discard the fruit, stir in the sugar and, when it is dissolved, pour the must into a jar. Top up with cold boiled water, fit an airlock and ferment out to dryness.

5. Rack into a clean jar, add one Campden tablet, top up, bung tight, label and store until the wine is bright.

6. Rack again and store for at least one year before bottling. Serve this deep red table wine free from chill, with red meats.

Bilberry 2

A light red made with tinned bilberries

bilberries in sugar syrup	900g	*2lb*
concentrated red grape juice	*approx.* 250g	*9oz*
sugar	800g	*1¾lb*
water	2.8 litres	*5 pints*
citric acid	10ml	*2 tsp*
tannin	5ml	*1 tsp*
pectic enzyme		
nutrient		
Burgundy yeast		

1. Empty the fruit and syrup into a mashing bin, and crush the berries. Pour hot water over them, cover and leave to cool.

2. Stir in the concentrated grape juice, citric acid, pectic enzyme, tannin, nutrient and an activated yeast.

3. Replace the cover and ferment on the pulp for three days, keeping the fruit submerged.

4. Strain out, press dry and discard the fruit. Stir in the sugar and when it is dissolved, pour the must into a sterilised jar, top up with cold boiled water, fit an airlock and ferment out to dryness.

5. Move the wine to a cold place for a few days to encourage clarification, then rack it into a clean jar, top up and add one Campden tablet. Bung tight, label and store until the wine is bright, then rack again.

6. Mature this wine for six months before bottling. Serve as a light table wine with red meats.

Blackberry 1

A dry red made with fresh blackberries

fresh or frozen blackberries	1.6kg	*3½lb*
concentrated red grape juice	*approx.* 250g	*9oz*
sugar	900g	*2lb*
water	2.8 litres	*5 pints*
citric acid	10ml	*2 tsp*
tannin	5ml	*1 tsp*
pectic enzyme		
Campden tablets		
nutrient		
Burgundy yeast		

1. Stalk, wash clean, drain and crush the blackberries. Pour hot water over them, cover and leave to cool.

2. Stir in the pectic enzyme, acid and one crushed Campden tablet, cover and leave for twenty-four hours.

3. Stir in the concentrated grape juice, tannin, nutrient and an activated yeast. Ferment on the pulp for four days, keeping the fruit submerged and the vessel covered.

4. Strain out, press dry and discard the pulp. Stir in the sugar, and, when it is dissolved, pour the must into a sterilised jar, top up with cold boiled water, fit an airlock and ferment out to dryness.

5. Rack into a clean jar, top up, add one Campden tablet, bung tight, label and store in a cold place until the wine is bright.

6. Rack again and keep this dry red table wine cool until it is at least one year old and preferably two, then bottle it. Serve it free from chill with beef, lamb, game and cheese.

Blackberry 2

A dry red made with tinned blackberries

blackberries in sugar syrup	1.35kg	*3lb*
concentrated red grape juice	*approx.* 250g	*9oz*
sugar	800g	*1¾lb*
water	2.8 litres	*5 pints*
citric acid	10ml	*2 tsp*
tannin	5ml	*1 tsp*
pectic enzyme		
nutrient		
Burgundy yeast		

1. Empty the blackberries and syrup into a mashing bin, and crush them. Pour hot water over them, cover and leave to cool.

2. Stir in the concentrated grape juice, citric acid, pectic enzyme, tannin, nutrient and an activated yeast.

3. Ferment on the pulp for three days, keeping the fruit submerged and the vessel covered.

4. Strain out, press dry and discard the fruit. Stir in the sugar and, when it is dissolved, pour the must into a jar, top up with cold boiled water, fit an airlock and ferment out to dryness.

5. Move the wine to a cold place for a few days to encourage clarification then rack it into a clean jar, top up and add one Campden tablet. Bung tight, label and store until the wine is bright, then rack again.

6. Mature this wine for six months before bottling. Serve it as a dry red table wine with red meats or cheese.

NOTE:
Blackberry wine tends to lose some of its colour when left in the light. Keep the fermentation and storage jars covered with black cloth or thick brown paper at all times and then use brown or green bottles.

Blackberry & Banana

A strong, sweet dessert wine

fresh or frozen blackberries	2.5kg *5½lb*
ripe bananas	2
concentrated red grape juice	*approx.* 250g *9oz*
brown sugar	1.13kg *2½lb*
water	1.7 litres *3 pints*
citric acid	10ml *2 tsp*
tannin	5ml *1 tsp*
pectic enzyme	
Campden tablets	
nutrient	
Madeira yeast	

1. Stalk, wash and clean, drain and crush the blackberries. Peel and mash the ripe bananas, pour hot water over all the fruit, cover and leave to cool.

2. Stir in the pectic enzyme, acid and one crushed Campden tablet, cover and leave for twenty-four hours.

3. Stir in the concentrated grape juice, tannin, nutrient and an activated yeast. Ferment on the pulp for five days, keeping the fruit submerged and the container loosely covered.

4. Strain out, press dry and discard the pulp, stir in one third of the sugar, leaving enough room for the remaining sugar. Fit an airlock and ferment in a warm place until the S.G. reaches 1.004 (10–14 days).

5. Remove half the must, and stir in half the remaining sugar. Return the sweetened must to the jar, replace the airlock and continue the fermentation for a further seven days.

6. Repeat the process with the last of the sugar and leave the must to finish fermenting, check the S.G. and if needs be sweeten it to 1.016.

7. Move the jar to a cold place for a few days to aid clarification, then rack the wine into a clean jar, add finings, bung tight and keep for a few more days in the cold until the wine is bright.

8. Rack again, then **store this wine in a warm place** for one year before bottling it. It develops the caramelised flavour of Madeira and is a strong, sweet dessert wine, ideal with Madeira cake.

Blackberry & Elderberry 1

A sweet wine with added prunes

blackberries	2kg *4½lb*
elderberries	680g *1½lb*
concentrated red grape juice	*approx.* 250g *9oz*
prunes in syrup	340g *12oz*
sugar	1kg *2½lb*
boiling water	2.8 litres *5 pints*
citric acid	10ml *2 tsp*
no tannin	
pectic enzyme	
Campden tablets	
nutrient	
Port yeast	

1. Stalk, wash and crush the blackberries and elderberries. Put them into a bin, pour on the boiling water, stir well, cover and leave to cool.

2. Add the prunes in syrup, first removing the stones, the concentrated grape juice, acid, pectic enzyme and one crushed Campden tablet. Cover and leave for twenty-four hours.

3. Add the nutrient and an active yeast. Cover and ferment on the pulp for four days, keeping the fruit submerged.

4. Strain out, press dry and discard the pulp. Add half the sugar to the must, and stir until it is dissolved. Pour it into a jar, fit an airlock and ferment down to S.G. 1.010.

5. Add the rest of the sugar by removing one third of the must, stirring in the sugar until it is dissolved, then returning it to the jar. Continue fermentation until it stops. If the S.G. is below 1.020 stir in sufficient sugar to bring the reading up to this figure. 113g (4oz) sugar increases the reading by about 8 units.

6. Rack the wine into a clean jar, top up, add one Campden tablet, bung tight and store in a cold place until the wine is bright.

7. Rack again and mature this wine for at least one year in bulk before bottling, then store for another year. Serve it after the dessert course of a meal.

Blackberry & Elderberry 2

A dry wine with added bananas

blackberries	680g	*1¼lb*
elderberries	225g	*8oz*
ripe bananas	2	
concentrated red grape juice	*approx.* 250g	*9oz*
sugar	800g	*1¾lb*
citric acid	10ml	*2 tsp*
hot water	4 litres	*7 pints*
no tannin		
pectic enzyme		
Campden tablets		
nutrient		
Bordeaux yeast		

1. Stalk, wash, peel and crush the fruit. Pour on hot water, stir well, cover and leave to cool.

2. Stir in the pectic enzyme, acid and one crushed Campden tablet, cover and leave for twenty-four hours.

3. Stir in the concentrated grape juice, nutrient and an activated yeast. Ferment on the pulp for three days, keeping the fruit submerged.

4. Strain out, press and discard the solids, and stir in the sugar. Pour the must into a jar, fit an airlock and ferment out.

5. Rack the wine into a clean jar, top up, and add one Campden tablet. Bung tight and store in a cold place until the wine is bright.

6. Rack again and keep until the wine is eight months old before bottling, then keep it for a further four months. Serve it free from chill as a dry red table wine with red meats, game or cheese.

Blackcurrant

A strong, medium sweet wine

blackcurrants in sugar syrup	1.35kg	*3lb*
concentrated red grape juice	*approx.* 500g	*18oz*
sugar	1kg	*2¼lb*
water	2.25 litres	*4 pints*
citric acid	5ml	*1 tsp*
tannin	2.5ml	*½ tsp*
pectic enzyme		
Campden tablets		
nutrient		
Port yeast		

1. Empty the blackcurrants and syrup into a polythene bin, crush them, add the water, acid, pectic enzyme and one crushed Campden tablet. Cover and leave for twenty-four hours.

2. Stir in the concentrated grape juice, tannin, nutrient and an active yeast. Cover and ferment on the pulp for three days, keeping the skins submerged.

3. Strain out and press the pulp, and stir in half the sugar. Pour the must into a jar leaving space for the rest of the sugar, fit an airlock and ferment in a warm place for ten days.

4. Remove half the must, stir in half the remaining sugar and, when it is dissolved, return it to the jar. Replace the airlock and continue fermentation.

5. After seven days repeat this process with the rest of the sugar and continue the fermentation to the end.

6. Move the jar to a cold place for a few days, then rack the wine into a clean jar, add one Campden tablet, and top up. Bung tight, label and leave the wine in a cold place until it is bright.

7. Rack again and store for ten months before bottling. Serve this well flavoured, strong, slightly sweet wine, free from chill, with cheese or nuts.

Blackcurrant & Banana 1

A sweet wine made with blackcurrant syrup

blackcurrant syrup	480ml	*17fl oz*
concentrated red grape juice	*approx.* 500g	*18oz*
ripe bananas	2	
brown sugar	900g	*2lb*
water	3.1 litres	*5½ pints*
citric acid	5ml	*1 tsp*
no tannin		
nutrient		
Madeira yeast		

1. Peel and slice the bananas, place them in a pan with the acid and 1¾ pints (*1 litre*) water. Bring to the boil, cover and simmer for half an hour then leave to cool.

2. Strain the banana liquor into a jar containing the blackcurrant syrup, concentrated grape juice, the rest of the water and an activated yeast and nutrient. Fit an airlock and ferment for ten days in a warm place.

3. Take out half the must, stir in half the sugar and when it is completely dissolved, return it to the jar. Replace the airlock and ferment on.

4. One week later repeat this process with the rest of the sugar.

5. When fermentation finishes, rack into a clean jar, top up, bung tight, and store until the wine is bright, then rack again. Keep for six months and serve free from chill as a sweet social wine.

Blackcurrant & Banana 2

A sweet wine made with fresh blackcurrants

fresh or frozen blackcurrants	1kg	*2¼lb*
ripe bananas	4	
concentrated red grape juice	*approx.* 250g	*9oz*
sugar	1.25kg	*2¾lb*
water	2.8 litres	*5 pints*
tannin	5ml	*1 tsp*
no acid		
pectic enzyme		
Campden tablets		
nutrient		
Port yeast		
wine finings		

1. Stalk, wash and crush the blackcurrants, peel and mash the bananas. Pour hot water over them, cover and leave to cool.

2. Stir in the pectic enzyme and one crushed Campden tablet. Cover and leave for twenty-four hours.

3. Stir in the concentrated grape juice, tannin, nutrient and an activated yeast. Cover and ferment on the pulp for three days, keeping the fruit submerged.

4. Strain out, press and discard the pulp, stir in one third of the sugar and, when it is dissolved, pour the must into a jar. Fit an airlock and ferment for ten days.

5. Remove half the must, stir in half the remaining sugar and, when it is dissolved, return the must to the jar. Replace the airlock and continue the fermentation for a further seven days.

6. Repeat this process with the last of the sugar and continue the fermentation to its end.

7. Move the jar to a cold place for a few days while the sediment settles, then rack the clearing wine into a clean jar. Add wine finings, top up, bung tight, label and leave in a cold place for a few more days until the wine is bright. Rack again and store in bulk until the wine is one year old. Serve it free from chill with nuts or cheese.

Blackcurrant & Bilberry

A dry wine made with tinned fruit

blackcurrants in syrup	450g	*1lb*
bilberries in syrup	450g	*1lb*
ripe bananas	2	
concentrated red grape juice	*approx.* 250g	*9oz*
sugar	800g	*1¾lb*
water	3 litres	*5½ pints*
tannin	5ml	*1 tsp*
citric acid	5ml	*1 tsp*
pectic enzyme		
Campden tablets		
nutrient		
Burgundy yeast		

1. Empty the contents of the cans into a bin and crush the fruit. Add the peeled and mashed bananas, water, acid, concentrated grape juice, pectic enzyme and one crushed Campden tablet. Cover and leave for twenty-four hours.

2. Add the tannin, nutrient and activated yeast and ferment on the pulp for three days, keeping the fruit submerged.

3. Strain out, press dry and discard the pulp, and stir in the sugar. Pour the must into a jar, top up with cold boiled water, fit an airlock and ferment out.

4. Rack the wine into a storage jar, add one Campden tablet, top up and store the wine until it is bright.

5. Rack again and keep for ten months before bottling, then keep it for a further five months. Serve it free from chill with meat or cheese.

Blackcurrant & Cherry

A dry wine made with tinned fruit

blackcurrants in sugar syrup	900g	*2lb*
black cherries in sugar syrup	450g	*1lb*
concentrated red grape juice	*approx.* 250g	*9oz*
sugar	900g	*2lb*
water	2.25 litres	*4 pints*
citric acid	5ml	*1 tsp*
tannin	2.5ml	*½ tsp*
pectic enzyme		
Campden tablets		
nutrient		
Burgundy yeast		

1. Empty the currants, cherries and syrup into a bin and crush the fruit, removing and discarding the cherry stones. Add the water, concentrated grape juice, citric acid, pectic enzyme and one crushed Campden tablet. Cover and leave for twenty-four hours.

2. Add the tannin, activated yeast and nutrient. Cover and ferment on the pulp for three days, keeping the fruit skins submerged.

3. Strain out, press dry and discard the pulp, and stir in the sugar. Pour the must into a jar, top up with cold boiled water, fit an airlock and ferment out.

4. Rack the wine into a storage jar, add one Campden tablet, top up, seal and store until it is bright. Rack again and keep for ten months before bottling. Serve it free from chill with cold meat or cheese.

Bramble 1

A dry rosé made with bramble jelly

bramble jelly	450g *1lb*
apple juice	1 litre *1¾ pints*
concentrated rosé grape juice	*approx.* 250g *9oz*
sugar	680g *1½ lb*
water	2.8 litres *5 pints*
citric acid	5ml *1 tsp*
tannin	2.5ml *½ tsp*
pectic enzyme (double dose)	
Campden tablets	
nutrient	
Bordeaux yeast	

1. Dissolve the bramble jelly in warm water and when cool add the apple juice, concentrated grape juice, acid, pectic enzyme and one crushed Campden tablet. Cover and leave for twenty-four hours.

2. Stir in the tannin, nutrient and active yeast, then pour the must into a fermentation jar. Leave space for the sugar, fit an airlock and ferment for ten days.

3. Remove some of the must, stir in the sugar and return it to the jar. Refit the airlock and continue fermentation to dryness.

4. Rack the wine into a clean jar, add one Campden tablet, and top up. Bung tight, label and store until the wine is bright.

5. Rack again and when the wine is six months old, syphon it into clean bottles each containing one saccharin pellet. Cork, label and keep for one month then serve cold with picnic meals.

Bramble 2

A dry white made with bramble tips

blackberry shoots	2.5kg *5¼ lb*
bananas	2
concentrated white grape juice	*approx.* 250g *9oz*
sugar	800g *1¾ lb*
water	4 litres *7 pints*
citric acid	14g *½oz*
tannin	2.5ml *½ tsp*
nutrient	
Graves yeast	

1. Wash the shoots, chop them up and place them in a pan for boiling. Peel and thinly slice the bananas and add to the pan. Pour on the water, bring to the boil, cover and simmer for thirty minutes, then leave to cool.

2. Strain out, drain and discard the solids. Stir in the concentrated grape juice, sugar, acid, tannin, nutrient and an active yeast. Pour the must into a fermentation jar, top up if necessary, fit an airlock and ferment out to dryness.

3. Rack the wine into a clean jar, top up, add one Campden tablet, bung tight, label and store until it is bright.

4. Rack again and store for one year before bottling. Serve cold as a dry white table wine.

Broad Bean

A dry white table wine

shelled broad beans at end of season	2kg *4½ lb*
bananas	2
concentrated white grape juice *approx.*	250g *9oz*
sugar	800g *1¾ lb*
water	4 litres *7 pints*
citric acid	15ml *3 tsp*
tannin	2.5ml *½ tsp*
nutrient	
Campden tablets	
Graves yeast	

1. Wash and chop up the broad beans and place them in a pan for boiling. Peel and thinly slice the bananas and add to the pan. Pour on the water, bring to the boil, cover and simmer until the beans are soft, then leave to cool.

2. Strain out, drain and discard the solids. Stir in the concentrated grape juice, sugar, acid, tannin, nutrient and an active yeast. Pour the must into a jar, top up if necessary, fit an airlock and ferment out to dryness.

3. Rack into a clean jar, top up, add one Campden tablet, bung tight and store until the wine is bright.

4. Rack again and store for one year before bottling. Serve cold as a dry white table wine.

Bullace

A sweet social wine

ripe bullaces	1.6kg *3½ lb*
concentrated red grape juice *approx.*	250g *9oz*
sugar	1.13kg *2½ lb*
water	3.4 litres *6 pints*
citric acid	10ml *2 tsp*
tannin	2.5ml *½ tsp*
pectic enzyme	
Campden tablets	
nutrient	
G.P. yeast	
potassium sorbate	

1. Wash and stalk the bullaces, place them in a polythene bin and pour boiling water over them. Cover and leave to cool.

2. Mash the fruit, and remove the stones. Add the pectic enzyme, acid and one crushed Campden tablet. Replace the cover and leave for twenty-four hours.

3. Stir in the concentrated grape juice, tannin, nutrient and active yeast, then ferment on the pulp for four days, keeping the fruit submerged.

4. Strain out, press dry and discard the pulp, and stir in the sugar. Pour the must into a jar, top up if necessary, fit an airlock and ferment down to S. G. 1.010.

5. Rack into a clean jar containing 1g potassium sorbate and one crushed Campden tablet to terminate fermentation.

6. Store in a cold place until the wine is bright, then rack again.

7. Mature this wine in bulk until it is one year old then bottle it. Serve it free from chill as a social wine.

Carrot 1

A sweet wine, made with fresh carrots

carrots	2kg *4½lb*
concentrated white grape juice	*approx.* 250g *9oz*
sugar	1.13kg *2½lb*
water	3.7 litres *6½ pints*
citric acid	20ml *4 tsp*
tannin	2.5ml *½ tsp*
nutrient	
Campden tablet	
G.P. yeast	
potassium sorbate	

1. Select good quality, mid-season carrots, scrub them clean, top and tail them and chop into small, dice-sized pieces. Boil them in a covered pan until they are quite tender, then leave them to cool.

2. Strain them into a suitable container, discard the carrots and use only the liquor to make the wine. Stir in the concentrated grape juice, half the sugar, the acid, tannin, nutrient and an active yeast.

3. Pour the must into a jar, leaving room for the rest of the sugar, fit an airlock and ferment for ten days.

4. Remove half the must, stir in half the remaining sugar, return it to the jar, replace the airlock and continue fermentation for another five days.

5. Repeat this process with the remaining sugar, top up, and after five days start checking the specific gravity.

6. As soon as 1.010 is reached, rack the wine into a clean jar containing 1g potassium sorbate and one Campden tablet. Top up, bung tight and store in a cold place until the wine is bright, then rack again.

7. Mature this wine for one year then bottle and serve cold as a social wine.

Carrot 2

A dry white made with carrot juice

carrot juice	560ml *1 pint*
concentrated white grape juice	*approx.* 250g *9oz*
sugar	1kg *2¼lb*
water	3.1 litres *5½ pints*
citric acid	20ml *4 tsp*
tannin	2.5ml *½ tsp*
Campden tablets	
nutrient	
G.P. yeast	

1. Carrot juice is available from 'health food' shops and similar outlets. Empty it into a sterilised fermentation jar, add the water, acid, tannin and concentrated grape juice and stir well or shake the jar so that the ingredients are thoroughly mixed.

2. Add an active yeast and nutrient, fit an airlock and ferment for three days.

3. Remove some of the must, stir in half the sugar, return it to the jar, refit the airlock and continue fermentation for eight days.

4. Repeat this process with the rest of the sugar and ferment to dryness.

5. Move the jar to a cold place for a few days, then syphon the clearing wine into a sterilised jar. Top up with white wine or cold boiled water, add one Campden tablet, bung tight, label and store until the wine is bright.

6. Rack again and mature this wine until it is one year old. Serve it cool as a white table wine with salads and vegetarian dishes.

Carrot & Orange 1

A dry wine with fresh carrots and oranges

carrots	1.6kg *3½lb*
Seville oranges	2
sweet oranges	2
concentrated white grape juice	*approx.* 250g *9oz*
sugar	1kg *2¼lb*
water	3.7 litres *6½ pints*
Campden tablets	
nutrient	
G.P. yeast	
no acid, tannin or pectic enzyme	

1. Top, tail, scrub and dice the carrots. Thinly pare the oranges avoiding all white pith. Place the diced carrots and chopped parings in a pan, add the water, cover and boil slowly in a covered pan until the carrots are tender.

2. Strain them into a suitable container, discard the carrots and use only the liquor to make the wine. Stir in the concentrated grape juice, half the sugar, the expressed and strained juice of the oranges, the nutrient and an active yeast.

3. Pour the must into a jar, leaving room for the rest of the sugar, fit an airlock and ferment for ten days.

4. Remove half the must, stir in the rest of the sugar, return this to the jar, replace the airlock and continue fermentation to the end.

5. Rack into a clean jar, add one Campden tablet, bung tight and store in a cold place until the wine is bright, then rack again.

6. Mature this wine for at least one year then bottle and serve it cold as a full bodied table wine that is splendid with roast poultry – especially ducklings.

NOTE:
No acid, tannin or pectic enzyme is required since this is a table wine of only around 12% alcohol.

Carrot & Orange 2

A medium sweet aperitif made with juices

carrot juice	560ml *1 pint*
unsweetened orange juice	1 litre *1¾ pints*
concentrated white grape juice	*approx.* 250g *9oz*
sugar	1.3kg *3lb*
water	2 litres *3½ pints*
malic acid	5ml *1 tsp*
tannin	5ml *1 tsp*
pectic enzyme	
Campden tablets	
nutrient	
Sherry yeast	

1. Mix together the carrot juice, orange juice, concentrated grape juice, the water, pectic enzyme, malic acid and one crushed Campden tablet. Stir well, cover and leave for twenty-four hours.

2. Add the tannin, nutrient and an active yeast, pour the must into a jar, leaving room for the sugar, fit an airlock and ferment in a warm place for five days.

3. Remove half the must, stir in one third of the sugar, return this to the jar, replace the airlock and continue fermentation for eight days.

4. Repeat this process with half the remaining sugar and after a further eight days stir in the last of the sugar. Stir well to admit air to the must and so encourage yeast formation.

5. When fermentation is finished, rack the wine into a clean jar leaving some head space, plug the neck of the jar with cotton wool and store the wine in a cold place until it is bright, then rack again.

6. Mature this wine for two years in a jar not quite full and plugged with cotton wool, so that a sherry-like flavour can be developed.

7. Serve it cold as a medium sweet aperitif.

NOTES:
1. The carrot juice can be obtained from fresh carrots via a juice extractor or ready prepared from a 'health food' shop. The orange juice must be canned or cartoned fresh orange juice free from sweetening and preservative.
2. If a dry aperitif is required, check the specific gravity before the addition of the last portion of sugar. Wait until the reading is down to 1.002 then add the sugar in 2oz (*56g*) doses every four days. It is important to keep the specific gravity hovering at this level until fermentation seems to have slowed right down, then give the wine a good stir and leave it to finish off.

Carrot & Orange 3

A medium sweet aperitif, fresh carrots and orange juice

carrots	1.6kg *3½lb*
unsweetened orange juice	1 litre *1¾ pints*
concentrated white grape juice	*approx.* 250g *9oz*
sugar	1.3kg *3lb*
water	2.25 litres *4 pints*
malic acid	5ml *1 tsp*
tannin	5ml *1 tsp*
pectic enzyme	
Campden tablets	
nutrient	
Sherry yeast	

1. Select small and young carrots, top, tail, scrub, dice and liquidise them. Add the orange juice from the carton, the concentrated grape juice, water, pectic enzyme, malic acid and one crushed Campden tablet. Stir well, cover and leave for twenty-four hours.

2. Add the tannin, nutrient and an active yeast, pour the must into a jar, leaving room for the sugar, fit an airlock and ferment in a warm place for five days.

3. Remove half the must, stir in one third of the sugar, return this to the jar, replace the airlock and continue fermentation for eight days.

4. Repeat this process with half the remaining sugar and after a further eight days stir in the last of the sugar. Stir well to admit air to the must and so encourage yeast formation.

5. When fermentation is finished, rack into a clean jar leaving some head space, plug the neck of the jar with cotton wool and store the wine in a cold place until it is bright, then rack again.

6. Mature this wine for two years in a jar not quite full and plugged with cotton wool, so that a sherry-like flavour can be developed.

7. Serve it cold as a medium sweet aperitif.

NOTE:
If a dry aperitif is required, check the specific gravity before the addition of the last portion of sugar. Wait until the reading is down to 1.002 then add the sugar in 2oz *(56g)* doses every four days. It is important to keep the specific gravity hovering at this level until fermentation seems to have slowed right down, then give the wine a good stir and leave it to finish off.

Celery

A dry white table wine

prepared celery	2kg *4½lb*
concentrated white grape juice	*approx.* 250g *9oz*
sugar	900g *2lb*
water	3.7 litres *6½ pint*
citric acid	15ml *3 tsp*
tannin	2.5ml *½ tsp*
Campden tablets	
nutrient	
Hock yeast	

1. Cut off the leaves, roots and any brown or damaged parts of several field or garden grown celeries. Hothouse grown celeries have less flavour. Scrub the stalks clean, then chop them up into small pieces.

2. Either boil the celery until tender and, when cool, strain and use only the liquid

OR

liquidise the celery and add this to cold water.

3. Stir in the concentrated grape juice, sugar, acid, tannin, nutrient and active yeast and pour the must into a jar. Fit an airlock and ferment out to dryness.

4. Rack into a clean jar, top up, add one Campden tablet, bung tight and store until the wine is bright, then rack again.

5. Mature this wine for one year before bottling, then serve it cold as a dry white table wine.

Celery & Apple

A dry social wine

prepared celery	1.35kg	*3lb*
cooking apples	900g	*2lb*
concentrated white grape juice	*approx.* 250g	*9oz*
sugar	900g	*2lb*
water	3.4 litres	*6 pints*
citric acid	10ml	*2 tsp*
tannin	2.5ml	*½ tsp*
pectic enzyme		
Campden tablets		
nutrient		
G.P. yeast		

1. Cut off the leaves, roots and any brown or damaged parts of several field or garden grown celeries. Hothouse celeries have less flavour. Scrub the stalks clean, then chop them up into small pieces.

2. Boil them in the water for thirty minutes then leave to cool.

3. Strain out, press and discard the pulp. Add the acid, pectic enzyme and one crushed Campden tablet.

4. Wash, crush or cut up the apples and drop them at once into the celery must. Cover and leave for twenty-four hours.

5. Add the concentrated grape juice, tannin, nutrient and active yeast. Cover and ferment on the pulp for five days, keeping the apples submerged.

6. Strain out, press dry and discard the fruit, and stir in the sugar. Pour the must into a jar, fit an airlock and ferment out.

7. Rack into a clean jar, top up, add one Campden tablet and store until the wine is bright.

8. Rack again and store for one year before bottling. Serve cool as a social wine. If it is too dry, slightly sweeten with one or two saccharin pellets per bottle.

Celery, Banana & Lemon

A medium sweet, full bodied white wine

prepared celery	1.35kg	*3lb*
ripe bananas	3	
fresh lemons	3	
concentrated white grape juice	*approx.* 250g	*9oz*
sugar	1kg	*2¼lb*
water	3.7 litres	*6½ pints*
tannin	2.5ml	*½ tsp*
no acid		
Campden tablets		
nutrient		
Sauternes yeast		

1. Cut off the leaves, roots and any brown or damaged parts of several field or garden grown celeries. Hothouse celeries have less flavour. Scrub the stalks clean, then chop them up into small pieces.

2. Peel the bananas, slice them and add to the celery.

3. Thinly pare the lemons, avoiding all white pith and add this to the celery.

4. Add the water, cover and boil for thirty minutes, then leave to cool.

5. Strain out, gently press the solids and discard them. Stir in the concentrated grape juice and sugar, the expressed and strained juice of the lemons, the tannin, nutrient and active yeast. Fit an airlock and ferment to a finish.

6. Rack the wine into a clean jar, add one Campden tablet, bung tight and store in a cold place until the wine is bright.

7. Rack again and mature the wine in bulk for nine months and in bottle for a further three months.

8. Serve cool as a medium sweet, full bodied, white social wine. If need be, slightly sweeten each bottle to your taste with one or two saccharin pellets.

Cherry 1

A dry white made with cooking cherries

cooking cherries	2kg *4½lb*
concentrated white grape juice	*approx.* 250g *9oz*
sugar	800g *1¾lb*
water	3.4 litres *6 pints*
citric acid	5ml *1 tsp*
tannin	2.5ml *½ tsp*
pectic enzyme	
Campden tablets	
nutrient	
Bordeaux yeast	

1. Wash and stalk the cherries and place them in a polythene bin. Pour on hot water and when it is cool, mash the cherries and remove all the stones.

2. Add the acid, pectic enzyme and one crushed Campden tablet. Cover and leave for twenty-four hours.

3. Stir in the concentrated grape juice, tannin, nutrient and activated yeast, then cover the bin and ferment on the pulp for three days keeping the cherries submerged.

4. Strain out, press and discard the fruit, stir in the sugar, pour the must into a jar, top up, fit an airlock and continue the fermentation to a finish.

5. Move the jar to a cold place for three days then syphon the clearing wine into a clean jar, top up with cold boiled water, add one Campden tablet, bung tight, label and store the wine in a cold place until it is bright.

6. Rack again and keep the wine until it is one year old before bottling it. Serve it as a dry white wine.

Cherry 2

A sweet dessert wine made with mixed cherries

mixed cherries	1.8kg *4lb*
Morello cherries	450g *1lb*
concentrated red grape juice	*approx.* 250g *9oz*
sugar	1.35kg *3lb*
water	3.1 litres *5¼ pints*
citric acid	10ml *2 tsp*
tannin	5ml *1 tsp*
pectic enzyme	
Campden tablets	
nutrient	
Port yeast	

1. Wash, stalk and stone the cherries and place them in a bin containing the water, acid, pectic enzyme and one crushed Campden tablet. Cover and leave for twenty-four hours.

2. Add the concentrated grape juice, tannin, nutrient and active yeast. Cover and ferment on the pulp for four days keeping the fruit submerged.

3. Strain out, press and discard the fruit, stir in 450g (*1lb*) sugar, pour the must into a jar leaving room for the rest of the sugar. Fit an airlock and ferment for seven days.

4. Take out some of the must, stir in 225g (*½lb*) sugar, return the must to the jar, re-fit the airlock and continue fermentation for another five days.

5. Repeat this process three more times until all the sugar has been added and fermentation has ceased.

6. Move the jar to a cold place for two days then rack the clearing wine into a sterilised storage jar. Top up with port wine, vodka, sweet red wine or cold boiled water. Bung tight and store until the wine is bright, then rack again and store for at least one year in bulk and another in bottle. Serve as a sweet dessert wine after a meal.

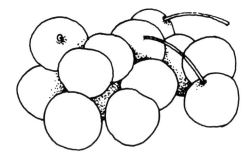

Cherry 3

A table wine made with pie filling

cherry pie filling	1.35kg *3lb*
concentrated red grape juice	*approx.* 250g *9oz*
sugar	680g *1½lb*
water	3.4 litres *6 pints*
citric acid	10ml *2 tsp*
tannin	5ml *1 tsp*
pectic enzyme	
amylase	
Campden tablets	
nutrient	
Bordeaux yeast	

1. Empty the pie filling into a polythene bin containing hot water and stir until the pulp is well dispersed. Cover and leave to cool.

2. Stir in the concentrated grape juice, citric acid, tannin, pectic enzyme and one crushed Campden tablet. Cover and leave for twenty-four hours.

3. If the labels indicate that the contents include 'edible starch', add the quantity of amylase recommended by the manufacturer – it varies. The amylase converts the starch to sugar. If it is omitted the wine may contain a starch haze.

An alternative is to use a cereal yeast (*Saccharomyces diastaticus*) which is able to ferment a small amount of starch.

4. Add the activated yeast and nutrient and ferment on the pulp for three days.

5. Strain the must through a fine meshed nylon straining bag to remove the solid particles. Stir in the sugar and when it is dissolved pour the must into a fermentation jar, top up if necessary, fit an airlock and ferment out to dryness.

6. Move the jar to a cold place for a few days, then rack the wine into a clean jar, and add one Campden tablet. Top up, bung tight and store until the wine is bright.

7. Syphon into bottles, cork and label them, and keep the wine until it is four months old. Serve as a table wine.

Cherry 4

A sweet social wine made with cherry jam

Morello cherry jam	1.35kg *3lb*
concentrated red grape juice	*approx.* 250g *9oz*
sugar	680g *1½lb*
water (see note)	3.4 litres *6 pints*
citric acid	10ml *2 tsp*
tannin	5ml *1 tsp*
pectic enzyme	
Campden tablets	
nutrient	
Port yeast	

1. Empty the jam into a polythene bin containing hot water and stir until the pulp is well dispersed. Cover and leave to cool.

2. Stir in the concentrated grape juice, citric acid, pectic enzyme and one crushed Campden tablet. Cover and leave for twenty-four hours.

3. Add the tannin, activated yeast and nutrient, cover and ferment on the pulp for three days, keeping the fruit submerged.

4. Strain the must through a fine meshed nylon straining bag to remove the solid particles. Stir in the sugar and when it is dissolved pour the must into a fermentation jar, top up if necessary, fit an airlock and ferment out.

5. Move the jar to a cold place for a few days, then rack the wine into a clean jar, top up, add one Campden tablet, bung tight and store until the wine is bright.

6. Syphon into bottles, cork and label them and keep the wine until it is nine months old. Serve it free from chill as a lovely flavoured social wine.

NOTE:
Two interesting variations are to use cider or strong ale instead of water. Stir one third of the sugar in at first, add the rest in 113g (*4oz*) quantities each time the specific gravity falls to 1.010. Finally sweeten to 1.020. You may not need all the sugar.

Cherry Plum

A medium sweet, white social wine

ripe cherry plums	2kg	*4½ lb*
ripe bananas	2	
concentrated white grape juice	*approx.* 250g	*9oz*
sugar	1kg	*2¼ lb*
water	3.4 litres	*6 pints*
citric acid	10ml	*2 tsp*
tannin	2.5ml	*½ tsp*
pectic enzyme		
Campden tablets		
nutrient		
Sauternes yeast		
potassium sorbate		

1. Stalk, wash and stone the cherry plums, peel and mash the bananas and add them to a bin containing the water, pectic enzyme, acid and one crushed Campden tablet. Cover and leave for twenty-four hours.

2. Stir in the grape juice, tannin, nutrient and active yeast. Cover and ferment on the pulp for four days keeping the fruit submerged.

3. Strain out, shake well and discard the pulp, stir in the sugar, pour the must into a jar, top up, fit an airlock and ferment down to 1.006.

4. Rack into a sterilised jar containing 1g potassium sorbate and one Campden tablet. Top up, bung tight and store until the wine is bright.

5. Rack again, store for one year in bulk and three months in bottle. Serve this medium sweet white wine cold as a social beverage.

Coffee

An unusual medium sweet wine

ground coffee	250g	*9oz*
and		
instant coffee	125g	*4½ oz*
or		
coffee essence	125g	*4½ oz*
concentrated white grape juice	*approx.* 250g	*9oz*
sugar	1kg	*2¼ lb*
water	3.7 litres	*6½ pin*
lemons	2	
bitter orange	1	
Campden tablet		
nutrient		
G.P. yeast		

no acid,* tannin or pectic enzyme

1. Thinly pare the lemons and orange, chop up the parings and pour boiling water over them. Add the coffee, stir well, cover and leave to cool.

2. Strain out and discard the solids, stir in the concentrated grape juice, half the sugar, the expressed and strained lemon and orange juice, the nutrient and yeast.

3. Pour the must into a sterilised jar, top up if necessary, fit an airlock and ferment for eight days before adding the rest of the sugar.

4. When fermentation is finished rack into a clean jar, add one Campden tablet and store in a cool place until the wine is bright. Syphon into bottles, sweetening each one with saccharin to suit your taste.

5. Keep this wine for three months before serving it chilled as an unusual social wine.

NOTE:
The different flavoured coffees make different flavoured wines. When using ground coffee ensure that freshly roasted beans have been ground for you.

*If chicory is included in the essence, omit the bitter orange and include one level 5ml spoonful of citric acid.

Coltsfoot

A medium sweet social wine

coltsfoot heads	2 litres *3½ pints*
concentrated white grape juice	*approx.* 250g *9oz*
sugar	1kg *2¼lb*
water	3.7 litres *6½ pints*
citric acid	15ml *3 tsp*
tannin	2.5ml *½ tsp*
Campden tablets	
nutrient	
Hock yeast	
potassium sorbate	

1. Remove all the green from the flower heads and use only the petals.

2. Place the petals in a suitable vessel, poor hot water over them and rub them against the side of the vessel with the back of a wooden spoon to extract the essence.

3. Cover and leave to cool, then add the acid and one crushed Campden tablet.

4. Macerate the petals as described twice each day for three days keeping the vessel closely covered.

5. Strain out, press dry and discard the petals. Stir in the grape juice, half the sugar, tannin, nutrient and an active yeast. Pour the must into a fermentation jar, fit an airlock and ferment for ten days.

6. Remove some must, stir in the rest of the sugar, return the must to the jar, re-fit the airlock and ferment to 1.006.

7. Rack the wine into a clean jar containing 1g potassium sorbate and one Campden tablet. Top up with cold boiled water, bung tight and store until the wine is bright.

8. Rack again and mature for six months before bottling. Serve it cold as a social wine.

Currant

A sweet wine

dried currants	2kg *4½lb*
concentrated white grape juice	*approx.* 250g *9oz*
lemon	1
hot water	4 litres *7 pints*
pectic enzyme	
Campden tablets	
All Purpose wine yeast	
no acid, tannin, nutrient or sugar	

1. Wash the currants, liquidise, mince or chop them up; thinly pare the lemon and add the parings only; pour hot water over them, cover and leave to cool. Add the expressed and strained juice of the lemon, the pectic enzyme and one crushed Campden tablet, cover and leave for twenty-four hours.

2. Add the concentrated grape juice and activated yeast and ferment on the pulp for ten days keeping the pulp submerged and the bin covered.

3. Strain out, press dry and discard the pulp. Pour the must into a sterilised jar, top up, fit an airlock and ferment out.

4. Syphon the clearing wine into a storage jar, top up, add one Campden tablet, bung tight and store until the wine is bright. Rack again and mature for one year.

Dandelion

A medium sweet, social wine

dandelion heads	2 litres *3½ pints*
concentrated white grape juice	*approx.* 500g *18oz*
sugar	900g *2lb*
hot water	3.4 litres *6 pints*
citric acid	15ml *3 tsp*
tannin	2.5ml *½ tsp*
Campden tablets	
nutrient	
Hock yeast	
potassium sorbate	

1. Remove all the green from the flower heads and use only the petals.

2. Place these in a suitable vessel, pour hot water over them and rub them against the side of the vessel with the back of a wooden spoon to extract the essence. Cover and leave to cool.

3. Add the acid and one crushed Campden tablet and macerate the petals twice each day for three days, keeping the vessel covered at other times.

4. Strain out, press dry and discard the petals, stir in the concentrated grape juice, sugar, tannin, nutrient and yeast. Pour the must into a fermentation jar, fit an airlock and ferment down to S.G. 1.006.

5. Rack into a clean jar, add 1g potassium sorbate and one Campden tablet, bung tight and as soon as the wine is clear, rack again and store for three months.

6. Syphon into bottles, cork, label and store for a further three to six months. Serve cold as a medium sweet social wine.

Dried Fruit

A strong, sweet dessert wine

raisins	450g *1lb*
dates	225g *½lb*
prunes	225g *½lb*
figs	112.5g *¼lb*
apricots	112.5g *¼lb*
brown sugar	900g *2lb*
water	3.4 litres *6 pints*
citric, malic and tartaric acid . . . of each	25g *2 sm. tsp*
tannin	2.5ml *½ tsp*
pectic enzyme, Campden tablets	
nutrient, Madeira yeast	

1. Wash the fruit, place it in a bin and pour hot water over it. Cover and leave overnight.

2. Break up or liquidise the fruit, first removing the prune stones.

3. Add the acids, pectic enzyme and one crushed Campden tablet, cover and leave for twenty-four hours in a warm place.

4. Add the tannin, nutrient and active yeast, then cover and ferment on the pulp for three days, keeping the fruit submerged.

5. Strain out and press the fruit dry, and stir in one third of the sugar. Pour into a sterilised jar, leave space for the rest of the sugar, fit an airlock and ferment for ten days.

6. Remove some of the must, stir in half the remaining sugar and return it to the jar. Replace the airlock and continue fermentation for a further ten days.

7. Add the remaining sugar as previously described and if need be top up with cold boiled water. Replace the airlock and continue the fermentation.

8. When the wine is quite still move the jar to a cool place for a few days, then rack into a clean jar. Plug the neck with cotton wool, label and store in a cool place until the wine is bright.

9. Rack again and mature in a warm place for at least one year in bulk and six months in bottle. This is a strong, sweet dessert wine with the caramelised flavour of Madeira.

Dried fruits make excellent wines in their own right, as well as being useful additives to other wines. The table on page 252 gives some important comparisons between the sugar, acid, tannin and water content of dried and fresh fruit.

Elderberry

A dry red table wine

elderberries	1kg	2¼ lb
ripe bananas	3	
concentrated red grape juice	*approx.* 250g	9oz
sugar	1kg	2¼ lb
water	3.4 litres	6 pints
citric acid	15ml	3 tsp
pectic enzyme		
Campden tablets		
nutrient		
Burgundy yeast		

1. Stalk and wash the elderberries, and crush or liquidise them. Peel and mash the bananas. Place the fruit in a polythene bin and pour boiling water over it. Cover and leave to cool.

2. Add the pectic enzyme, acid and one crushed Campden tablet. Replace the cover and leave for twenty-four hours.

3. Stir in the concentrated grape juice, nutrient and active yeast; cover and ferment on the pulp for three days keeping the fruit submerged.

4. Strain out, drain dry and discard the pulp, and stir in the sugar. Pour the must into a fermentation jar, top up if necessary, fit an airlock and ferment out.

5. Rack into a clean jar, top up, add one crushed Campden tablet, bung tight and label.

6. Store the jar in a cold place until the wine is bright, then rack again.

7. Mature this wine in bulk until it is one year old, then bottle it and keep it for a further six months. Serve it free from chill as a red table wine with casseroles and similar well flavoured dishes.

Elderberry & Banana

A dry red table wine

ripe elderberries	900g	2lb
bananas	450g	1lb
concentrated red grape juice	*approx.* 250g	9oz
sugar	800g	1¾ lb
water	2.8 litres	5 pints
citric acid	15ml	3 tsp
tannin	2.5ml	½ tsp
pectic enzyme		
Campden tablets		
nutrient		
Burgundy yeast		

1. Stalk, wash and crush the elderberries, peel and mash the bananas and place them in a bin. Pour hot water over them, cover and leave to cool.

2. Stir in the concentrated grape juice, citric acid and pectic enzyme. Re-cover and leave in a warm place for twenty-four hours.

3. Add the tannin, nutrient and an activated yeast, then ferment on the pulp for three days, keeping the fruit submerged.

4. Strain out, press dry and discard the fruit. Stir in the sugar and, when it is dissolved, pour the must into a jar, top up with cold boiled water, fit an airlock and ferment out to dryness.

5. Move the wine to a cold place for a few days to encourage clarification then rack it into a clean jar, top up and add one Campden tablet. Bung tight, label and store until the wine is bright, then rack again.

6. Mature this wine for twelve months before bottling, then keep it for another six months. Serve as a dry red table wine with red meats, game and cheese.

Elderberry & Bilberry

A dry red table wine

ripe elderberries	900g *2lb*
bilberries	450g *1lb*
ripe banana	1
concentrated red grape juice	*approx.* 250g *9oz*
sugar	800g *1¾lb*
water	2.8 litres *5 pints*
citric acid	10ml *2 tsp*
tannin	2.5ml *½ tsp*
pectic enzyme	
Campden tablets	
nutrient	
Burgundy yeast	

1. Stalk, wash and crush the berries, peel and mash the banana, place in a bin. Pour hot water over them, cover and leave to cool.

2. Stir in the concentrated grape juice, citric acid and pectic enzyme. Re-cover and leave in a warm place for twenty-four hours.

3. Add the tannin, nutrient and an activated yeast, then ferment on the pulp for three days, keeping the fruit submerged.

4. Strain out, press dry and discard the fruit, stir in the sugar and when it is dissolved, pour the must into a jar, top up with cold boiled water, fit an air-lock and ferment out to dryness.

5. Move the wine to a cold place for a few days to encourage clarification then rack it into a clean jar, top up and add one Campden tablet. Bung tight, label and store until the wine is bright, then rack again.

6. Mature this wine for twelve months before bottling then keep it for another six months. Serve as a dry red table wine with red meats, game and cheese.

Elderberry & Blackberry 1

A dry red table wine

ripe elderberries	900g *2lb*
ripe blackberries	900g *2lb*
concentrated red grape juice	*approx.* 250g *9oz*
sugar	800g *1¾lb*
water	2.8 litres *5 pints*
citric acid	10ml *2 tsp*
tannin	2.5ml *½ tsp*
pectic enzyme	
Campden tablets	
nutrient	
Burgundy yeast	

1. Stalk, wash and crush the berries, and place them in a mashing bin. Pour hot water over them, cover and leave to cool.

2. Stir in the concentrated grape juice, citric acid and pectic enzyme. Re-cover and leave in a warm place for twenty-four hours.

3. Add the tannin, nutrient and an activated yeast, then ferment on the pulp for three days, keeping the fruit submerged.

4. Strain out, press dry and discard the fruit. Stir in the sugar and, when it is dissolved, pour the must into a jar, top up with cold boiled water, fit an air-lock and ferment out to dryness.

5. Move the wine to a cold place for a few days to encourage clarification then rack it into a clean jar, top up and add one Campden tablet. Bung tight, label and store until the wine is bright, then rack again.

6. Mature this wine for twelve months before bottling, then keep it for another six months. Serve as a dry red table wine with red meats, game and cheese.

Elderberry & Blackberry 2

A dessert wine made with rose hip syrup

elderberries	680g *1¼lb*
blackberries	680g *1¼*lb
rose hip syrup	340ml *12 fl oz*
concentrated red grape juice	*approx.* 250g *9oz*
sugar	900g *2lb*
water	3 litres *5½ pints*
citric acid	10ml *2 tsp*
pectic enzyme	
nutrient	
Port yeast	
Campden tablets	
no tannin	

1. Stalk, wash and crush the fruit. Pour hot water over it, cover and leave to cool.

2. Stir in the rose hip syrup and grape juice concentrate, one crushed Campden tablet, the acid and pectic enzyme. Cover and leave for twenty-four hours.

3. Add the nutrient and an active yeast. Ferment on the pulp for four days, keeping the fruit submerged.

4. Strain out, press dry and discard the fruit. Stir in half the sugar and pour the must into a fermentation jar, fit an airlock and ferment down to S.G. 1.010.

5. Stir in half the remaining sugar and, when S.G. 1.010 is reached again, stir in the rest.

6. When fermentation finishes, check the S.G. and if need be increase it to 1.020 with more sugar.

7. As soon as the wine begins to clear, syphon it into a clean jar, top up, add one Campden tablet, bung tight, label and store until the wine is bright.

8. Rack again and store for one year, then bottle and store for a further year. Serve with cheese.

Elderberry & Blackcurrant

A dry red table wine

ripe elderberries	900g *2lb*
ripe blackcurrants	450g *1lb*
ripe bananas	2
concentrated red grape juice	*approx.* 250g *9oz*
sugar	800g *1¾lb*
water	2.8 litres *5 pints*
citric acid	5ml *1 tsp*
tannin	2.5ml *½ tsp*
pectic enzyme	
Campden tablets	
nutrient	
Burgundy yeast	

1. Stalk, wash and crush the berries, peel and mash the bananas, and place them in a mashing bin. Pour hot water over them, cover and leave to cool.

2. Stir in the concentrated grape juice, citric acid and pectic enzyme. Re-cover and leave in a warm place for twenty-four hours.

3. Add the tannin, nutrient and an activated yeast, then ferment on the pulp for three days, keeping the fruit submerged.

4. Strain out, press dry and discard the fruit. Stir in the sugar and when it is dissolved, pour the must into a jar, top up with cold boiled water, fit an airlock and ferment out to dryness.

5. Move the wine to a cold place for a few days to encourage clarification then rack it into a clean jar, top up and add one Campden tablet. Bung tight, label and store until the wine is bright, then rack again.

6. Mature this wine for twelve months before bottling, then keep it for another six months. Serve as a dry red table wine with red meats, game and cheese.

Elderberry & Damson

A dry red table wine

ripe elderberries	900g	*2lb*
ripe damsons	900g	*2lb*
ripe banana		1
concentrated red grape juice	*approx.* 250g	*9oz*
sugar	800g	*1¾lb*
water	2.8 litres	*5 pints*
citric acid	10ml	*2 tsp*
tannin	2.5ml	*½ tsp*
pectic enzyme		
Campden tablets		
nutrient		
Burgundy yeast		

1. Stalk, wash and stone the damsons, crush the elderberries, peel and mash the banana and place them all in a bin. Pour hot water over them, cover and leave to cool.

2. Stir in the concentrated grape juice, citric acid and pectic enzyme. Re-cover and leave in a warm place for twenty-four hours.

3. Add the tannin, nutrient and an activated yeast, then ferment on the pulp for three days, keeping the fruit submerged.

4. Strain out, press dry and discard the fruit. Stir in the sugar and when it is dissolved, pour the must into a jar, top up with cold boiled water, fit an airlock and ferment out to dryness.

5. Move the wine to a cold place for a few days to encourage clarification then rack it into a clean jar, top up and add one Campden tablet. Bung tight, label and store until the wine is bright, then rack again.

6. Mature this wine for twelve months before bottling then keep it for another six months. Serve as a dry red table wine with red meats, game and cheese.

Elderberry & Runner Bean

A dry red table wine

ripe elderberries	900g	*2lb*
runner beans	450g	*1lb*
concentrated red grape juice	*approx.* 250g	*9oz*
sugar	800g	*1¾lb*
water	2.8 litres	*5 pints*
citric acid	15ml	*3 tsp*
tannin	2.5ml	*½ tsp*
pectic enzyme		
Campden tablets		
nutrient		
Burgundy yeast		

1. Wash and thinly slice the beans, place them in a pan, pour on boiling water, bring to the boil and simmer for thirty minutes.

2. Stalk, wash and crush the elderberries, place them in a mashing bin and strain the runner bean liquor on to them. Cover and leave to cool.

3. Stir in the concentrated grape juice, citric acid and pectic enzyme. Re-cover and leave in a warm place for twenty-four hours.

4. Add the tannin, nutrient and an activated yeast, then ferment on the pulp for three days, keeping the fruit submerged.

5. Strain out, press dry and discard the fruit. Stir in the sugar and when it is dissolved, pour the must into a jar, top up with cold boiled water, fit an airlock and ferment out to dryness.

6. Move the wine to a cold place for a few days to encourage clarification then rack it into a clean jar, top up and add one Campden tablet. Bung tight, label and store until the wine is bright, then rack again.

7. Mature this wine for twelve months before bottling then keep it for another six months. Serve as a dry red table wine with red meats, game and cheese.

Elderflower

A fragrant, medium sweet social wine

elderflowers	560ml	*1 pint*
concentrated white grape juice	*approx.* 1kg	*2¼ lb*
sugar	170g	*6oz*
hot water	3.4 litres	*6 pints*
Campden tablets		
nutrient		
Hock yeast		
no acid, tannin or pectic enzyme		

1. Pick the flowers on a fine sunny day from several different trees. Take them home in paper *not* plastic bags, since the latter cause 'sweating'. Remove every trace of leaf and stem, because the green causes bitterness. Place the florets in a suitable measure, shake them down but do not press them.

2. Empty the florets into a ceramic bowl or small polythene bin, pour hot water over them and rub them against the side of the vessel with the back of a wooden spoon to extract the essence. Cover and leave to cool.

3. Add one crushed Campden tablet and macerate the florets twice a day for two days. Strain out, press dry and discard the petals, stir in the concentrated grape juice, sugar, nutrient and yeast. Pour the must into a fermentation jar, fit an airlock and ferment out.

4. Rack into a clean jar, add one crushed Campden tablet, top up, bung tight and store the wine until bright.

5. Syphon into bottles, add two saccharin pellets to each and store until the wine is six months old. Serve it cold as a delightfully fragrant social wine.

Folly

A dry white table wine

young vine shoots, leaves and prunings	2.5kg	*5½ lb*
bananas	2	
concentrated white grape juice	*approx.* 250g	*9oz*
sugar	800g	*1¾ lb*
water	4 litres	*7 pints*
citric acid	15ml	*3 tsp*
tannin	2.5ml	*½ tsp*
nutrient		
Graves yeast		

1. Wash the shoots, chop them up and place them in a pan for boiling. Peel and thinly slice the bananas and add to the pan. Pour on the water, bring to the boil, cover and simmer for thirty minutes then leave to cool.

2. Strain out, drain and discard the solids. Stir in the concentrated grape juice, sugar, acid, tannin, nutrient and an active yeast. Pour the must into a jar, top up if necessary, fit an airlock and ferment out to dryness.

3. Rack into a clean jar, top up, add one Campden tablet, bung tight and store until the wine is bright.

4. Rack again and store for one year before bottling. Serve cold as a dry white table wine.

NOTE:
This wine is named after the French word for a leaf – *feuille.*

Gooseberry 1

Light and dry, made with fresh gooseberries

gooseberries (careless var.)	1.35kg	*3lb*
concentrated white grape juice	*approx.* 250g	*9oz*
sugar	800g	*1¼lb*
water	3.7 litres	*6½ pints*
citric acid	5ml	*1 tsp*
tannin	2.5ml	*½ tsp*
pectic enzyme		
Campden tablets		
nutrient		
Hock yeast		

1. Top, tail and wash the gooseberries, pour hot water over them and leave to cool.

2. Crush the now softened berries, add the acid, pectic enzyme and one crushed Campden tablet, cover and leave twenty-four hours.

3. Stir in the concentrated grape juice, tannin, nutrient and active yeast and ferment on the pulp for three days, keeping the fruit submerged.

4. Strain out, press and discard the fruit. Stir in the sugar, pour the must into a sterilised jar, top up, fit an airlock and ferment out.

5. Move the jar to a cool place for a few days, then rack into a clean jar, and add one Campden tablet. Bung tight, label and store until the wine is bright.

6. Syphon into bottles and store this wine for twelve months before serving it cold, as a light dry table wine.

Gooseberry 2

A dry wine made with tinned gooseberries

gooseberries in sugar syrup	1.35kg	*3lb*
concentrated white grape juice	*approx.* 250g	*9oz*
sugar	800g	*1¼lb*
water	2.8 litres	*5 pints*
citric acid	10ml	*2 tsp*
tannin	2.5ml	*½ tsp*
pectic enzyme		
Campden tablets		
nutrient		
Hock yeast		

1. Separate the fruit from the syrup, and set aside the syrup for use later.

2. Mash the fruit and place it in a bin with 2 litres (*3½ pints*) water, the acid, pectic enzyme and one crushed Campden tablet. Cover and leave for twenty-four hours.

3. Add the fruit syrup, concentrated grape juice, tannin, nutrient and active yeast. Ferment for three days keeping the fruit submerged.

4. Strain out the pulp, stir in the sugar, and pour the must into a fermentation jar. Top up, fit an airlock and ferment to dryness.

5. Rack, add one Campden tablet and as soon as the wine is bright, syphon it into bottles and store for three months.

Gooseberry & Banana

A sweet social or dessert wine

yellow/green gooseberries	1.8kg *4lb*
ripe bananas	450g *1lb*
concentrated white grape juice	*approx.* 250g *9oz*
sugar	900g *2lb*
water	2.5 litres *4½ pints*
tannin	2.5ml *½ tsp*
citric acid	10ml *2 tsp*
pectic enzyme	
Campden tablets	
nutrient	
Sauternes yeast	
potassium sorbate	

1. Wash, top and tail gooseberries and place them in a bin with the peeled and thinly sliced bananas. Pour hot water over them, cover, and leave until cool. Then crush the fruit ensuring that each berry is broken.

2. Add the pectic enzyme, acid and one crushed Campden tablet, cover and leave for twenty-four hours.

3. Stir in the concentrated grape juice, tannin, nutrient and activated yeast, replace the cover and ferment on the pulp for four days, keeping the fruit submerged.

4. Strain out, press and discard the fruit pulp, stir in the sugar and, when it is dissolved, pour the must into jar. Top up with cold boiled water if necessary, fit an airlock and ferment down to S.G. 1.016.

5. Rack the wine into a clean jar containing 1g potassium sorbate and one crushed Campden tablet to end the fermentation. Top up, bung tight and store in a cold place until the wine is bright.

6. Rack again and store until the wine is one year old. Serve cold with the sweet course of a meal or as a social wine with sweet cake or biscuits.

Grape 1

A medium sweet English rosé

black and white grapes
pectic enzyme
Campden tablets
sugar as necessary
Bordeaux yeast

1. Use three measures of white grapes to one of black. Stalk, wash and crush them, add one 5ml spoonful of pectic enzyme and one crushed Campden tablet per 15lb. Cover and leave for twenty-four hours.

2. Strain out some of the juice, check the specific gravity and calculate how much sugar will be required to increase the reading to 1.078.

3. If the colour of the juice is already a pretty pink, strain out and press the pulp dry and add the yeast. If not add the yeast and ferment on the pulp for a day or two, keeping the skins submerged.

4. When the colour of the juice pleases you, strain out and press the pulp dry, stir in the sugar, pour the must into jars, fit airlocks and ferment out.

5. Rack into clean jars, add one Campden tablet per gallon, bung tight and store until the wine is bright.

6. Rack into bottles, sweeten each with one or two saccharin tablets per bottle and keep for six to nine months. Serve this attractive rosé wine cold.

NOTE:
As a guide to quantity 15lb of grapes, well pressed, produces about one gallon of juice.

Grape 2

A dry English red

black grapes (mixed varieties if possible)
pectic enzyme
Campden tablets
sugar as necessary
Burgundy yeast

1. Leave the grapes on the vines as long as you can so that they develop as much sugar as possible.

2. Stalk, wash and crush them, add one 5ml spoonful of pectic enzyme, and one crushed Campden tablet per 15lb. Cover and leave for twenty-four hours.

3. Strain out some of the juice, check the specific gravity and calculate how much sugar will be required to raise the gravity to 1.086, but do not add it yet.

4. Stir in an activated wine yeast and ferment in a covered bin for eight to ten days keeping the skins submerged.

5. Check the specific gravity daily after six days and when the reading is down to 1.006 strain out, press dry and discard the skins. Stir in the sugar, pour the must into jars, fit airlocks and ferment out.

6. Rack into clean jars, add one Campden tablet per gallon, bung tight and store in a cool place until the wine is bright.

7. Rack again and store for eighteen months or so.

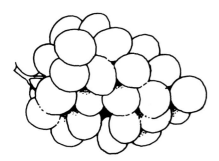

Grape 3

A dry English white

white grapes (mixed varieties if possible)
pectic enzyme
Campden tablets
sugar as necessary
Hock yeast

1. Leave the grapes on the vines as long as you can so that they develop as much sugar as possible.

2. Stalk, wash and crush them, add one 5ml spoonful of pectic enzyme, and one crushed Campden tablet per 15lb. Cover and leave for twenty-four hours.

3. Strain out and press the pulp dry, check the specific gravity and stir in enough sugar to raise the reading to around 1.074.

4. Add an activated yeast, pour the must into jars, fit airlocks and ferment out in a coolish place, 60°F *(15.5°C)*.

5. Rack into clean jars, add one Campden tablet per gallon, bung tight and store until the wine is bright.

6. Syphon the wine into bottles, add one or two saccharin tablets to each and keep it for six to nine months. Serve it cold.

Grape 4

Red, white or rosé from imported grapes

grapes
pectic enzyme
Campden tablets
citric acid
Bordeaux yeast

Grapefruit

A dry aperitif

large fresh grapefruit	4
concentrated white grape juice	*approx.* 500g *18oz*
sugar	800g *1¼lb*
water	3.4 litres *6 pints*
Campden tablets	
nutrient	
Hock yeast	

no acid, tannin or pectic enzyme

Apart from flavour the difference between imported and English grapes is the higher sugar and lower acid content of the imported varieties. These are dessert grapes more suitable for eating rather than making into wine.

Successful wine has been made from the little seedless sultana grapes obtainable from the greengrocer in August and from the larger black and white Almeria grapes available in the autumn.

They are most successful when blended measure for measure with English grapes when the acids and sugars compensate.

If you use imported grapes exclusively, leave out any that are brown or mouldy. Stalk, wash and crush the rest. Add one 5ml spoonful of citric acid per 15lb grapes and make red, white or rosé wines in the manner described for English grape wines.

1. Thinly pare the grapefruit avoiding all white pith, chop up the parings and place them in a polythene bin containing the water.

2. Cut each grapefruit in half, squeeze out and strain the juice, add it to the parings.

3. Add the concentrated grape juice, nutrient and yeast and ferment for three days, keeping the parings moist and the bin covered.

4. Strain out and press the parings. Stir in the sugar, and pour the must into a fermentation jar, fit an airlock and ferment out.

5. Rack into a clean jar, add one Campden tablet, top up, bung tight and store until the wine is bright.

6. Rack again and store for nine months before bottling. Take the edge off the dryness with one saccharin pellet per bottle if so desired. Serve cold as an aperitif.

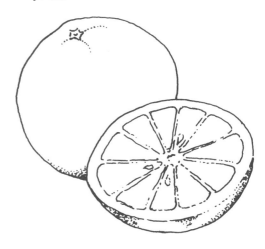

Greengage & Banana

A sweet social or dessert wine

fresh greengages	1.8kg *4lb*
ripe bananas	450g *1lb*
concentrated white grape juice	*approx.* 250g *9oz*
sugar	900g *2lb*
water	2.5 litres *4½ pints*
citric acid	5ml *1 tsp*
tannin	2.5ml *½ tsp*
pectic enzyme	
Campden tablets	
nutrient	
Sauternes yeast	
potassium sorbate	

1. Wash and stalk the greengages and place them in a bin with the peeled and thinly sliced bananas. Pour hot water over them, cover and, when cool, remove and discard the stones.

2. Add the acid, pectic enzyme and one crushed Campden tablet. Cover and leave for twenty-four hours.

3. Stir in the concentrated grape juice, tannin, nutrient and activated yeast, replace the cover and ferment on the pulp for four days, keeping the fruit submerged.

4. Strain out, press and discard the fruit pulp, stir in the sugar and, when it is dissolved, pour the must into a jar. Top up with cold boiled water if necessary, fit an airlock and ferment down to S.G. 1.016.

5. Rack the wine into a clean jar containing 1g potassium sorbate and one crushed Campden tablet to end the fermentation. Top up, bung tight and store in a cold place until the wine is bright.

6. Rack again and store until the wine is one year old. Serve cold with the sweet course of a meal or as a social wine with sweet cake or biscuits.

Grocer's Red 1

A dry table wine made with tinned fruits

blackberries, black cherries, damsons and prunes in sugar syrup . . . of each	450g *1lb*
concentrated red grape juice	*approx.* 250g *9oz*
water	2.8 litres *5 pints*
sugar	900g *2lb*
citric acid	10ml *2 tsp*
tannin	5ml *1 tsp*
pectic enzyme	
nutrient	
Bordeaux yeast	
Campden tablets	

1. Separate the fruit from the syrup which should be set aside. Remove and discard the stones, mash the fruit and add to the bin containing the water, pectic enzyme, acid and one crushed Campden tablet. Cover and leave for twenty-four hours.

2. Add the fruit syrup, grape juice, tannin, nutrient and activated wine yeast. Ferment on the pulp for four days keeping the fruit submerged and the bin covered.

3. Strain out, press dry and discard the fruit, and stir in the sugar. Pour the must into a sterilised jar, top up, fit an airlock and ferment out to dryness.

4. Rack into a storage jar, top up, add one Campden tablet, bung tight and store until the wine is bright, then rack again. Mature for six months in bulk and three months in bottle. Serve free from chill as a red table wine.

Grocer's Red 2

Robust and dry, made from mixed jams

bramble jelly, blackcurrant jam		
and damson jam . . . of each	450g	*1lb*
concentrated red grape juice *approx.*	250g	*9oz*
sugar	225g	*½lb*
citric acid	10ml	*2 tsp*
tannin	5ml	*1 tsp*
water	2.8 litres	*5 pints*
pectic enzyme (double dose)		
Campden tablets		
nutrient		
Bordeaux yeast		

1. Dissolve the bramble jelly, blackcurrant and damson jams in hot water. Cover and leave to cool, then remove any damson stones.

2. Stir in the pectic enzyme, acid and one crushed Campden tablet. Cover and leave for twenty-four hours.

3. Stir in the concentrated grape juice, tannin, nutrient and an activated yeast. Cover and ferment on the pulp for three days, keeping the fruit skins submerged.

4. Strain out, press dry and discard the solids, and stir in the sugar. Pour the must into a sterilised jar, top up with cold boiled water, fit an airlock and ferment out to dryness.

5. Rack the wine into a clean jar, top up, add one crushed Campden tablet, bung tight and store in a cold place until the wine is bright.

6. Rack again and keep the wine in bulk for six months before bottling. Serve it free from chill as a robust, dry red table wine with red meats, game or cheese.

Grocer's Rosé

A dry wine made with tinned fruits

raspberries, strawberries and		
red plums in sugar syrup . . . of each	450g	*1lb*
concentrated rosé grape juice *approx.*	250g	*9oz*
sugar	800g	*1¾lb*
water	2.8 litres	*5 pints*
citric acid	10ml	*2 tsp*
tannin	2.5ml	*½ tsp*
pectic enzyme		
nutrient		
Campden tablets		
Bordeaux yeast		

1. Separate the fruit from the syrup, which should be set aside. Remove and discard the stones, mash the fruit and add to the bin containing the water, pectic enzyme, acid and one crushed Campden tablet, cover and leave for twenty-four hours.

2. Add the fruit syrup, grape juice, tannin, nutrient and activated wine yeast. Ferment on the pulp for three days keeping the fruit submerged.

3. Strain out, press dry and discard the pulp, and stir in the sugar. Pour the must into a fermentation jar, top up, fit an airlock and ferment to dryness.

4. Rack, add one Campden tablet and, as soon as the wine is bright, syphon it into bottles, sweeten to taste with saccharin and mature until it is four months old.

Hedgerow flowers and fruits, such as the crab apples, elderberries, sloes and blackberries shown here, reduce the cost of winemaking substantially and produce excellent country wines. Crab apples also improve cider if included in a mixture of apples, and sloes can be used to make sloe gin.

Grocer's White 1

Light and dry, quickly mature, tinned fruit

gooseberries, apricots and golden plums in sugar syrup . . . of each	450g	*1 lb*
concentrated white grape juice *approx.*	250g	*9oz*
sugar	800g	*1¾ lb*
water	2.8 litres	*5 pints*
citric acid	10ml	*2 tsp*
tannin	2.5ml	*½ tsp*
pectic enzyme		
Campden tablets		
nutrient		
Hock yeast		

1. Separate the fruit from the syrup, which should be set aside.

2. Mash the fruit, discard the stones, and place it in a bin containing 3½ pints water, the acid, pectic enzyme, tannin and one crushed Campden tablet. Cover and leave for twenty-four hours.

3. Add the fruit syrup, concentrated grape juice, nutrient and yeast, then cover and ferment for three days, keeping the fruit submerged.

4. Strain out, press dry and discard the pulp, and stir in the sugar. Pour the must into a fermentation jar, top up, fit an airlock and ferment to dryness.

5. Rack, add one Campden tablet and, as soon as the wine is bright, syphon it into bottles.

Grocer's White 2

Dry and slightly tropical, tinned fruit

pears, peaches and pineapple in sugar syrup . . . of each	450g	*1 lb*
concentrated white grape juice *approx.*	250g	*9oz*
sugar	800g	*1¾ lb*
water	2.8 litres	*5 pints*
citric acid	10ml	*2 tsp*
tannin	2.5ml	*½ tsp*
pectic enzyme		
Campden tablets		
nutrient		
Hock yeast		

1. Separate the fruit from the syrup, which should be set aside.

2. Mash the fruit, discard the stones, and place it in a bin containing 3½ pints water, the acid, pectic enzyme, tannin and one crushed Campden tablet. Cover and leave for twenty-four hours.

3. Add the fruit syrup, concentrated grape juice, nutrient and yeast, then cover and ferment for three days, keeping the fruit submerged.

4. Strain out, press dry and discard the pulp, and stir in the sugar. Pour the must into a fermentation jar, top up, fit an airlock and ferment to dryness.

5. Rack, add one Campden tablet, and, as soon as the wine is bright, syphon it into bottles and store for three months.

NOTE:
This excellent light wine is ready for drinking when three months old.

Grocer's White 3

Dry and almost oriental, tinned fruit

grapefruit segments, guava halves and
mandarin segments in syrup . . .

of each	450g *1lb*
concentrated white grape juice	*approx.* 250g *9oz*
sugar	800g *1¼lb*
water	2.8 litres *5 pints*
citric acid	10ml *2 tsp*
tannin	2.5ml *½ tsp*

pectic enzyme
Campden tablets
nutrient
Hock yeast

1. Separate the fruit from the syrup, which should be set aside.

2. Mash the fruit, discard the stones, and place it in a bin containing 3½ pints water, the acid, pectic enzyme, tannin and one crushed Campden tablet. Cover and leave for twenty-four hours.

3. Add the fruit syrup, concentrated grape juice, nutrient and yeast, then cover and ferment for three days, keeping the fruit submerged.

4. Strain out, press dry and discard the pulp, and stir in the sugar. Pour the must into a fermentation jar, top up, fit an airlock and ferment to dryness.

5. Rack, add one Campden tablet and, as soon as the wine is bright, syphon it into bottles and store for three months.

Guava

A dry white table wine

guavas in sugar syrup	1.35kg *3lb*
concentrated white grape juice	*approx.* 250g *9oz*
sugar	800g *1¼lb*
water	3.1 litres *5½ pints*
citric acid	10ml *2 tsp*
tannin	2.5ml *½ tsp*

pectic enzyme
Campden tablets
nutrient
All Purpose wine yeast

1. Strain out the guavas from the syrup, which should be set aside. Mash the fruit, add the water, citric acid, pectic enzyme and one crushed Campden tablet. Cover and leave for twenty-four hours.

2. Stir in the syrup, concentrated grape juice, tannin, nutrient and active wine yeast. Cover and ferment on the pulp for three days keeping the fruit submerged.

3. Strain out the pulp through a nylon sieve and roll it around until all the juice has been extracted. Stir in the sugar, pour the must into a sterilised jar, fit an airlock and ferment out to dryness.

4. Rack the wine into a storage jar, and add one Campden tablet. Top up, bung tight, label and store until it is bright.

5. Bottle at once and keep until the wine is four months old. Serve it cold as a white table wine.

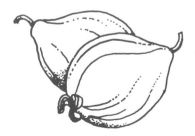

Loganberry

A sweet, strong dessert wine

fresh or frozen loganberries	2kg	*4½lb*
concentrated red grape juice	*approx.* 500g	*18oz*
sugar	1kg	*2¼lb*
water	2.8 litres	*5 pints*
citric acid	5ml	*1 tsp*
tannin	2.5ml	*½ tsp*
pectic enzyme		
Campden tablets		
nutrient		
Port yeast		
finings		

1. Stalk, wash clean, drain and crush the loganberries, pour hot water over them, cover and leave to cool.

2. Add the pectic enzyme, acid and one crushed Campden tablet. Replace the cover and leave for twenty-four hours.

3. Stir in the concentrated grape juice, tannin, nutrient and an activated yeast. Ferment on the pulp for four days, keeping the fruit submerged.

4. Strain out, press dry and discard the pulp. Stir in the sugar and top up. Fit an airlock and ferment in a warm place.

5. When fermentation is finished, check the S.G. and if need be sweeten the wine with sugar to 1.016.

6. Move the jar to a cold place for a few days to aid clarification, then rack the wine into a clean jar, add finings, bung tight and keep for a few more days in the cold until the wine is bright.

7. Rack again and store this wine for at least one year before bottling it. It develops a fine flavour and is a strong and sweet dessert wine.

Lychee

A dry white table wine

lychees in sugar syrup	900g	*2lb*
concentrated white grape juice	*approx.* 250g	*9oz*
sugar	800g	*1¾lb*
water	2.8 litres	*5 pints*
citric acid	10ml	*2 tsp*
tannin	2.5ml	*½ tsp*
pectic enzyme		
Campden tablets		
nutrient		
All Purpose wine yeast		

1. Strain out the lychees from the syrup, which should be set aside. Mash the fruit, add the water, citric acid, pectic enzyme and one crushed Campden tablet. Cover and leave for twenty-four hours.

2. Stir in the syrup, concentrated grape juice, tannin, nutrient and active wine yeast. Cover and ferment on the pulp for three days, keeping the fruit submerged.

3. Strain out the pulp through a nylon sieve and roll it around until all the juice has been extracted. Stir in the sugar, pour the must into a sterilised jar, fit an airlock and ferment out to dryness.

4. Rack the wine into a storage jar, add one Campden tablet, top up, bung tight, label and store until it is bright.

5. Bottle at once and keep until the wine is four months old. Serve it cold as a white table wine.

Mango

A dry white table wine

mangoes in sugar syrup	1.35kg *3lb*
concentrated white grape juice	*approx.* 250g *9oz*
sugar	800g *1¾lb*
water	3.1 litres *5½ pints*
citric acid	10ml *2 tsp*
tannin	2.5ml *½ tsp*
pectic enzyme	
Campden tablets	
nutrient	
All Purpose wine yeast	

1. Strain out the mangoes from the syrup, which should be set aside. Mash the fruit, add the water, citric acid, pectic enzyme and one crushed Campden tablet. Cover and leave for twenty-four hours.

2. Stir in the syrup, concentrated grape juice, tannin, nutrient and active wine yeast. Cover and ferment on the pulp for three days, keeping the fruit submerged.

3. Strain out the pulp through a nylon sieve and roll it around until all the juice has been extracted. Stir in the sugar, pour the must into a sterilised jar, fit an airlock and ferment out to dryness.

4. Rack the wine into a storage jar, add one Campden tablet, and top up. Bung tight, label and store until it is bright.

5. Bottle at once and keep until the wine is four months old. Serve it cold as a white table wine.

Marrow

A medium sweet social wine

marrow	3.2kg *7lb*
bruised root ginger	28g *1oz*
concentrated white grape juice	*approx.* 250g *9oz*
sugar	900g *2lb*
hot water	4 litres *7 pints*
citric acid	15ml *3 tsp*
tannin	2.5ml *½ tsp*
Campden tablets	
nutrient	
Hock yeast	

1. Wipe an old marrow at the end of the season with a sulphited cloth. Cut the flesh up into thin slices, being careful not to cut any pips. Place all the marrow, skin, flesh and pips into a bin with the bruised root ginger. Pour on five pints hot water, cover and leave to cool, but stir frequently to extract flavour and nutrients.

2. Boil together the sugar, acid and the rest of the water for twenty minutes, then leave to cool.

3. Strain out the marrow and ginger, pour the liquor into the syrup, then add the concentrated grape juice, the tannin, nutrient and yeast.

4. Pour the must into a sterilised jar, fit an airlock and ferment out.

5. Rack the wine into a clean storage jar, add one Campden tablet, bung tight and store until it is bright.

6. Rack again and store in bulk for six months before bottling and sweetening to taste with saccharin. Serve as a social wine.

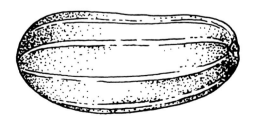

Medlars

A sweet social wine

mellow medlars	2kg *4¼lb*
concentrated white grape juice *approx.*	250g *9oz*
sugar	1kg *2¼lb*
water	3 litres *5¼ pints*
citric acid	10ml *2 tsp*
tannin	2.5ml *½ tsp*
pectic enzyme	
Campden tablets	
nutrient	
Sauternes yeast	
potassium sorbate	

1. Wash, crush or cut up the medlars and drop them into a bin containing the water, acid, pectic enzyme and one crushed Campden tablet. Cover and leave for twenty-four hours.

2. Stir in the concentrated grape juice, tannin, nutrient and yeast. Ferment on the pulp for five days, keeping the fruit submerged and the bin covered.

3. Strain out, press dry and discard the medlars. Stir in the sugar, pour the must into a fermentation jar, fit an airlock and ferment down to S.G. 1.010.

4. Syphon the wine into a clean jar, add 1g potassium sorbate and one Campden tablet, bung tight and store in a cool place.

5. As soon as the wine is bright, rack again and store under a safety bung for nine months.

6. Bottle and keep for a further three months before serving cold as a social wine.

Melon

A medium sweet social wine

melon	2kg *4¼lb*
bruised root ginger	28g *1oz*
concentrated white grape juice *approx.*	250g *9oz*
sugar	900g *2lb*
hot water	4 litres *7 pints*
citric acid	15ml *3 tsp*
tannin	2.5ml *½ tsp*
Campden tablets	
nutrient	
Hock yeast	

1. Wipe melon with a sulphited cloth. Cut the flesh up into thin slices, being careful not to cut any pips. Place all the melon, skin, flesh and pips into bin with the bruised root ginger. Pour on five pints hot water, cover and leave to cool, but stir frequently to extract flavour and nutrients.

2. Boil together the sugar, acid and the rest of the water for twenty minutes, then leave to cool.

3. Strain out the melon and ginger, pour the liquor into the syrup, then add the concentrated grape juice, tannin, nutrient and yeast.

4. Pour the must into a sterilised jar, fit an airlock and ferment out.

5. Rack the wine into a clean storage jar, add one Campden tablet, bung tight and store until it is bright.

6. Rack again and store in bulk for six months before bottling and sweetening to taste with saccharin. Serve as a social wine.

Mixed Soft Fruit

A medium dry rosé

*mixed soft fruit as available	1.5kg *3¼lb*
concentrated rosé grape juice	*approx.* 250g *9oz*
sugar	900g *2lb*
water	2.8 litres *5 pints*
citric acid	5ml *1 tsp*
tannin	2.5ml *½ tsp*
pectic enzyme	
Campden tablets	
nutrient	
Bordeaux yeast	

1. Stalk, wash and crush the fruit, place it in a suitable bin and pour hot water over it. Cover and leave to cool.

2. Add the acid, pectic enzyme and one crushed Campden tablet, cover and leave for twenty-four hours.

3. Stir in the concentrated grape juice, tannin, nutrient and yeast. Ferment on the pulp for three days, keeping the fruit submerged and the bin covered.

4. Strain out, press dry and discard the fruit, stir in the sugar, pour the must into a fermentation jar and ferment out.

5. Rack into a clean jar, add one Campden tablet, top up, bung tight and store until the wine is bright.

6. Rack again and store for nine months, then bottle. Add one saccharin tablet to each and store for a further three months. Serve this wine cold as a rosé wine with ham, snacks or picnics.

*Use a mixture of black, red and whitecurrants, raspberries, strawberries, loganberries, early blackberries, cherries, early plums and gooseberries, but do not let any one fruit predominate. 170g – 227g (*6oz – 8oz*) of each fruit is enough.

Mixed Vegetable

A medium sweet, white social wine

carrots, parsnips and swedes	2kg *4¼lb*
concentrated white grape juice	*approx.* 250g *9oz*
sugar	1.1kg *2¼lb*
citric acid	20ml *4 tsp*
tannin	2.5ml *½ tsp*
water	3.7 litres *6¼ pints*
Campden tablets	
nutrient	
Cereal or G.P. yeast	

1. Top, tail, scrub clean, cut up the vegetables into small dice-sized pieces, add the water, and bring to the boil. Cover and simmer until all the vegetables are tender.

2. Strain on to the sugar and acid, stir well until both are dissolved then cover and leave to cool.

3. Add the concentrated grape juice, tannin, nutrient and active yeast. Pour the must into a jar, fit an airlock and ferment out.

4. Move the jar to a cold place for a few days, then rack into a clean jar, add one Campden tablet, bung tight and store until the wine is bright.

5. Rack again and mature this wine for eighteen months. Serve it cold as a medium sweet white social wine. If it is not sweet enough for your palate, add one or two saccharin pellets per bottle.

NOTE:
The cereal yeast is able to ferment a small amount of starch and helps to produce a haze free wine from vegetables.

151

Mulberry

A strong, sweet dessert wine

fresh or frozen mulberries	2kg *4½lb*
concentrated red grape juice	*approx.* 500g *18oz*
sugar	1kg *2½lb*
water	2.8 litres *5 pints*
citric acid	5ml *1 tsp*
tannin	2.5ml *½ tsp*
pectic enzyme	
Campden tablets	
nutrient	
Port yeast	
finings	

1. Stalk, wash clean, drain and crush the mulberries, pour hot water over them, cover and leave to cool.

2. Add the pectic enzyme, acid and one crushed Campden tablet. Replace the cover and leave for twenty-four hours.

3. Stir in the concentrated grape juice, tannin, nutrient and an activated yeast. Ferment on the pulp for four days, keeping the fruit submerged.

4. Strain out, press dry and discard the pulp, stir in the sugar and top up. Fit an airlock and ferment in a warm place.

5. When fermentation is finished, check the S.G. and if need be sweeten the wine with sugar to 1.016.

6. Move the jar to a cold place for a few days to aid clarification, then rack the wine into a clean jar. Add finings, bung tight and keep for a few more days in the cold until the wine is bright.

7. Rack again and store this wine for at least one year before bottling it. It develops a fine flavour and is a strong and sweet dessert wine.

Muscatel

A sweet dessert or social wine

muscatel raisins	2kg *4½lb*
dark brown sugar	250g *9oz*
citric acid	10ml *2 tsp*
tannin	2.5ml *½ tsp*
water	4 litres *7 pints*
pectic enzyme	
Campden tablet	
nutrient	
Sherry yeast	

1. Wash and chop the raisins, place them in a bin and pour hot water over them. Cover and leave to cool.

2. Stir in the acid, pectic enzyme and one crushed Campden tablet. Cover and leave for twenty-four hours.

3. Stir in the nutrient, tannin and active yeast and ferment on the pulp for ten days, keeping the pulp submerged and the bin covered. Give the must a stir every other day.

4. Strain out, press dry and discard the pulp (or add it to another must for a few days). Stir in the sugar, pour the must into a fermentation jar, fit an airlock and ferment to a finish.

5. Check that the wine is still sweet, then rack into a clean jar, plug the neck with cotton wool and store until the wine is bright.

6. Rack again and store this sweet sherry style wine for at least one year under cotton wool and preferably longer. Bottle and keep for a further six months, then serve it cold as a dessert or social wine.

Orange 1

A smooth, sweet dessert wine

sweet oranges	8
mandarins	2
ripe bananas	2
concentrated sweet white grape juice	*approx.* 250g *9oz*
sugar	1.25kg *2¼lb*
water	3.4 litres *6 pints*
nutrient	
Sauternes yeast	
Campden tablet	
no acid, tannin or pectic enzyme	
potassium sorbate	
half bottle of gin (optional)	

1. Thinly pare the oranges, avoiding the white pith and saving the fruit. Peel and mash the bananas, discarding the skins. Place orange parings and mashed bananas in a bin. Pour on hot water, cover and leave to cool.

2. Stir in the concentrated grape juice, the expressed and strained juice of the fruit, the nutrient and yeast. Ferment on the pulp for three days keeping the fruit submerged and the bin covered.

3. Strain out and drain the fruit, stir in the sugar, pour the must into a fermentation jar, top up, fit an airlock and ferment down to S.G. 1.016.

4. Rack into a clean jar, add 1g potassium sorbate and one Campden tablet, fit a safety bung and store in a cold place until clear.

5. Rack again, add the gin if available and store for at least one year before bottling. Alternatively the gin may be added at the bottling stage and stored for a further six months. This is a very smooth, sweet wine to serve cold as a dessert wine.

Orange 2

A dry aperitif

Seville oranges	4
sweet oranges	4
ripe bananas	2
concentrated white grape juice	*approx.* 250g *9oz*
sugar	1.25kg *2¼lb*
hot water	3.4 litres *6 pints*
calcium sulphate	10ml *2 tsp*
nutrient	
Sherry flor yeast	
no acid, tannin or pectic enzyme	

1. Very thinly pare the oranges, removing no white pith and saving the fruit. Peel and mash the bananas, discarding the skins. Place the orange parings and mashed bananas in a bin. Pour on hot water, add the calcium sulphate, cover and leave to cool.

2. Stir in the grape juice (dry sherry style for preference), the expressed and strained juice of the oranges, the nutrient and active yeast. Ferment for three days, keeping the floating pulp submerged and the bin covered.

3. Strain out, drain and discard the pulp, and stir in half the sugar. Pour the must into a fermentation jar, fit an airlock and ferment in a warm place, 20°C to 21°C *(68°F to 70°F)*, for ten days.

4. Remove some of the must, stir in half the remaining sugar, return it to the jar and continue fermentation for another five days.

5. Repeat this process with the last of the sugar, stir well and ferment out to dryness.

6. Rack into a clean jar, do not top up nor add a Campden tablet, but plug the neck of the jar with cotton wool. Label and store in a cool place until clear.

7. Rack again and mature this wine under cotton wool for at least one year before bottling and keep for a further six months. Alternatively blend this with another dry sherry style wine to improve both. Serve cold as an aperitif.

Orange & Rosehip

A dry social wine

unsweetened orange juice	1 litre	*1¼ pints*
rosehip syrup	340ml	*12fl oz*
concentrated white grape juice	*approx.* 250g	*9oz*
sugar	900g	*2lb*
water	2.25 litres	*4 pints*
nutrient		
no acid or tannin		
G.P. yeast		

1. Mix all the ingredients together. Pour the must into a sterilised jar, fit an airlock and ferment out to dryness.

2. Rack into a clean jar, add one Campden tablet and store until the wine is bright.

3. Syphon into bottles, adding one saccharin pellet to each bottle if desired.

This makes an attractive social wine when served slightly chilled.

Parsley

A dry aperitif

freshly-gathered parsley	450g	*1lb*
concentrated white grape juice	*approx.* 250g	*9oz*
sugar	1kg	*2¼lb*
boiling water	4 litres	*7 pints*
citric acid	20ml	*4 tsp*
Campden tablets		
nutrient		
Sherry yeast		
no tannin		

1. Wash the parsley in running cold water, shake off the surplus moisture, chop it up, place it in a bin and pour six pints boiling water over it. Stir well, then cover and leave for one hour.

2. Boil the sugar, acid and one pint of water together for twenty minutes, then cover and leave in a cold place.

3. Strain out, press dry and discard the parsley and, when cool, mix in the concentrated grape juice, the nutrient and the yeast. Pour the must into a fermentation jar and fit an airlock.

4. After two days, mix in half the sugar syrup, and after a further four days add the rest.

5. When fermentation is finished, rack into a clean jar, add one Campden tablet and, as soon as the wine is bright, rack again.

6. Store for six months before bottling. Serve it cold as an aperitif.

Parsnip

A strong, sweet dessert wine

fresh parsnips	2kg *4½lb*
concentrated white grape juice	*approx.* 500g *18oz*
sugar	1.25kg *2¾lb*
water	3.4 litres *6 pints*
citric acid	20ml *4 tsp*
tannin	5ml *1 tsp*
nutrient	
Tokay yeast	

1. Select tender, freshly dug parsnips, and scrub them carefully to remove every trace of soil. Top and tail them, cut into small cubes, place them in a pan together with as much of the water as you can. Bring to the boil, cover and simmer until the parsnips are quite tender, but not mushy. Leave to cool.

2. Strain out, drain well and discard the parsnips. Stir the concentrated grape juice into the liquor together with the acid, tannin, nutrient and an activated yeast. Pour the must into a jar leaving room for the sugar. Fit an airlock and ferment for seven days in a warm place, 24°C *(75°F)*.

3. Remove half the must, stir in one third of the sugar and, when it is completely dissolved, return the must to the jar, replace the airlock and continue the fermentation.

4. After a further seven days, repeat the process with half the remaining sugar and, seven days later still, add the remaining portion in the same way.

5. When fermentation is finished, move the wine to a cold place for a few days to help it to clear, then rack it into a clean jar, top up, if possible with vodka, if not with another white wine or cold boiled water.

6. Store this strong, sweet, dessert wine for at least one year in a warm place and, preferably, after bottling, keep it for a further year.

Passion Fruit

A medium sweet social wine

passion fruit juice	560 ml *1 pint*
concentrated white grape juice	*approx.* 250g *9oz*
sugar	900g *2lb*
water	3.1 litres *5½ pints*
citric acid	5ml *1 tsp*
tannin	2.5ml *½ tsp*
pectic enzyme	
Campden tablets	
All Purpose wine yeast	
potassium sorbate	

1. Mix together the passion fruit juice, grape juice, water, acid, pectic enzyme and one crushed Campden tablet. Pour the must into a sterilised jar, bung tight and leave for twenty-four hours.

2. Add the tannin, nutrient and active yeast, fit an airlock and ferment for five days.

3. Remove some of the must, stir in the sugar, and return the must to the jar. Re-fit the airlock and ferment down to 1.006.

4. Rack the wine into a clean jar, add 1 g potassium sorbate and one Campden tablet, top up with cold boiled water, bung tight and store until the wine is bright.

5 Rack again and mature the wine for six months before bottling. Serve it cold as a social wine with a magnificent bouquet and flavour.

NOTES:
1. Passion fruit juice also makes a splendid sparkling wine. Use ½lb less sugar and a Champagne yeast. After six months, re-ferment in bottle.

2. Passion fruits grow only in sub-tropical climates, especially in Australia and the U.S.A. The best variety to use for wine is the granadillo. It has a purplish tough and crinkled skin when ripe. Use the soft fruit pulp within.

Peach

A medium sweet white wine

fresh peaches	2kg	*4½ lb*
concentrated white grape juice	*approx.* 250g	*9oz*
sugar	900g	*2lb*
water	3.4 litres	*6 pints*
citric acid	10ml	*2 tsp*
tannin	2.5ml	*½ tsp*
pectic enzyme		
Campden tablets		
nutrient		
Hock yeast		

1. Peel the peaches, remove and discard the stones, cut up or crush the fruit and place in a bin containing the water, acid, pectic enzyme and one crushed Campden tablet. Cover and leave for twenty-four hours.

2. Stir in the concentrated grape juice, tannin, nutrient and active yeast. Ferment on the pulp for three days, keeping the fruit submerged and the bin loosely covered.

3. Strain out, gently press and discard the fruit, and stir in the sugar. Pour the must into a sterilised jar, top up, fit an airlock and ferment out.

4. Move the jar to a cool place for a few days, then rack into a clean jar, add one Campden tablet, bung tight, label and store until the wine is bright.

5. Syphon into bottles and store the wine for six months before sweetening it to taste with saccharin. Serve it chilled as a light white wine.

Peapod

A dry white table wine

empty pea pods, fresh green and tender	2kg	*4½ lb*
concentrated white grape juice	*approx.* 250g	*9oz*
sugar	900g	*2lb*
water	3.7 litres	*6½ pint*
citric acid	15ml	*3 tsp*
tannin	2.5ml	*½ tsp*
Campden tablets		
nutrient		
G.P. yeast		

1. Select good quality freshly picked peapods after they have been shelled. Chop them into small pieces and boil them in a covered pan until they are quite tender, then leave them to cool.

2. Strain into a suitable container, discard the peapods and use only the liquor to make the wine. Stir in the concentrated grape juice, sugar, acid, tannin, nutrient and an active yeast.

3. Pour the must into a jar, topping up if necessary, fit an airlock and ferment out.

4. Rack the clearing wine into a clean jar, add one Campden tablet, top up, bung tight and store in a cold place until the wine is bright, then rack again.

5. Mature this wine for one year, then bottle and serve it cold as a white table wine.

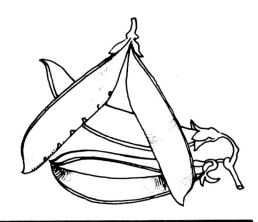

Pear

A sparkling dry aperitif

hard pears	2kg	4½lb
concentrated white grape juice	*approx.* 250g	9oz
sugar	800g	1¾lb
citric acid	10ml	2 tsp
cold water	3.4 litres	6 pints
pectic enzyme		
Campden tablets		
nutrient		
Champagne yeast (for two fermentations)		
Castor sugar	70g	2½oz

1. Stalk, wash, crush or cut up the pears into small pieces and drop them into a bin containing the acid, pectic enzyme and one crushed Campden tablet. Cover and leave for twenty-four hours.

2. Stir in the concentrated grape juice, nutrient and yeast. Ferment on the pulp for five days, keeping the fruit submerged and the bin covered.

3. Strain out, press dry and discard the pulp, and stir in the sugar. Pour the must into a fermentation jar, top up, fit an airlock and ferment right out to dryness.

4. Rack into a storage jar, add one Campden tablet, bung tight and store until the wine is bright.

5. Rack again and store until the wine is six to eight months old.

6. Stir in the caster sugar and fresh yeast, fit an airlock and as soon as the wine is fermenting again syphon it into six sterilised champagne bottles.

7. Seal with hollow domed plastic stoppers or blister stoppers, wire them on and lay the bottles on their sides in a warm room for one week.

8. Move the bottles to a cool store and mature them on their sides for at least another eight months before disgorging the sediment.

9. Add one saccharin pellet to each bottle before serving this sparkling wine, well chilled, as an aperitif.

Pineapple

A dry white table wine, or aperitif

fresh pineapple	2kg	4½lb
concentrated white grape juice	*approx.* 250g	9oz
sugar	1kg	2¼lb
water	2.8 litres	5 pints
citric acid	5ml	1 tsp
tannin	2.5ml	½ tsp
pectic enzyme		
Campden tablets		
nutrient		
Chablis yeast		

1. Top and tail the pineapple, chop it up into small pieces including the skin and crush it as much as you can.

2. Pour on cold water, acid, pectic enzyme and one crushed Campden tablet. Cover and leave for twenty-four hours.

3. Add the concentrated grape juice, tannin, nutrient and yeast. Cover and ferment for three days keeping the fruit submerged.

4. Strain out, press dry and discard the pulp, stir in the sugar, pour the must into a fermentation jar, top up, fit an airlock and ferment to dryness.

5. Rack the clearing wine into a sterilised jar, top up with cold boiled water, and add one Campden tablet. Bung tight, label, and store until the wine is bright.

6. Rack again and store in bulk for twelve months and in bottle for a further six months. Serve as a dry white table wine or as an aperitif.

Pineapple & Gooseberry

A dry white table wine

unsweetened pineapple juice	1 litre *1¾ pints*
gooseberries in syrup	450g *1lb*
concentrated white grape juice	*approx.* 250g *9oz*
sugar	900g *2 lb*
water	2.8 litres *5 pints*
citric acid	5ml *1 tsp*
tannin	2.5ml *½ tsp*
pectic enzyme	
Campden tablets	
nutrient	
Hock yeast	

1. Empty the pineapple juice into a bin containing cold water, citric acid, pectic enzyme and one Campden tablet. Strain the gooseberries from their syrup (saving this for later addition), crush the fruit and add to the bin. Cover and leave for twenty-four hours.

2. Stir in the concentrated grape juice, fruit syrup, tannin, nutrient and active yeast. Ferment on the pulp for three days, keeping the fruit submerged and the bin covered.

3. Strain out, press and discard the pulp, and stir in the sugar. Pour the must into a sterilised jar, top up if necessary, fit an airlock and ferment out to dryness.

4. Rack into a clean jar, add one Campden tablet and store in a cool place until the wine is bright. Syphon into bottles, sweetening each one with one saccharin pellet if desired.

5. Keep this wine for three months before serving it nicely chilled.

Plum 1

A dry white made with golden plums

golden plums	2kg *4½lb*
concentrated white grape juice	*approx.* 250g *9oz*
sugar	800g *1¾lb*
water	2.8 litres *5 pints*
citric acid	5ml *1 tsp*
tannin	2.5ml *½ tsp*
pectic enzyme	
Campden tablets	
nutrient	
Graves yeast	

1. Stalk, wash, stone and crush the fruit. Pour on hot water, cover and leave to cool.

2. Stir in the pectic enzyme, acid and one crushed Campden tablet. Cover and leave for twenty-four hours.

3. Stir in the concentrated grape juice, tannin, nutrient and an activated yeast. Ferment on the pulp for three days, keeping the fruit submerged.

4. Strain out, press dry and discard the pulp. Stir in the sugar, and when it is dissolved, pour the must into a jar, top up, fit an airlock and ferment to dryness.

5. Rack into a clean jar, top up, add one Campden tablet, bung tight and stand in a cold place until the wine is bright.

6. Rack again and keep this dry white table wine for six months before bottling and for six months afterwards.

Plum 2

A dry social wine, with tinned golden plums

golden plums in sugar syrup	1.35kg	*3lb*
concentrated white grape juice	*approx.* 250g	*9oz*
sugar	800g	*1¾lb*
water	2.8 litres	*5 pints*
citric acid	10ml	*2 tsp*
tannin	2.5ml	*½ tsp*
pectic enzyme		
Campden tablets		
nutrient		
Hock yeast		

1. Separate the fruit from the syrup, which should be set aside.

2. Mash the fruit, discard the stones, and place the pulp in a bin with 3½ pints water, the acid, pectic enzyme and one crushed Campden tablet. Cover and leave for twenty-four hours.

3. Add the fruit syrup, concentrated grape juice, tannin, nutrient and activated yeast. Cover and ferment for three days, keeping the fruit submerged.

4. Strain out the pulp, stir in the sugar, and pour the must into a fermentation jar. Top up, fit an airlock and ferment to dryness.

5. Rack, add one Campden tablet and as soon as the wine is bright, syphon it into bottles.

6. Store this wine until it is three months old, then serve it chilled as an aperitif, social or picnic wine.

Plum 3

A dry red made with red or black plums

red/black plums	2kg	*4¼lb*
concentrated red grape juice	*approx.* 250g	*9oz*
sugar	900g	*2lb*
water	2.8 litres	*5 pints*
citric acid	5ml	*1 tsp*
tannin	2.5ml	*½ tsp*
pectic enzyme		
Campden tablets		
nutrient		
Burgundy yeast		

1. Stalk, wash and stone the plums.

2. Mash the fruit, place it in a bin and pour on hot water. When cool, add the acid, pectic enzyme and one crushed Campden tablet. Cover and leave for twenty-four hours.

3. Add the concentrated grape juice, tannin, nutrient and activated yeast. Cover and ferment for four days, keeping the fruit submerged.

4. Strain out the pulp, stir in the sugar, pour the must into a fermentation jar, top up, fit an airlock and ferment to dryness.

5. Rack, add one Campden tablet and as soon as the wine is bright, rack again. Store it for twelve months in bulk and six months in bottle.

Serve it free from chill as a dry red table wine.

Plum 4

A light dry red made with tinned red plums

red plums in sugar syrup	1.35kg *3lb*
concentrated rosé grape juice	*approx.* 250g *9oz*
sugar	800g *1¾lb*
water	2.8 litres *5 pints*
citric acid	10ml *2 tsp*
tannin	5 ml *1 tsp*
pectic enzyme	
Campden tablets	
nutrient	
Bordeaux yeast	

1. Separate the fruit from the syrup, which should be set aside.

2. Mash the fruit, discard the stones and place the pulp in a bin with 3½ pints water, the acid, pectic enzyme and one crushed Campden tablet. Cover and leave for twenty-four hours.

3. Add the fruit syrup, concentrated grape juice, tannin, nutrient and yeast. Cover and ferment for three days, keeping the fruit submerged.

4. Strain out the pulp, stir in the sugar, and pour the must into a fermentation jar. Top up, fit an airlock and ferment to dryness.

5. Rack the wine into a sterilised storage jar, top up, add one Campden tablet and as soon as the wine is bright, syphon it into bottles. Store for six months, then serve it as a light table wine with mild cheeses, cold meats etc.

Plum 5

A dry sherry-style wine, Victoria plums

Victoria plums	2kg *4½lb*
concentrated sherry type grape juice	*approx.* 250g *9oz*
sugar	1.25kg *2¾lb*
water	3.5 litres *6 pints*
citric acid	10ml *2 tsp*
tannin	5ml *1 tsp*
pectic enzyme	
Campden tablets	
nutrient	
Sherry flor yeast	

1. Stalk, wash, stone and mash the fruit. Place it in a bin containing the water, acid, pectic enzyme, tannin and one crushed Campden tablet. Cover and leave for twenty-four hours.

2. Add the concentrated grape juice, nutrient and yeast. Ferment for three days, keeping the fruit submerged.

3. Strain out, press dry and discard the pulp, and stir in half the sugar. Pour the must into a fermentation jar, plug the neck with cotton wool and ferment in a warm atmosphere.

4. After ten days remove some of the must, stir in half the remaining sugar, return it to the jar, replace the cotton wool and continue the fermentation.

5. After a further seven days stir in the rest of the sugar and ferment out.

6. Rack, add one Campden tablet, store until the wine is bright, then rack again.

7. Mature this wine for at least one year in a jar not quite full and fitted with a cotton wool plug instead of a bung.

8. If possible blend this dry sherry style wine with another – say made from Seville oranges. Keep for a further six months in bulk, then bottle.

Potato

A very strong, sweet dessert wine

old potatoes	1kg	2¼lb
muscatel raisins	500g	18oz
wheat flakes	250g	9oz
light brown sugar	1kg	2¼lb
hot water	4 litres	7 pints
citric acid	15ml	3 tsp
tannin	2.5ml	½ tsp
fungal amylase	5ml	1 tsp
Campden tablet		
nutrient		
Madeira yeast		

1. Scrub the potatoes clean, but do not peel them. Cut them up into thin slices and place them in a bin with the washed and chopped raisins and wheat flakes. Pour on hot water, stir well, cover and leave to cool.

2. Stir in the acid, amylase and one crushed Campden tablet. Cover and leave for twenty-four hours.

3. Add the tannin, nutrient and active yeast and ferment on the pulp for seven days, keeping the pulp submerged and the bin covered.

4. Strain out, press dry and discard the pulp, and stir in half the sugar. Pour the must into a fermentation jar leaving room for the rest of the sugar, fit an airlock and ferment in a warm place for seven days.

5. Remove some of the must, stir in half the remaining sugar and return this to the jar. Continue fermentation for another seven days.

6. Repeat this process with the rest of the sugar and continue the fermentation until it stops.

7. Syphon the clearing wine into a clean jar. Top up, bung tight, label, and store until the wine is bright.

8. Rack again and store this wine in as warm a place as possible (up to 50°C/122°F) for six months. Return the wine to a cool store for a further two years, then bottle and keep for a further six months. Serve it cool with sponge cakes. It is very strong and sweet.

Prune

A sweet, golden dessert wine

prunes	900g	2lb
concentrated muscatel grape juice *approx.*	500g	18oz
ripe bananas	4	
brown sugar	680g	1½lb
clover honey	225g	½lb
water	3.4 litres	6 pints
citric acid	15ml	3 tsp
tannin	2.5ml	½ tsp
pectic enzyme		
Campden tablets		
nutrient		
Madeira yeast		

1. Wash and stone the prunes, peel and slice the bananas and simmer them in the water for about thirty minutes, together with the acid and honey. Skim off any scum from the honey. Empty into a bin and leave to cool.

2. Add the pectic enzyme and one crushed Campden tablet, cover and leave for twenty-four hours.

3. Add the concentrated grape juice, tannin, nutrient and yeast, then cover and ferment on the pulp for five days, keeping the fruit well submerged.

4. Strain out, press dry and discard the fruit, and stir in half the sugar. Pour the must into a jar, fit an airlock and ferment down to S.G. 1.010. Stir in the rest of the sugar and continue fermentation to the end. If necessary, increase the gravity to 1.016 with additional brown sugar, stir well and leave for a few days until the wine begins to clear.

5. Rack into a clean jar, top up, add one Campden tablet and store in a cold place until the wine is bright, then rack again.

6. Mature this strong, golden dessert wine for one year in a warm place before bottling, then keep for a further year. Serve it cool with plain sponge cake.

Quince 1

A sweet dessert wine, with fresh quince

mellow quince	2kg 4½ lb
concentrated white grape juice	approx. 250g 9oz
sugar	1kg 2¼ lb
water	2.8 litres 5 pints
citric acid	10ml 2 tsp
tannin	2.5ml ½ tsp
pectic enzyme	
Campden tablets	
nutrient	
Sauternes yeast	
potassium sorbate	

1. Wash and quarter the ripe yellow quinces, remove and discard the seeds and tough core membranes. Crush the fruit or cut it up into small pieces and drop them at once into a bin containing the water, acid, pectic enzyme and one crushed Campden tablet. Cover and leave for twenty-four hours.

2. Add the concentrated grape juice, tannin, nutrient and active yeast and ferment on the pulp for five days keeping the fruit submerged.

3. Strain out, press dry, remove the fruit and add the sugar to the must, stir until it is dissolved, then pour it into a jar, top up if necessary, fit an airlock and ferment down to S.G. 1.010. (If you wish seal the pulp in a polythene bag or box, label and store it in the freezer or refrigerator.)

4. Rack into a clean jar containing 1g potassium sorbate and one Campden tablet; bung tight and store in a cold place until the wine is bright.

5. Rack again and mature this wine for one year in bulk before bottling. Serve it cold with the dessert course of a meal – especially apple pie or apple crumble.

Quince 2

A subtle, dry aperitif from quince pulp

quince pulp from previous recipe	
eating and cooking apples	4kg 9lb
concentrated white grape juice	approx. 250g 9oz
sugar	800g 1¾ lb
water	2.25 litres 4 pints
citric acid	10ml 2 tsp
tannin	2.5ml ½ tsp
pectic enzyme	
Campden tablets	
nutrient	
Champagne yeast	

1. Wash and crush the apples, removing and discarding any bruised or damaged parts, and drop them at once into a bin containing the water, acid, pectic enzyme and one crushed Campden tablet.

2. Mix in the quince pulp from the previous recipe, cover and leave for twenty-four hours.

3. Add the concentrated grape juice, tannin, nutrient and yeast and ferment on the pulp for five days, keeping the fruit well submerged.

4. Strain out, press dry and discard the fruit, and stir in the sugar. Pour the must into a jar, top up if necessary, fit an airlock and ferment out to dryness.

5. Rack into a clean jar, top up, add one Campden tablet and store in a cold place until the wine is bright, then rack again.

6. Mature this dry white table wine for one year before bottling. It has a delightful and subtle bouquet and flavour and is equally enjoyable drunk as an aperitif or as a social wine. Add one saccharin pellet per bottle if the wine is too dry for your palate.

NOTE:
A jar of quince jelly may be used instead of the pulp. Double the pectic enzyme and use a little less sugar, depending on the sweetness of the apples. A total S.G. of 1.080 is recommended.

Raisin

A sweet, golden dessert wine

raisins	2kg *4½lb*
citric acid	10ml *2 tsp*
tannin	2.5ml *¼ tsp*
water	4 litres *7 pints*
pectic enzyme	
Campden tablet	
nutrient	
Sauternes yeast	

1. Wash and chop the raisins, place them in a bin and pour hot water over them. Cover and leave to cool.

2. Stir in the acid, pectic enzyme and one crushed Campden tablet. Cover and leave for twenty-four hours.

3. Stir in the nutrient, tannin and active yeast and ferment on the pulp for ten days, keeping the pulp submerged and the bin covered. Give the must a stir every other day.

4. Strain out, press dry and discard the pulp or add to another must for a few days. Pour the must into a fermentation jar, fit an airlock and ferment to a finish.

5. Check that the wine is still sweet, then rack into a clean jar, plug the neck with a safety bung and store until the wine is bright.

6. Rack again, top up, add one Campden tablet and store this sweet golden wine for at least one year before bottling. Serve it cold with the dessert course of a meal.

Raspberry 1

A medium sweet rosé

fresh raspberries	1.35kg *3lb*
concentrated rosé grape juice	*approx.* 250g *9oz*
sugar	900g *2lb*
water	3.4 litres *6 pints*
citric acid	2.5ml *¼ tsp*
tannin	2.5ml *¼ tsp*
pectic enzyme	
Campden tablets	
nutrient	
Bordeaux yeast	

1. Stalk, wash and crush the raspberries. Drop them at once into a bin containing the water, acid, pectic enzyme and one crushed Campden tablet. Cover and leave for twenty-four hours.

2. Stir in the concentrated grape juice, tannin, activated yeast and nutrient. Cover and ferment on the pulp for three days, keeping the fruit submerged.

3. Strain out, press dry and discard the pulp, and stir in the sugar. Pour the must into a jar, top up, fit an airlock and ferment out to dryness.

4. Move the jar to a cold place for two days, then rack the wine into a clean jar. Top up, add one Campden tablet, bung tight, label and store until the wine is bright.

5. Rack again and store for six months before sweetening with two saccharin tablets per bottle and serving cold as a rosé wine.

NOTE:
Two mashed ripe bananas may be added to the raspberries to improve the body of this wine but they are not essential.

Raspberry 2

A sweet rosé

fresh or frozen raspberries	2kg	*4½lb*
concentrated rosé grape juice	*approx.* 250g	*9oz*
sugar	1kg	*2½lb*
water	3.4 litres	*6 pints*
citric acid	5ml	*1 tsp*
tannin	2.5ml	*½ tsp*
pectic enzyme		
Campden tablets		
nutrient		
Sauternes yeast		

1. Clean, wash and crush the raspberries and put them into a bin containing the water, acid, pectic enzyme and one crushed Campden tablet. Cover and leave for twenty-four hours.

2. Stir in the concentrated grape juice, tannin, nutrient and an activated yeast. Ferment for four days, keeping the fruit submerged and the bin covered.

3. Strain out the pulp through a fine mesh straining bag, stir in the sugar. Pour the must into a fermentation jar, top up, fit an airlock and ferment out.

4. Rack into a clean jar containing one crushed Campden tablet. Top up, bung tight, label and store in a cold place until the wine is bright.

5. Rack again and store for one year before bottling and sweetening to taste with saccharin. Serve this wine cold with sweet cakes.

Raspberry 3

A dry rosé made with pie filling

raspberry pie filling	1.35kg	*3lb*
concentrated rosé grape juice	*approx.* 250g	*9oz*
sugar	680g	*1½lb*
water	3.4 litres	*6 pints*
citric acid	10ml	*2 tsp*
tannin	5 ml	*1 tsp*
pectic enzyme		
amylase		
Campden tablets		
nutrient		
Bordeaux yeast		

1. Empty the pie filling into a polythene bin containing hot water and stir until the pulp is well dispersed. Cover and leave to cool.

2. If the label indicates that the contents include 'edible starch', add the quantity of amylase recommended by the manufacturer – it varies. The amylase converts the starch to sugar. If it is omitted the wine may contain a starch haze.
   An alternative is to use a cereal yeast (*Saccharomyces diastaticus*) which is able to ferment a small amount of starch.

3. Stir in the concentrated grape juice, citric acid, tannin, pectic enzyme and one crushed Campden tablet. Cover and leave for twenty-four hours.

4. Add the activated yeast and nutrient, cover and ferment on the pulp for three days.

5. Strain the must through a fine meshed nylon straining bag to remove the solid particles. Stir in the sugar and when it is dissolved pour the must into a fermentation jar, top up if necessary, fit an airlock and ferment out to dryness.

6. Move the jar to a cold place for a few days, then rack into a clean jar, add one Campden tablet and store until the wine is bright.

7. Syphon into bottles, cork and label them and keep the wine until it is four months old.

A medium sweet rosé

redcurrants	1.35kg *3lb*
concentrated rosé grape juice	*approx.* 250g *9oz*
sugar	900g *2lb*
water	3.4 litres *6 pints*
tannin	2.5ml ½ *tsp*
citric acid	2.5ml ½ *tsp*
pectic enzyme	
Campden tablets	
nutrient	
Bordeaux yeast	

1. Stalk, wash and crush the redcurrants. Drop them at once into a bin containing the water, acid, pectic enzyme and one crushed Campden tablet. Cover and leave for twenty-four hours.

2. Stir in the concentrated grape juice, tannin, activated yeast and nutrient. Cover and ferment on the pulp for three days keeping the fruit submerged.

3. Strain out, press dry and discard the pulp, stir in the sugar, pour the must into a jar, top up, fit an air-lock and ferment out to dryness.

4. Move the jar to a cold place for two days, then rack the wine into a clean jar. Top up, add one Campden tablet, bung tight, label and store until the wine is bright.

5. Rack again and store for six months before sweetening with two saccharin tablets per bottle and serving cold as a rosé wine.

A medium dry rosé

redcurrants	1.3kg *3lb*
concentrated red grape juice	*approx.* 250g *9oz*
sugar	800g *1¼lb*
water	2.8 litres *5 pints*
tannin	2.5ml ½ *tsp*
pectic enzyme	
no acid	
Campden tablets	
nutrient	
Bordeaux yeast	

1. Stalk, wash and crush the redcurrants, and pour hot water over them. Cover and leave to cool.

2. Stir in the pectic enzyme and one crushed Campden tablet, cover and leave for twenty-four hours.

3. Stir in the concentrated grape juice, tannin, nutrient and an activated yeast. Ferment on the pulp for three days, keeping the fruit submerged.

4. Strain out, press and discard the pulp, and stir in the sugar. Pour the must into a jar, top up, fit an air-lock and ferment to dryness.

5. Move the jar to a cold place for a few days then rack the clearing wine into a clean jar. Add one Campden tablet, bung tight, leave until the wine is bright, then rack again.

6. Store in bulk for six months, then sweeten slightly with saccharin, bottle and keep until the wine is one year old. Serve it chilled as a fresh rosé wine.

NOTE:
Two mashed ripe bananas may be added to the redcurrants to improve the body of this wine but they are not essential.

Rhubarb

A sweet, dessert or social wine.

fresh rhubarb	2kg 4½ lb
orange	1
concentrated white grape juice	*approx.* 250g *9oz*
sugar	1.13kg 2½ lb
water	3.4 litres *6 pints*
tannin	2.5ml ½ *tsp*
pectic enzyme	
Campden tablets	
nutrient	
Sauternes yeast	
potassium sorbate	

1. Top and tail the rhubarb, and wipe the stalks and orange with a sulphited cloth. Cut up or crush the stalks, thinly pare the orange, using only the parings at this stage. Pour hot water over them and fit a cover.

2. When cool, add the expressed and strained juice of the orange, the pectic enzyme and one crushed Campden tablet. Replace the cover and leave for twenty-four hours.

3. Stir in the concentrated grape juice, tannin, nutrient and active yeast. Ferment on the pulp for three days, keeping the fruit submerged and the bin loosely covered.

4. Strain out, press and discard the fruit, and stir in the sugar. Pour the must into a sterilised jar, top up, fit an airlock and ferment down to S.G. 1.016.

5. Rack the wine into a clean jar, add 1g potassium sorbate and one crushed Campden tablet. Top up, replace the airlock and leave in a cool place.

6. When the wine is bright, rack again, top up, bung tight, label and store in bulk for six months before bottling. Serve this wine cold with the dessert course of a meal or as a social wine.

Rhubarb & Banana

A full bodied dry white

rhubarb	2kg 4½ lb
ripe bananas	4
lemon	1
concentrated white grape juice	*approx.* 250g *9oz*
sugar	900g *2lb*
water	3.5 litres *6 pints*
tannin	2.5ml ½ *tsp*
pectic enzyme	
Campden tablets	
nutrient	
G.P. yeast	
no acid	

1. Top and tail the rhubarb, wipe the stalks clean and cut them up into small pieces. Peel and mash the bananas and add to the rhubarb. Thinly pare the lemon, chop and add the parings.

2. Pour boiling water over the fruit, cover and leave to cool.

3. Add the expressed juice of the lemon, the pectic enzyme and one crushed Campden tablet. Cover and leave for twenty-four hours.

4. Stir in the concentrated grape juice, tannin, nutrient and active yeast and ferment on the pulp for five days keeping the fruit submerged.

5. Strain out, press and discard the fruit, and stir in the sugar. Pour the must into a sterilised jar, top up, fit an airlock and ferment out to dryness.

6. Move the jar to a cold place for a few days, then rack the clearing wine into a clean jar. Add one Campden tablet, top up, bung tight and store until the wine is clear.

7. Rack again and keep this wine until it is one year old before bottling. This makes a full bodied dry white table wine, but it may be sweetened with saccharin at the bottling stage to produce a social wine.

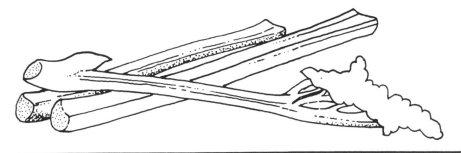

Rhubarb & Date

A dry aperitif

rhubarb	2kg *4½ lb*
dates	225g *½ lb*
raisins	225g *½ lb*
dried apricots	113g *¼ lb*
lemon	1
sugar	1kg *2¼ lb*
water	3.7 litres *6½ pints*
tannin	2.5ml *½ tsp*
pectic enzyme	
Campden tablets	
nutrient	
Sherry yeast, **no acid**	

1. Top and tail the rhubarb, and wipe the stalks clean. Cut them up into small pieces and place them in a polythene bin containing the washed and chopped raisins and apricots, the chopped dates and very thinly pared rind of the lemon.

2. Pour boiling water over the fruit, cover the bin and leave it to cool.

3. Add the pectic enzyme, the expressed juice of the lemon and one Campden tablet. Re-cover the bin and leave for twenty-four hours.

4. Add the tannin, nutrient and activated yeast and ferment on the pulp for five days, keeping the fruit submerged.

5. Strain out, press dry and discard the fruit, and stir in one third of the sugar. Pour the must into a sterilised jar, plug the neck with cotton wool and continue the fermentation for ten days.

6. Remove some of the must, stir in half the remaining sugar, replace the cotton wool and continue the fermentation. Ten days later repeat the process with the last of the sugar.

7. When fermentation finishes, rack the wine into a clean jar. Leave some air space by not quite filling the jar, plug the neck with cotton wool and store until the wine is bright. Rack again and continue storage in the same way for one year.

8. The wine may now be bottled and kept for a further six months. Alternatively before bottling, blend the wine with one bottle of a commercial sherry of your choice and, if you so wish, sweeten to suit your palate. Serve this wine cool as an aperitif.

Rhubarb & Orange

A dry aperitif

rhubarb in syrup	1.6kg *3½ lb*
unsweetened orange juice	140ml *5fl oz*
concentrated white grape juice	*approx.* 250g *9oz*
water	2.8 litres *5 pints*
sugar	800g *1¼ lb*
tannin	2.5ml *½ tsp*
pectic enzyme	
Campden tablets	
nutrient	
All Purpose wine yeast	
no acid	

1. Separate the rhubarb from the syrup, which should be set aside. Crush the fruit and place it in a bin containing the water, orange juice, pectic enzyme and one crushed Campden tablet. Cover and leave for twenty-four hours.

2. Add the tannin, concentrated grape juice, nutrient and activated yeast. Ferment on the pulp for three days, keeping the fruit submerged and the bin covered.

3. Strain out, press dry and discard the fruit. Stir in the sugar, pour the must into a fermentation jar, top up, fit an airlock and ferment out.

4. Rack into a storage jar, add one Campden tablet and store until the wine is bright. Rack into bottles and mature this wine until it is four months old. Serve it cold as an aperitif.

Rice & Raisin

A medium sweet social wine

rice	450g *1lb*
raisins	1kg *2¼lb*
sugar	450g *1lb*
water	4 litres *7 pints*
citric acid	10ml *2 tsp*
tannin	2.5ml *½ tsp*
Campden tablet	
nutrient	
G.P. yeast	

1. Wash the rice and place it in a pan. Add the water, bring to the boil, cover and simmer for thirty minutes.

2. Strain out, drain and discard the rice. Pour the liquor over the washed and chopped raisins, cover and leave to cool.

3. Stir in the acid, tannin, nutrient, and an activated yeast and ferment for eight days, keeping the fruit submerged.

4. Strain out, press dry and discard the raisins. Stir in the sugar, pour the must into a fermentation jar, top up, fit an airlock and ferment out.

5. Rack into a clean jar, add one Campden tablet, bung tight, label and store in a cold place until the wine is bright.

6. Rack again and store for one year. If need be, sweeten slightly and serve cold as a social wine.

Rosehip

A sweet social wine

freshly gathered rosehips	2kg *4½lb*
concentrated white grape juice *approx.*	250g *9oz*
citric acid	15ml *3 tsp*
tannin	2.5ml *½ tsp*
sugar	1kg *2¼lb*
water	3.7litres *6½ pints*
nutrient	
Sauternes yeast	
potassium sorbate	

1. Top, tail, wash and crush the rosehips. Place them in a large pan, cover them with water, bring to the boil and simmer for half an hour. Leave to cool.

2. Strain out, press the hips dry and discard them. Stir in the concentrated grape juice, acid, tannin. sugar, nutrient and yeast.

3. Pour the must into a fermentation jar, fit an airlock and ferment down to S. G. 1.010.

4. Rack into a clean jar, top up, add one Campden tablet and 1g potassium sorbate, fit a safety bung and store in a cold place until the wine is bright.

5. Rack again and mature for one year before bottling. Keep for at least a further three months then serve cold as a social wine with sweet biscuits.

NOTES:
1. 500 g *(1 lb 2 oz)* dried rosehip shells may be used instead of fresh hips.
2. Rosehips and dried rosehip shells may be used in conjunction with many other ingredients to provide body. 250 g *(9 oz)* per gallon is usually enough.
3. Rosehip purée may be bought and made into wine in accordance with the instructions provided by the manufacturer.

Rosehips are rich in vitamins, make good dessert wine and blend well with other fruits such as figs.

Rosehip & Fig

A medium sweet aperitif

rosehip syrup	340g *12oz*
dried figs	250g *9oz*
concentrated white grape juice	*approx.* 250g *9oz*
sugar	1kg *2¼lb*
water	3.4 litres *6 pints*
citric acid	15ml *3 tsp*
tannin	2.5ml *½ tsp*
pectic enzyme	
Campden tablet	
nutrient	
Sherry yeast	

1. Wash and chop the figs, pour four pints boiling water over them, cover and leave overnight. Next day, bring them to the boil in the same water and simmer for thirty minutes.

2. Strain out, press dry and discard the figs and leave the liquor to cool. Stir in the rosehip syrup, concentrated grape juice, half the acid, the pectic enzyme and one crushed Campden tablet. Cover and leave for twenty-four hours.

3. Meanwhile, boil the sugar and the rest of the acid in two pints of water for twenty minutes, then cover. Leave to cool, bottle and store in the cool until required.

4. Pour the must into a sterilised jar, add the tannin, nutrient and yeast, fit an airlock, ferment for five days then add the sugar syrup in three equal portions at five day intervals.

5. When fermentation finishes, move the jar to a cold place for a few days, then rack the clearing wine into a clean jar. Plug the neck of the jar with cotton wool and store until the wine is bright.

6. Rack again and keep this wine under a cotton wool plug until it is one year old before bottling, then keep it for a further six months. Serve it cold. This makes an attractive aperitif that may be sweetened with saccharin at the bottling stage to suit your palate.

NOTES:
1. A concentrated rosehip and fig purée is available from some home brew shops.
2. 1.3 kg *(3lb)* rosehips may be used instead of the syrup: top and tail, crush and boil them with the figs.
Alternatively, 450g *(1lb)* dried rosehip shells may be washed and boiled with the figs.

Rose Petal

A medium sweet social wine

scented rose petals	2 litres *3½ pints*
concentrated rosé grape juice	*approx.* 500g *18oz*
sugar	680g *1½lb*
hot water	3.4 litres *6 pints*
citric acid	5ml *1 tsp*
Campden tablets	
nutrient	
Bordeaux yeast	
no tannin	

1. Pick the roses when fully blown and just before petal fall. Place them in a suitable measure and shake them down – but do not press them.

2. Empty the petals into a ceramic bowl or small polythene bin, pour hot water over them and rub them against the side of the vessel with the back of a wooden spoon to extract the essence. Cover and leave to cool.

3. Add one crushed Campden tablet and the acid, macerate the petals twice a day for two days. Strain out, press dry and discard the petals. Stir in the concentrated grape juice, sugar, nutrient and yeast. Pour the must into a fermentation jar and ferment out.

4. Rack into a clean jar, add one Campden tablet, top up, bung tight and store the wine until bright.

5. Syphon into bottles, add two saccharin pellets to each and store until the wine is six months old. Serve it cold as a delightfully fragrant social wine.

Sloe

A dry red table wine

fresh sloes	1.35kg *3lb*
concentrated red grape juice	*approx.* 250g *9oz*
sugar	900g *2lb*
water	3.7 litres *6½ pints*
citric acid	10ml *2 tsp*
tannin	5ml *1 tsp*
pectic enzyme	
nutrient	
Campden tablets	
Burgundy yeast	

1. Stalk, wash and crush the sloes, and pour hot water over them. Cover and leave to cool.

2. Add the pectic enzyme, acid and one crushed Campden tablet, cover and leave for twenty-four hours.

3. Stir in the concentrated grape juice, tannin, nutrient and activated yeast. Ferment on the pulp for four days, keeping the fruit submerged.

4. Strain out, press dry and discard the fruit. Stir in the sugar and when it is dissolved, pour the must into a jar, top it up with cold boiled water, fit an airlock and ferment out to dryness.

5. Rack into a clean jar, add one Campden tablet and store until the wine is bright.

6. Rack again and store for at least one year before bottling. Serve this dry red table wine, free from chill, with red meats.

Not everyone knows what sloes look like, but the close-up picture overleaf, taken by the author on one of his rambles among the hedgerows, should help the beginner to recognise this free fruit. Another picture on page 144 shows how they appear from a distance.

Strawberry 1

A medium sweet rosé

fresh strawberries	1.35kg *3lb*
concentrated rosé grape juice	*approx.* 250g *9oz*
sugar	900g *2lb*
water	3.4 litres *6 pints*
citric acid	2.5ml *½ tsp*
tannin	2.5ml *½ tsp*
pectic enzyme	
Campden tablets	
nutrient	
Bordeaux yeast	

1. Hull, wash and crush the strawberries. Drop them at once into a bin containing the water, acid, pectic enzyme and one crushed Campden tablet. Cover and leave for twenty-four hours.

2. Stir in the concentrated grape juice, tannin, activated yeast and nutrient. Cover and ferment on the pulp for three days keeping the fruit submerged.

3. Strain out, press dry and discard the pulp, and stir in the sugar. Pour the must into a jar, top up, fit an airlock and ferment out to dryness.

4. Move the jar to a cold place for two days, then rack the wine into a clean jar. Top up, add one Campden tablet, bung tight, label and store until the wine is bright.

5. Rack again and store for six months before sweetening with two saccharin tablets per bottle and serving cold as a rosé wine.

NOTE:
Two mashed bananas may be added to the strawberries to improve the body of this wine, but they are not essential.

Strawberry 2

A dry picnic wine made with pie filling

strawberry pie filling | 1.35kg *3lb*
concentrated rosé grape juice *approx.* 250g *9oz*
sugar | 680g *1½lb*
water | 3.4 litres *6 pints*
citric acid | 10ml *2 tsp*
tannin | 5ml *1 tsp*
pectic enzyme
amylase
Campden tablets
nutrient
Bordeaux yeast
no acid

1. Empty the pie filling into a polythene bin containing hot water and stir until the pulp is well dispersed. Cover and leave to cool.

2. If the labels on the cans indicate that the contents include 'edible starch', add the quantity of amylase recommended by the manufacturer – it varies. The amylase converts the starch to sugar. If it is omitted the wine may contain a starch haze.

An alternative is to use a cereal yeast *(Saccharomyces diastaticus)* which is able to ferment a small amount of starch.

3. Stir in the concentrated grape juice, citric acid, tannin, pectic enzyme and one crushed Campden tablet. Cover and leave for twenty-four hours.

4. Add the activated yeast and nutrient, then cover and ferment on the pulp for three days.

5. Strain the must through a fine meshed nylon straining bag to remove the solid particles. Stir in the sugar and, when it is dissolved, pour the must into a fermentation jar, top up if necessary, fit an airlock and ferment out to dryness.

6. Move the jar to a cold place for a few days, then rack the wine into a clean jar. Top up. add one Campden tablet, bung tight and store until the wine is bright.

7. Syphon into bottles, cork and label them and keep the wine until it is four months old. Serve chilled as a luncheon or picnic wine.

Pick sloes when they are ripe and soft, preferably after the first frost of the autumn.

Strawberry 3

A medium dry rosé made with jam

strawberry jam | 1.35kg *3lb*
concentrated rosé grape juice *approx.* 250g *9oz*
sugar | 450g *1lb*
water | 3.4 litres *6 pints*
citric acid | 15ml *3 tsp*
tannin | 2.5ml *½ tsp*
pectic enzyme (double dose)
Campden tablets
nutrient
Bordeaux yeast

1. Dissolve the jam in warm water and when cool add the pectic enzyme, acid and one crushed Campden tablet. Cover and leave for two days.

2. Stir in the concentrated grape juice, tannin, nutrient and active yeast. Replace the cover and ferment for two days.

3. Strain the must through a fine mesh nylon bag, stir in the sugar and pour the must into a sterilised jar. Top up with cold boiled water if necessary, fit an airlock and ferment out.

4. Rack the wine into a sterilised jar containing one crushed Campden tablet, top up, bung tight, label and store in a cold place until the wine is bright.

5. Syphon the clear wine into bottles and store for six months, sweetening it with one saccharin pellet per bottle. This is a light, pleasantly flavoured rosé wine. Serve it cold with picnic lunches or sandwich snacks.

NOTE:
Use a jam containing no additional pectin or preservative.

Sultana

A medium sweet social wine

sultanas	1.6kg *3½lb*
water	4.5 litres *8 pints*
citric acid	5ml *1 tsp*
tannin	2.5ml *½ tsp*
pectic enzyme	
Campden tablets	
nutrient	
Hock yeast	
Potassium sorbate	

1. Wash and chop the sultanas, place them in a bin and pour hot water over them. Cover and leave to cool.

2. Stir in the acid, pectic enzyme and one crushed Campden tablet, cover and leave for twenty-four hours.

3. Stir in the nutrient, tannin and active yeast and ferment on the pulp for ten days keeping the pulp submerged and the bin covered. Give the must a stir every other day.

4. Strain out, press dry and discard the pulp or add to another must for a few days. Pour the must into a fermentation jar, fit an airlock and ferment down to S.G. 1.006.

5. Rack into a clean jar, add 1g potassium sorbate and one Campden tablet. Fit a safety bung and store in a cold place until the wine is bright.

6. Rack again and mature for nine months in bulk and three in bottle. Serve cold as a social wine.

Supermarket White

A dry aperitif or table wine

unsweetened apple juice	2 litres *3½ pints*
unsweetened grapefruit juice	1 litre *1¾ pints*
concentrated white grape juice	*approx.* 250g *9oz*
cold water	1 litre *1¾ pints*
sugar	900g *2lb*
pectic enzyme	5ml *1 tsp*
tannin	2.5ml *½ tsp*
Campden tablets	
nutrient	
Moselle wine yeast	
no acid	

1. Empty the fruit juice into a jar containing the water, pectic enzyme and one Campden tablet. Fit an airlock and leave for twenty-four hours.

2. Stir in the grape juice, tannin, nutrient and active yeast, then ferment for three days.

3. Remove some of the must, stir in the sugar, return it to the jar and continue fermentation to dryness.

4. Rack the wine into a storage jar, top up, add one Campden tablet, bung tight and store until the wine is bright. Rack into bottles, add one saccharin pellet to each and store until the wine is four months old. Serve it cold as an aperitif or white table wine.

NOTE:
Different wines can be made in the same way by substituting orange or pineapple juice for the grapefruit juice. These are very attractive wines costing around one fifth of their commercial equivalent.

Whitecurrant

A medium sweet social wine

fresh white currants	1.35kg	*3lb*
concentrated white grape juice	*approx.* 250g	*9oz*
sugar	900g	*2lb*
water	3.4 litres	*6 pints*
citric acid	2.5ml	*½ tsp*
tannin	2.5ml	*½ tsp*
pectic enzyme		
Campden tablets		
nutrient		
Hock yeast		

1. Stalk, wash and crush the white currants. Drop them at once into a bin containing the water, acid, pectic enzyme and one crushed Campden tablet. Cover and leave for twenty-four hours.

2. Stir in the concentrated grape juice, tannin, activated yeast and nutrient. Cover and ferment on the pulp for three days keeping the fruit submerged.

3. Strain out, press dry and discard the pulp, and stir in the sugar. Pour the must into a jar, top up, fit an airlock and ferment out to dryness.

4. Move the jar to a cold place for two days, then rack the wine into a clean jar. Top up, add one Campden tablet, bung tight, label and store until the wine is bright.

5. Rack again and store for six months before sweetening with two saccharin tablets per bottle and serving as a social wine.

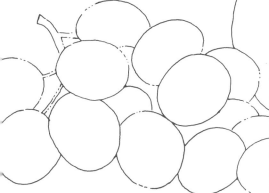

NOTE:
Two mashed bananas may be added to the white currants to improve the body of this wine, but they are not essential.

CHAPTER SEVENTEEN

Brewing beer

Mankind has been brewing beer for several thousand years. The slaves who built the Pyramids of Egypt drank it, as did the Romans, who called it 'cerevese'. The Anglo Saxons were also great beer drinkers, using the long horns from their cattle as drinking vessels. For centuries beer, or ale as it was then called, was brewed by women. It was drunk by the whole family including the children. A thin light ale, often unflavoured, was drunk in the morning and a somewhat better one, sometimes flavoured with herbs, in the evening. The first tax was imposed in the twelfth century and it has remained ever since with varying degrees of severity.

In the fifteenth century brewing began to move away from the home to small local breweries and this steadily increased until the beginning of the eighteenth century when the great brewing names of today started their businesses.

In 1880 an Act was passed requiring home brewers not only to obtain a licence to brew but also to pay duty on the beer brewed. Brewing at home virtually ceased and remained dormant until the early 1950s. The awakening interest in making fruit and other wines at home led the way for a revival in home brewing, stimulated in 1963 by the repeal of the Act of 1880. During the late 1960s, Boots and other firms began marketing home brew kits consisting of a can of hop flavoured malt extract, a sachet of dried yeast granules, and detailed brewing instructions. Home brewing began to make great progress. A vast new group of home

Traditional English pies, cheese and bread make a splendid meal – with beer.

Two fermenting bins, one with a tap, and a glass beer hydrometer, as described in the text.

brewers was formed since these kits eliminated much of the work from home beermaking, although some experienced home brewers also continue to brew from a plain malt extract and hops, or direct from grains.

Equipment

The equipment needed for home brewing is similar to that used for winemaking. Whether you are going to brew kit beers, malt extract and hop beers or grain mashed beers, you will need a **polythene bin and lid.** Since you always use a size rather larger than the quantity you brew, having a range of bins is very useful. For example, you need a 25 litre bin to brew 40 pints and a 15 litre bin for 16 pints.

The finished beer can be syphoned from its sediment but the 25 litre bin with a draw off tap is extremely useful, especially for the 40 pint brews.

A long handled **polypropylene paddle** is ideal for stirring the brews but one that is spoon shaped is also available. For those who have to ferment their beers in cold places a **thermostatic heater** is available. An **electrically heated belt** to put around the bin may be used as an alternative.

The original gravity is an important factor in brewing beers of a particular style and a **hydrometer** should always be available, likewise a **thermometer,** since temperatures are such an important factor in brewing.

Proper dark brown, strong, unblemished **bottles** are essential for the safe storage of beers. Mineral water and cider bottles are not suitable, nor are the 'one-way' disposable beer bottles. During the conditioning period in bottle, pressures are generated that could burst any but a purpose made beer bottle, especially when handled in a way that disturbs the gas.

Crown corks should be used with a Boots **crown corker** to seal the bottles with a gas proof finish. A wide selection of tools are available. Select one that will match your output. What is suitable for the odd gallon is not adequate for a frequent forty pint sealing session. Bottles can also be sealed with re-usable polythene reclosure caps.

A **bottle brush** should be used for cleaning bottles that are to be used again.

For draught beers use Boots **pressure barrel** fitted with a draw off tap at the bottom and a carbon dioxide pressure injector

The right sort of bottles to use for beer, a thermostatic heater in a bin of fermenting beer, a barrel with a pressure injector and the simple-to-use crown corker.

at the top. An occasional squirt of gas maintains the pressure and keeps the beer in good condition.

Attractive **labels** not only remind you of the bottle contents and the date it was brewed but also impart a professional finish to your work.

Hygiene

Cleanliness is just as important in brewing beer at home as it is in making wine. All the equipment used should be kept clean and sterilised immediately before use, and the brew should be kept covered at all times. Dead yeast should be removed by skimming off the fermentation froth and racking the beer from its sediment at the end of fermentation. Storage vessels and bottles should also be sterilised before use and this includes crown caps. Ingredients should be kept covered in airtight containers and stored in a cool place. Attention to these details prevents off-flavours and ensures a clean taste in the finished beers.

Beer styles

Bitter beers dominate the drinking habits of both men and women, young and old. They include light ale, pale ale and export ale.

Light ale is as its name suggests a fairly weak beer that is only lightly hopped. The colour is that of ripe straw. It is usually bottled and can be regarded as a thirst-quenching beer, ideal after strenuous exercise.

Pale ale is a little stronger, with rather more flavour. The colour is somewhat darker, varying between that of golden straw to a light amber. It is also usually bottled and makes a pleasant luncheon drink.

Export ale is sometimes described as Burton bitter, best bitter or India Pale Ale. Originally a beer of this type was exported to British troops stationed in India during the days of the Empire. It is a stronger beer, well hopped and brewed from hard water. It has a malty/tangy taste and a beautiful copper colour that is very appealing to the eye. While some versions of this beer are bottled, a draught version is the most popular.

Brown ales are now much less popular than once they were and the style differs to some extent between the North and the South of England. The colour ranges from a dark amber to a blackish brown. The alcohol content is not high but the hop flavour is more pronounced in the North than the South. There is usually a sweetish finish to this full bodied beer due to a higher dextrin content. Brown ales are usually sold in bottles.

Stouts also come in several varieties. The very dry version, or Irish stout, is domino black in colour and pours with a remarkably close knit head that remains on top of the beer to the last mouthful. Stout is brewed from soft water and gets its flavour both from the black malt, which also gives it colour, and from the bitter hops that are used. Dry stout is stronger than sweet stout, which often contains some lactose. Oatmeal is occasionally added to make yet another flavour. Most stouts are bottled although a draught stout can also be bought.

Barley wine is sold in small bottles sometimes called nips. It is a very strong beer containing around 10% alcohol. It is highly malted and needs long maturation. The colour ranges from gold to brown, the texture is remarkably smooth and full bodied and the beer is extremely satisfying.

Lager is made from different barleys, different hops and different yeast, is mashed at different temperatures, fermented at a lower temperature than normal and matured for much longer than other beers. The colour varies from very light to very dark gold. They have a noticeable and appealing bouquet. The lighter lagers are tangy, crisp, sharp and thirst quenching. The darker varieties are stronger and very smooth. Lager should always be brewed from soft water, an appropriate malt syrup flavoured with Styrian, Saaz or Hallertau hops and slowly fermented with a *carlsbergensis* yeast at a temperature of 11° or 12°C *(low 50s F)*.

CHAPTER EIGHTEEN

The ingredients for beer

Although wheat, maize and other cereals have been used as the basis for beer, and are still used as adjuncts, malted barley has long been preferred. Similarly, hops have been preferred for the past five centuries over all other herbs and flavourings. The water, too, plays an important part in determining the character of the finished beer and certain towns, notably Burton-on-Trent, have become famous for their beer because of the mineral salts in their water. Beer cannot be brewed without yeast, as Pasteur proved. Malted barley, hops, water and yeast, then, are the basic ingredients of all beers.

Malt

Many farmers grow certain varieties of barley solely for the brewing industries. After harvesting, the grains are sent to a maltster and placed in a warm damp atmosphere for a while to encourage germination. This breaks down the protective wall around the starch and causes the development of enzymes that can convert the starch into maltose. As soon as the grain begins to sprout, further growth is stopped by heating the grain to 50°C (122°F). This produces the pale malt which is the basis of all beers. Some of the malted barley is roasted at higher temperatures and produces crystal, chocolate and black malts. The latter two impart flavour but no fermentable sugar to the mash.

For good results, always use the best quality ingredients when brewing from malt extract and hops.

Enthusiasts who wish to brew their beer from grains are advised to buy them from a reputable source to ensure that they are fresh

Crystal
Malt Grains
for use in recipes to add flavour and colour
1 kg 2.2 lb

Goldings Hops
for use in recipes to make Bitter, Pale Ale and Barley Wine
100 gram 3.5 oz

Custom Brew
Malt Extract

Fuggles Hops
for use in recipes to make Brown Ale and Strong Ale
100 gram 3.5 oz

Custom Brew

Hallertau Hops
for use in recipes to make Lager
100 gram 3.5 oz

Custom Brew
Malt
Extract
1.8 kg 3.97 lb
for use in recipes to make
Bitter and Brown Ale

Custom Brew
Brewers Yeast
in Suspension
Contains three sachets

Boots
Custom Brew
Pale
Malt Extract
1.8 kg 3.97 lb
for use in recipes to make
Pale Ale and Lager
THE BOOTS COMPANY LTD NOTTINGHAM ENGLAND

Custom Brew
Dried
Yeast
80 gram 2.8 oz
contains eight sachets

Custom Brew
Root
Ginger
100 gram 3.5 oz

and in good condition. If malted barley is left open to the air it soon becomes slack and stale and unsuitable for brewing good beer. It is best bought as required, but if a larger purchase is made, the grains should be kept well wrapped, in an airtight container stored in a cool dry place.

Before use, the grains have to be cracked and this is best done just before you buy them. If you have to crush your own be careful not to grind the grains too small since this will make them difficult to mash. You may have to soak them in water for an hour to soften them before crushing between a rolling pin and a marble or formica surface. Always use pale and crystal malt to provide adequate fermentable sugar in your mash. As a rule of thumb, 450 g *(1 lb)* pale malt mashed in 4.5 litres *(1 gallon)* of water will produce an S.G. of 1.024.

Malt syrup is made by preparing a wort from a mash of mixed grains. This is then heated to evaporate most of the water. The resultant toffee-like syrup contains approximately 80% solids and 20% water. 450 g *(1 lb)* of malt syrup dissolved in 4.5 litres *(1 gallon)* of water produces a specific gravity around 1.028. Malt syrup can be produced to retain a number of the diastase enzymes so that these can convert the starch in a small quantity of flaked rice or flaked maize or wheat flour into maltose. It is known as a diastatic malt syrup or DMS.

The malt syrup can be further dried and spun into flour. This is very sensitive to moisture, however, and must be kept well wrapped up in an absolutely airtight container otherwise it will absorb moisture from the air and revert to its toffee-like state.

Hops

The hop plant grows up strings to a height of two or three metres. The flower consists of a number of overlapping petals that look rather like miniature fir cones. At the base of the cone there is a small quantity of a golden coloured powder called lupulin. This is the bittering substance. Oils and resin are also produced in the petals which are water repellent – no doubt to keep the powder dry. When adding hops to water it is necessary to wet them thoroughly by squeezing them in your hand in the water to force them to absorb the moisture.

There are different varieties of hops that are used for the different styles of beer. East Kent Goldings, now largely superseded by Wye Challenger, are mainly used for the various styles of bitter beers. Fuggles, or the new Wye Northdown hops, are mostly used for brown ales and stouts. Hallertau, the Continental hop, is used for lager.

Modern technology has discovered ways of grinding up the hops, discarding unwanted stalks, etc and compressing the product into pellets. These can be stored in vapour proof, polythene-lined foil containers and keep perfectly fresh until required. They are particularly useful for adding to a fermenting brew to impart a fresh hoppy tang – a process known as dry hopping. Hop oil may also be used for this purpose but it is very strong and only a few drops per gallon are needed.

Water

All tap water in the United Kingdom is safe to use for brewing. Its hardness or softness depends to a large extent on the area. Experience over the centuries shows that hard water is best for brewing bitter style beers and barley wine; while soft water is best for brewing brown ales, stouts and lagers. This is particularly important in the mashing of the grains and the preparation of the wort. It has a lesser significance with malt syrup beers since the minerals will have already been absorbed in the preparation of the syrup.

Hard water can be softened by boiling to precipitate the temporary hardness (calcium carbonate) and by the addition of up to 2.5 ml (½ tsp) of ordinary table salt per gallon depending on the degree of hardness.

Soft water can be hardened by the addition of 2.5 ml (½ tsp) per gallon of a mixture of calcium sulphate and magnesium sulphate in the ratio of four to one for pale ales and eight to one for best bitters and barley wine. Sachets of ready mixed hardening salts can be bought from shops specialising in the supply of home brew ingredients. It is best to boil all the water used in brewing in case it is chlorinated or fluorided. The boiling drives off the additives and leaves it free from unwanted flavours.

Yeast

The granulated yeast, *Saccharomyces cerevisiae*, seems to be the most effective for the home brewing of beer since it can be sprinkled on and it very soon starts fermenting. Good results have been obtained from some liquid yeasts that have first been made up into starter bottles. Sediment in bottled fine ales can also be made into a starter. Sometimes one can buy granulated yeast prepared from a stout fermentation, alternatively the sediment in good bottled stout can be used to form a starter. These specialised yeasts from fine ales and stouts enhance the flavour of the beers brewed at home. They are both top fermenting yeasts and produce a substantial froth which has to be skimmed off and discarded.

Lager yeast, *Saccharomyces carlsbergensis*, on the other hand is a different variety that ferments from the bottom. It ferments slowly at a low temperature and imparts a good flavour.

Sugar

It is customary to add some sugar when brewing because sugar is cheaper than malt. Sugar produces alcohol, but alcohol alone does not make good beer. The sugar content should never produce more than one-third of the alcohol content and preferably less than one-quarter.

Granulated white sugar is mostly used but brown sugars are sometimes used to add colour and a little flavour. Golden syrup may be used with success but best of all is glucose – whether in the form of a powder or small solid pieces called chips.

Castor sugar, or better still glucose powder, should be used for priming because it dissolves more readily.

Commercial brewers use invert sugar but this is not so necessary in the small quantities of beer brewed at home. It can be quickly and easily made by boiling 1 kg granulated sugar in 620 ml of water *(2 lb in 1 pint)* with a 5 ml spoonful of citric acid for twenty minutes. The advantage is that the inverted sugar syrup is readily dispersable in the wort and immediately fermentable.

Adjuncts

A number of different ingredients may be added to enhance the flavour and texture of a beer. They should be used in moderation and should never exceed in weight one-fifth of the total grains used – one-tenth is an even more desirable proportion.

The range includes raw barley, roasted barley, torrefied barley, brewing flour *(wheat flour)*, wheat syrup, wheat flakes *("Weetabix")*, flaked maize, flaked rice and porridge oats. Lactose is added to sweeten some brown ales and stouts.

Finings

Carragheen moss, sometimes called Irish moss, may be added at the boiling stage to help clear the wort prior to fermentation. Gelatine is often used after fermentation, and isinglass, too. A number of proprietary brands of finings are marketed for this purpose, but it should be said that most beers clear to brilliance on their own if properly brewed and stored in a cool place for long enough.

Many different kinds of beer can be simply and successfully brewed by using these beer kits. This is the best way for beginners to start.

Heading agents

These are added to a brew to improve the retention of a good head after the beer has been poured into a glass. They are marketed in both liquid and powder form and should be used in accordance with the manufacturer's recommendations. Again, it must be said that properly brewed beer from good and fresh ingredients rarely needs the support of a heading agent.

Only good ingredients will produce good beer. It must be repeated that to use inferior ingredients is wasteful of your effort and time. Saving one or two pence per pint by buying poor but cheap ingredients is not important compared with the saving on Excise Duty, V.A.T., brewers' costs and publicans' costs. The best bargain to be obtained is the purchase of the very best ingredients.

CHAPTER NINETEEN

Brewing from kits

The vast majority of the beer brewed at home is from kits. There are two kinds – the wet and the dry. The wet kit consists of a hopped malt extract in a can or plastic container. Full instructions are given on the label for converting the extract into a highly palatable and enjoyable beer. A sachet of yeast is attached. All you have to add is the water and a small quantity of sugar.

The dry kit consists of a carton container, a muslin bag of hops and grains, a sealed plastic bag of malt flour and a sachet of yeast. Full instructions are printed on the carton and, again, all you have to add is the sugar and water.

If you have never brewed beer before, you are strongly recommended to begin by making up several kits. They are sold in a variety of sizes and styles by a dozen or more manufacturers. The trial size of eight pints has many advantages for the absolute beginner, but a successful brew is soon consumed! Other kits are available for brewing sixteen, twenty-four, thirty-two or forty pints. The larger kits involve a lot of bottling, so the beers from these kits are often put into plastic casks and served as draught – expecially the favourite, bitter beer. Stouts, brown ales, lagers and barley wines are the most popular styles available but there are quite a number of others including Northern Brown, pale ale, mild, shandy, etc.

A picture guide is on pages 190–191, full description on pages 192–193.

1. Stir the malt extract into two pints of hot water, and keep stirring till it's dissolved.

2. Stir in the sugar, bring to the boil and simmer for five minutes.

3. Empty the hot wort into a sterilised bin containing eight pints of cold water, then top up with more cold water to make a total of sixteen pints.

4. Check the temperature (with a special thermometer, not a medical one) till it falls below 75°F (24°C).

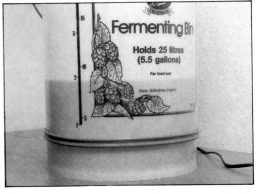

5. When the temperature is right sprinkle on the yeast granules or pitch in the contents of a yeast starter bottle and put the lid on.

6. A heating belt helps to maintain an even warmth. On the second and third days skim off any froth and give the beer a good stir.

A step-by-step guide

7. When the surface is still and no bubbles are bursting the fermentation is finished.

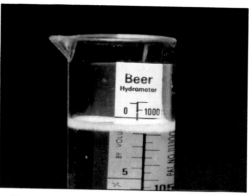

8. If the hydrometer reading confirms this (it should be 1.000 or just above) move the bin, with the lid firmly in place, to a cool room to clear.

9. Syphon the beer into one-pint sterilised beer bottles to within 1¼ inches of the top.

10. Add the priming sugar at the rate of half a level 5 ml spoonful per pint.

11. Seal each bottle with a sterilised cap, securely crimped on, then shake the bottle gently to dissolve the sugar and test the seal. Leave in a warm room for a few days while the sugar ferments.

12. Store in a cool place for two weeks or so to mature, chill slightly before serving, then drink.

The wet kit method

The instructions vary slightly from one manufacturer to another but each begins with an exhortation to cleanliness and urges the sterilisation of all equipment before use. This point can never be over emphasised. Lack of care in this regard causes all sorts of nasty smells and flavours that can put you off ever brewing beer again. Make equally sure, too, that you keep your brew well covered at all times to prevent infection from airborne bacteria, moulds and fungi.

The following method for brewing sixteen pints of beer from a wet kit has been found very successful over many years and is illustrated in the sequence of step-by-step pictures.

1. Place two pints of water in an aluminium or stainless steel pan and bring it to the boil.

2. Pour in the hopped malt extract stirring gently until it is dissolved. Rinse out the container with some of the wort to ensure that none is wasted.

3. Stir in the recommended quantity of sugar, bring to the boil and simmer for five minutes.

4. Meanwhile, pour eight pints of cold water into a sterilised polythene bin capable of holding $3\frac{1}{2}$ gallons *(15 litres)*.

5. Pour the hot wort from the pan into the bin and add another four pints or so of cold water to make up a total of sixteen pints.

6. Check the temperature of the wort and provided it is not higher than 24°C *(75°F)* sprinkle on the yeast and cover the bin with its lid or a clean thick cloth.

If the wort is too hot, and it may well be, leave it covered in a cool place until the temperature has fallen.

7. Leave the brew to ferment but skim off any froth on the second and third days and give the beer a good stir.

8. When the surface of the beer is clear and no bubbles can be seen bursting, check the specific gravity of the brew with a hydrometer or beerometer. If the reading is 1.008 or above leave the brew in a warm place to finish fermenting. If the reading is 1.000 or just above, give the beer a gentle stir, move the bin to a cool place to aid clarification but ensure that it is very closely covered.

9. Syphon the beer into sterilised orthodox returnable beer bottles, leaving an air space of approximately $1\frac{1}{4}$ in *(3.2 cm)* beneath the cap or screw stopper.

DO NOT use non-returnable, or mineral water bottles. It is possible that these could be burst by the pressure caused by the priming sugar.

10. Prime each bottle with castor sugar at the rate of one level 5 ml spoonful per quart. Do not exceed this quantity but do not omit it. If you use more, the beer will gush and lift up the sediment when the bottle is unsealed. If you use less or omit the sugar, the beer will be flat and lifeless when poured.

11. Seal each bottle securely with a sterilised crown cap or screw stopper, then shake the bottle gently to dissolve the sugar and test the seal.

12. Leave the bottles in a warm room for a few days while the sugar is fermented, then store them in a cool place for two weeks or longer to mature. Chill them slightly before serving.

Larger quantities are brewed in exactly the same way. If you prefer draught beer, syphon the finished beer into a sterilised plastic cask, stir in priming sugar at the rate of $\frac{1}{2}$ oz *(15g)* per gallon, seal the cask and leave it in a cool place but in a position where the beer can be drawn off without moving the cask. Draught beer does not keep as well as bottled beer even under pressure from a CO_2 injector. The contents of the cask are best consumed over a period of seven to ten weeks, starting some two weeks after priming.

Starting a dry kit

1. Pour four pints of water into a pan, empty the hops and grains into the water and squeeze the hops with your hand until they are wet. This ensures a better extraction than leaving the hops and grains in the muslin bag.

2. Bring the water to the boil and continue this vigorously under a cover for thirty to sixty minutes. Dissolve the malt flour in two pints of hot water, then stir in the sugar.

3. Strain the hop and grain liquor into the malt and sugar solution and top up with cold water. Check the temperature and continue as from item 6 of the wet kit process.

Brewing from kits soon becomes as easy as making a pot of tea. The quality of the hopped malt extracts is now very high and good, cheap beer can be brewed each time.

For a change, use less water than is recommended, say 20 pints instead of 24. This will give you less beer, but it will be stronger in alcohol and flavour.

CHAPTER TWENTY

Brewing from malt extract and hops

Before kits were marketed most home brewing was with plain malt syrup and hops. The introduction of kits diminished the interest in this aspect of brewing for a while. A number of home brewers who began with kits, however, are now moving on to brewing from malt syrup, hops and adjuncts so that they can brew more individual beers.

Manufacturers recognise this market demand by producing malt syrups of a specific kind, e.g. dark syrups for stouts, high dextrin syrup for best bitters and pale syrups for lager and so on. They also market malt syrups containing diastase for use with adjuncts. Varied types and amounts of hops can be used, together with adjuncts, to produce your own individual beers.

When making up your own recipes, care should be taken not to use too much sugar nor too many adjuncts. The quantity of sugar used should never produce much more than one-third of the alcohol and preferably no more than one-quarter. The adjuncts, too, should never exceed more than one-fifth of the weight of the malt and preferably no more than one-tenth. Subtlety in flavour and texture is sought in the finest beers.

While it is not essential to do so, there is a growing tendency to boil the malt syrup with the hops and adjuncts. A rolling boil is called for and this is best achieved in a large covered stainless steel or aluminium pan to avoid too much wastage of volatile flavourings by evaporation. The flavour can be enhanced by beginning the boil with, say, three-quarters of the hops and adding the remainder for the last five minutes or so. This ensures that there is a good extraction of the essential oils and resin but provides for a fresh hoppy taste. Alternatively, a different variety of hop may be added for the last period of the boil.

Dry hopping is also available when brewing beer in this manner. A handful of hops or a few hop pellets are added after the final skimming and stirring of the fermenting wort. The action of the alcohol on the hops and the movement caused by the bubbles of carbon dioxide extract a hoppy tang that adds additional appeal to a beer.

Malt syrup, hops and adjunct beers are best fermented in an atmospheric temperature around 20° to 21°C *(68° to 70°F)*. Keep the brew well covered and if possible use a bin with a close fitting lid and an airlock. This ensures a safe and reasonably fast fermentation.

Skimming off and discarding the dirty froth is important since this removes potential off flavours caused by dead yeast cells. Also, wipe clean the deposit of dead cells and hop particles that cling to the side of the bin at the surface level of the brew.

After skimming, always rouse up or stir the brew to encourage the dissipation of carbon dioxide, which inhibits fermentation. Rousing also admits oxygen that enables the yeast cells to reproduce themselves and maintain a large colony able to ferment the sugars quickly.

When fermentation is finished and the surface of the beer clears, finings may be added, but it is usually sufficient to move the beer to a cold place for two days while the suspended solids settle on the bottom of the bin.

If the bin is not fitted with a tap through which the beer can be drawn off, it should be syphoned into sterilised bottles allowing some head space for the pressure caused by the priming fermentation. Alternatively of course, it can be put into a pressure barrel and subsequently served as draught beer.

You can prime the beer either by adding one level 5 ml spoonful of sugar per quart or by krausening. For the former method the sugar can be dissolved in some of the beer and then distributed equally among the bottles allowing twice as much for a quart as for a pint and twice as much for a pint as for a half pint.

Priming by krausening *(after the name of the man who invented the method)* must be determined before fermentation. One-twentieth of the volume of wort must be drawn off into a sterilised container and stored in a refrigerator until the beer is bottled or casked. It is then mixed into the bulk, or distributed among the bottles or added to the cask. The sugar in the unfermented wort is fermented by the yeast cells remaining in the beer after if has been racked from the sediment. This method aids head retention as well as improving condition.

These beers need rather longer to mature than kit beers and if well made will keep for up to one year, improving for most of that time.

There are countless experiments and variations that you can make to any recipe, both to suit your own taste and to utilise any ingredients that you may have by you. Changes are best made in moderation and during a period of experimentation it is recommended that you make up one gallon brews keeping good records of each. These brews can be used for comparison one with another. Some you will prefer to others. When you have found one that you particularly enjoy, you can brew it in larger quantities.

Best Bitter (5 gallons) O.G. 1.042 44

Custom Brew malt extract	1.8kg	*4lb*
Custom Brew crystal malt grains	500g	*18oz*
Wye Challenger or Golding hops	100g	*3½oz*
granulated sugar	900g	*2lb*
sachet of beer yeast granules		

1. Warm a gallon of water in a suitable boiling pan, slowly stir in the malt syrup and rinse out the can with the warm wort.

2. Add approximately three-quarters of the hops, saving the rest for later. Wet them thoroughly.

3. Stir in the malt grains, then fit a lid if possible, increase the heat and boil vigorously for half an hour, stirring occasionally to prevent the grains sticking to the bottom of the pan.

4. Add the remaining hops and continue the boil for a further five minutes or so.

5. Turn off the heat and leave for a quarter of an hour for the grains and hops to settle.

6. Sterilise a large *(25 litre)* polythene bin and strain the liquor into it through a nylon straining bag.

7. Rinse the grains and hops with a pint of tepid water, then discard them to the compost heap.

8. Stir in the sugar and when it is dissolved, add sufficient cold water to bring the level of the wort up to the 5 gallon mark.

9. Check the temperature of the wort and when it has fallen to around 20°C *(68°F)* check the specific gravity with a hydrometer or beerometer. If necessary, adjust to 1.042/44 with a little more sugar or water *(depending on whether you have to increase or decrease the reading).*

10. Sprinkle on the yeast, cover the bin and ferment out, skimming and stirring on the second and third days.

11. When fermentation appears to have finished and the specific gravity is down to 1.008 or below, move the bin to a cool place for two days.

12. Sterilise orthodox beer bottles and caps. Syphon the beer into the bottles leaving approximately 3.5 cm *(1½ in)* head space in each, add priming sugar at the rate of one level 5 ml spoonful per quart and seal securely.

13. Shake the bottles gently to dissolve the sugar and test the seals. Leave them in a warm room for four or five days, then store them in a cool place for three or four weeks.

Lager   (4 gallons)   O.G. 1.044

Custom Brew pale malt extract	1.8kg	*4lb*
light brown sugar	600g	*21oz*
Hallertau hops	100g	*3½oz*
sachet of *carlsbergensis* yeast		

Method as described in the previous recipe, using less water. When fermentation has started, move the bin to a cool place and ferment the wort slowly under an airlock. Mature for six to eight weeks.

Stout   (16 pints)   O.G. 1.042

Custom Brew malt extract	900g	*2lb*
crystal malt grains	200g	*7oz*
chocolate malt grains	200g	*7oz*
black malt grains	100g	*3½oz*
Wye Northdown or Fuggle hops	40g	*1½oz*
dark brown sugar	400g	*14oz*
sachet of beer yeast granules		

Method as for Best Bitter but using only two-fifths of the water.

Brown Ale (3 gallons) O.G. 1.032

Custom Brew malt extract	900g	*2lb*
crystal malt grains	200g	*7oz*
chocolate malt grains	200g	*7oz*
Wye Northdown or Fuggle hops	50g	*1¾oz*
brown sugar	450g	*1lb*
sachet of beer yeast granules		

Method as for Best Bitter but using only three-fifths of the water.

Barley Wine (8 pints) O.G. 1.096

Custom Brew malt extract	900g	*2lb*
crystal malt grains	500g	*18oz*
demerara sugar	125g	*4½oz*
Wye Challenger hops	30g	*1oz*
champagne wine yeast		

1. Dissolve the malt extract in four pints of warm water, add the malt grains and all but a handful of hops. Cover the pan and boil vigorously for half an hour.

2. Add the remaining hops and boil for a further five minutes. Leave to cool for fifteen minutes then strain into a small bin.

3. Stir in the sugar, make up to one gallon with cold water and when cool add the wine yeast.

4. Pour the wort into a fermentation jar, fit an airlock and leave in a warm place until fermentation is finished.

5. Rack into sterilised half pint bottles, prime with four level 5 ml spoonsful of castor sugar or glucose dissolved in a little of the beer and distributed evenly among the bottles.

6. Seal securely, leave in a warm room for one week and a cool store for one year.

Brown Ale (16 pints) O.G. 1.032

malt extract	900g	*2lb*
crystal malt grains	125g	*4½oz*
dark brown sugar	100g	*3½oz*
Fuggle hops	35g	*1¼oz*

After the malt extract has dissolved, and the crushed crystal malt grains have been added, the hops, which contain oil, need to be thoroughly wetted to prevent them floating on the wort. Squeeze them with your hand if necessary (but not in boiling water).

soft water — 8 litres *14 pints*
beer yeast

1. Dissolve the malt extract in hot water, add the crushed crystal malt grains and hops, well wetted, and boil for thirty minutes.

2. Leave covered for a further thirty minutes, then strain out the hops and grains and rinse them with one pint of warm water.

3. Stir in the dark brown sugar, top up to 16½ pints with cold water and when cool enough, add the yeast; cover loosely and leave in a temperature of around 18°C *(65°F)*

4. Skim and stir on the second and third days, then leave to ferment out.

5. Move the beer to a cold place for two days, then syphon into sterilised bottles. Prime with castor sugar at the rate of one level 5 ml spoonful per quart, seal securely, leave in a warm room for four days and a cool store for a further two weeks.

NOTE:
If a sweeter brown ale is required add two level 5 ml spoonsful lactose to each pint at the bottling stage.

Strong Ale 1 (20 pints) O.G. 1.054

hopped malt extract (bitter)	1.25kg	2¾lb
water	10 litres	18 pints
white sugar	450g	1lb
citric acid	2.5ml	½ tsp
beer yeast		

1. Boil the sugar and acid in two pints of water for twenty minutes; cover, leave to cool, then bottle and seal until required.

2. Dissolve the hopped malt extract in four pints of warm water, top up with 12 pints cold water and stir in the yeast. Cover and leave in a constant temperature.

3. Stir the beer well on the second and third days, first removing any scum.

4. On the fourth day, stir in half the sugar syrup and on the eighth day stir in the rest.

5. Continue fermentation, giving the beer a stir each day until fermentation finishes.

6. Move the beer to a cool place for two days, then bottle and prime with castor sugar at the rate of 2.5 ml (½ tsp) per pint. Seal securely and store for three months.

Strong Ale 2 (8 pints) O.G. 1.054

pale malt grains	1kg	*2¼lb*
hard water	4.5 litres	*8 pints*
Golding hops	28g	*1oz*
beer yeast		

1. Mash the crushed grains in 7 pints water and maintain at a temperature of 66.5°C *(152°F)* for four hours, stirring every hour.

2. Strain out the grains and sparge with a pint of warm water.

3. Mix in the hops, wetting them thoroughly and boil with one level teaspoonful of Irish Moss for one hour. Leave to cool.

4. Strain out, drain and discard the hops. Syphon half a pint of the wort into a sterilised bottle, seal it and store it in the refrigerator until required.

5. Pitch the yeast into the bulk of the wort, ferment in an even temperature around 17.5°C *(64°F)*

6. Skim and stir on the second, third and fourth days, then syphon the beer into a demijohn, fit an airlock and ferment out.

7. Move the jar to a cold place for two days and when the beer begins to clear, syphon it into sterilised beer bottles in which the reserved and unfermented wort has been evenly distributed.

8. Seal the bottles at once. Leave them in a warm room for four days, then store them for three months.

NOTE:
No priming sugar required.

Draught Bitter (4 gallons) O.G. 1.040

malt extract	1.8kg	*4lb*
crystal malt grains	350g	*12½oz*
Golding hops	100g	*3½oz*
glucose chips	500g	*1lb 2oz*
hard water	18 litres	*4 gallons*
beer yeast		
beer finings		

1. Dissolve the malt extract in one gallon of warm water, stir in the crushed crystal malt grains, add three quarters of the hops, wetting them thoroughly, bring to the boil and continue for thirty minutes.

2. Add all but a big handful of the remaining hops and continue the boil for a further ten minutes. Cover and leave to cool.

3. Strain out the hops and grains and rinse them with 4 pints of warm water. Stir in the glucose chips.

4. Top up with cold water to the 4 gallon mark and when the temperature has fallen to 21°C *(70°F)*, sprinkle on the yeast granules and loosely cover the bin.

5. Skim and stir on the second and third days, then add the rest of the hops, wet them thoroughly and leave the beer to ferment out.

6. Syphon the beer into demijohns, add finings, fit loose bungs, and leave in a cold place for four days.

7. Syphon the beer into a pressure keg, dissolve 71g *(2½ oz)* castor sugar in one pint of the beer and mix it into the whole.

8. Seal the keg and mature this tangy bitter for at least two weeks.

Draught Lager (5 gallons) O.G. 1.034

pale malt extract	1.8kg	*4lb*
Golden syrup	500g	*1lb 2oz*
Hallertau hops	100g	*3½oz*
soft water	18 litres	*4 gallons*
lager yeast (carlsbergensis)		

1. Place the hops in a large boiling pan, add up to one gallon of cold water and wet the hops thoroughly. Bring to the boil and continue for forty-five minutes.

2. Remove from the heat, stir in the malt extract, return to the heat and boil for a further five minutes.

3. Strain out the hops, rinse them with warm water, stir in the golden syrup, make up to 4 gallons with cold water and, when the temperature is down to below 21°C *(70°F)*, add the lager yeast.

4. Ferment in a polythene bin fitted with a lid, containing an air-lock. (This bottom fermenting yeast does not create a frothy head.) Once fermentation starts, move the bin to a cool place (59°F/15°C) and leave the beer to ferment out – ten days or more.

5. When fermentation is quite finished and the beer is clearing, syphon into a sterilised pressure keg, stir in 56 g *(2 oz)* castor sugar, seal the keg securely, and after four days in a warm room, store for three weeks in as cold a place as you can find and serve from there.

CHAPTER TWENTY-ONE

Brewing from grains

After successfully brewing from beer kits and then from malt syrup, hops and adjuncts, the keen brewer is anxious to mash his own grains and make a wort of his choice. Happily, it is now easy for him to do so. Fermenting bins can be bought which are already fitted with a draw off tap and a hole in the lid for the wire of an immersion heater. Sometimes they have a narrow mesh false bottom. Calico sparging bags fitted to a stand make this aspect of mashing equally easy.

When mashing from grains the hardness or softness of the water plays a major part. Pay adequate attention to the water you use if you want the best results. Draw off all the water you need for a particular brew and treat it appropriately (chapter 18). If your beer is unsuccessful for no apparent reason, look at your water supply and try to change it. This simple remedy usually proves effective.

Make sure the grains you use are really fresh. Slack or stale grains make poor beer. Buy them from a source that has a quick turnover, if you can. If you buy a large quantity for economy, keep your stock well covered, in a dry and dark store. The least humidity causes deterioration of the grains. Similarly, of course, with your hops and your yeast.

If possible, buy grains that are already crushed, since crushing them at home is a difficult task. You need a marble hard surface and a hardwood or ceramic rolling pin. Even so, you may find it helpful to soak the grains in warm water for an hour to soften them.

After a few brews you will not want to follow recipes, but in formulating your own, have regard to the likely specific gravity of the finished wort. An original gravity of 1.030 is adequate for mild and brown ales, 1.034 for light ales and sweet stouts, 1.040 for bitter beers, 1.044 for export ales and dry stouts and 1.086 for barley wine. Lagers can vary from the light and golden around 1.032 to the dark and heavy around 1.046.

Pale malt and crystal malt grains and flaked barley consist of around 70% fermentable sugar; flaked maize, flaked rice and flaked wheat consist of around 80%. Malt extract is also about 80%. Chocolate and black malts and roasted barley are virtually sugarless but convey good flavour and colour when used in moderation. As a safe guide make sure that you use 75% pale malt. The remaining 25% in pale beers could include 15% sugar and 10% other grains. In darker beers the black malt does not count in this calculation.

The specific gravity of the wort obtained from different barleys varies and you may find it necessary to increase the quantity of grain you use to achieve an adequate gravity. Some can yield as low as 1.020 and others as high as 1.030. Some of the model recipes that follow are calculated on an average of 1.024 and others on 1.027. The specific gravity can contain more unfermentable dextrin if the grain is mashed at a temperature above 66.5°C *(152° F)*. But the fermentable maltose will be less, resulting in a lower alcohol beer.

The extraction rate is also related to the stiffness of the mash. The stiffer the mash the more dextrin is produced. On the other hand too thin a mash results in the extraction of starch and albuminous matter that causes a hazy beer. The maximum amount of water to grain *(including sparging water)* is one gallon to 1½ lb. One gallon to 2½ lb is a much safer ratio.

Mashing time also affects the dextrin malto: tio. After two hours, four parts maltose to one part dextrin is roduced; after six hours, the ratio is six parts maltose to one part dextrin. Without dextrin a beer tastes very thin and watery, but the optimum ratio depends on the style of beer being brewed. Best bitters, export and strong ales need more dextrin than light or luncheon ales, brown ales and sweet stouts.

Whether you add your grains to the hot water or your hot water to the grains, depends on the facilities you have and the quantity of beer you are brewing. The important factors are to get the ratio of water to grains about right and to stir the mash thoroughly before covering it up.

Temperature can be maintained just by lagging the mashing bin or by using a thermostatic heater or heating belt or both. In either case, give the mash a stir every half hour. If you are using only the lagging method, a falling temperature can be increased by the addition of some very hot water. The actual quantity and temperature of the water to add will vary with the volume of the mash, its temperature and the number of degrees to be increased. One pint of water at 93°C *(200°F)* will raise the temperature of 20 pints of mash at 65°C *(150°F)* to 66.5°C *(152.5°F)*.

Mash for two hours at as constant a temperature as possible, then check to see whether all the starch has been converted. Remove a tablespoonful of the wort and empty it into a white saucer. Add a few drops of household iodine and if the wort turns blue or even darkens, then some starch still remains and mashing should be continued for another half hour.

This sounds easy in theory, but it is less easy in practice, especially if a darker beer is being brewed. It may be necessary to dilute the wort to lighten its colour. After a little practice, however, you can sense rather than see a change or no change. If in serious doubt, you can always remove enough to fill a trial jar, cool it as rapidly as you can to 15.5°C *(60°F)* and check its specific gravity. It is not vitally important for the home brewer to extract every last unit of maltose and dextrin from the grains, although it is for the commercial brewer.

Having satisfied yourself that the end point has been reached, or as good as, strain off the wort and pour, or better still spray, hot water of a slightly higher temperature than the mash, through the grains to wash off the molecules of maltose and dextrin clinging to the husks.

Pour the wort into a boiling pan, add all or most of the hops, wetting them thoroughly, cover the pan and boil vigorously for up to one hour.

The remaining hops may be added towards the end of the boiling to impart a fresh hop flavour to the bitterness.

The boiling precipitates protein from the mash and this should be allowed to settle for half an hour before straining out the hops. If you wish, some Irish Moss can be added with the hops to help coagulate all the suspended solids and so ensure a clean wort for fermentation.

When the wort is removed, stir in any sugar that is required. Glucose chips are the favourite, but Golden Syrup, invert sugar or granulated sugar may all be used. Cold water is then added and when the wort is cool enough the specific gravity should be checked and if necessary the wort adjusted with a little more sugar or water.

An activated yeast should now be pitched into the wort, the fermentation vessel covered with a cloth or a lid fitted with an airlock and the fermentation conducted in the same way as for kit beers, or malt syrup and hop beers. The quality of grain beers can be improved by a lower fermentation temperature, say between 14°C and 17.5°C *(58°F and 64°F)*. Don't forget to skim and stir, clear, prime and seal securely.

Summary

1. Use the correctly treated water for the style of beer.

2. Use only freshly bought grains, hops and yeast.

3. Balance the ratio of different grains to the pale malt to suit the style of beer.

4. Balance the ratio of maltose to dextrin to suit the style of beer. Remember that this depends on the stiffness of the mash, the mashing temperature and the length of the mash.

5. Check for end point after two hours, but perfection is not essential.

6. Sparge the grains with a little hot water so as not to waste any extracted maltose and dextrin.

7. Add the hops, boil vigorously, then leave for a while so the suspended solids can settle.

8. Stir in the sugar and make up to the required quantity with cold water, then adjust to achieve the appropriate specific gravity.

9. Add the yeast and ferment as usual, but at a lower temperature.

Recipes

It is not necessary to repeat all these details after each recipe, for grain mash brewers will well understand the method explained above. Only the suggested ingredients, mashing temperatures and original gravity figures will therefore be given in the recipes.

After straining out the grains, rinse them with hot water so that no malt sugar is left on them and wasted.

Light Ale (16 pints) O.G. 1.032

pale malt	900g	*2lb*
wheat flakes	115g	*4oz*
crystal malt	56g	*2oz*
Challenger hops	28g	*1oz*
hard water	9 litres	*2 gallons*
glucose chips if necessary		
beer yeast		

Mash at 64.5°C to 65.5°C *(148°F to 150°F)*. Boil for forty-five minutes. Adjust O.G. to 1.032. Condition for at least four weeks after bottling.

Best Bitter (16 pints) O.G. 1.044

pale malt	1.135kg	*2½lb*
crystal malt	225g	*8oz*
flaked maize	115g	*4oz*
wheat flakes	115g	*4oz*
Golding hops	56g	*2oz*
hard water	9 litres	*2 gallons*
glucose chips if necessary		
beer yeast		

Mash at 66.5°C *(152°F)*. Boil for one hour. Adjust O.G. to 1.044. Condition for at least six weeks after bottling.

Brown Ale 1 (16 pints) O.G. 1.034

pale malt	900g	*2lb*
crystal malt	170g	*6oz*
flaked oats	115g	*4oz*
black malt	56g	*2oz*
Fuggle hops	28g	*1oz*
soft water	9 litres	*2 gallons*
glucose chips if necessary		
beer yeast		

Mash at 60°C *(140°F)*. Boil for thirty minutes. Adjust O.G. to 1.034. If desired sweeten with 170g *(6oz)* lactose. Condition for at least four weeks after bottling.

Irish Stout (16 pints) O.G. 1.046

pale malt	1.135kg	2½lb
crystal malt	170g	6oz
chocolate malt	170g	6oz
black malt	115g	4oz
wheat flakes	115g	4oz
roasted barley	115g	4oz
brown sugar	115g	4oz
Fuggle hops	56g	2oz
soft water	9 litres	2 gallons
stout yeast		

Mash at 64.5°C *(148°F)*. Boil for forty-five minutes. Adjust O.G. to 1.046. Condition for at least six weeks after bottling.

Lager (16 pints) O.G. 1.044

lager or very pale malt	1.35kg	3lb
flaked maize	170g	6oz
Hallertau hops	56g	2oz
soft water	9 litres	2 gallons
table salt	2.5ml	½tsp
citric acid	2.5ml	½ tsp
Carlsbergensis yeast		

Start mash at 48.5°C *(120°F)* for thirty minutes. Increase to 60°C *(140°F)* for thirty minutes. Increase to 71°C *(160°F)* for thirty minutes. Allow temperature to fall until end point is reached. Boil three-quarters of the hops for thirty minutes, and add the rest and boil for a further fifteen minutes. Adjust O.G. to 1.044 with glucose. Ferment at 10°C *(50°F)* or as low as possible, under an airlock. Condition for at least three months after bottling.

Barley Wine (8 pints) O.G. 1.084

pale malt	1.135kg	2½lb
crystal malt	170g	6oz
Challenger hops	28g	1oz
hard water	4.5 litres	1 gallon
demerara sugar	170g	6oz
citric acid	1.25ml	¼ tsp
calcium sulphate	1.25ml	¼ tsp
Champagne wine yeast		

Mash between 65.5°C and 67.5°C *(150°F and 154°F)* in 7 pints water, sparge with 1 pint. Boil for forty-five minutes. Adjust O.G. to 1.084. Ferment in jar under airlock. Mature for at least one year after bottling in 280 ml *(10 fl oz)* beer bottles.

Daily Bitter (5 gallons) OG 1.040

crushed pale malt	2kg	*4½lb*
crushed crystal malt	500g	*18oz*
demerara sugar	500g	*18oz*
hard water	22.5 litres	*5 gallons*
Golding hops	100g	*3½oz*
beer yeast		
glucose chips	85g	*3oz*

Mash at 66.5°C *(152°F)* for six hours. Boil the hops with the wort for one hour. When cool and made up to five gallons adjust O.G. to 1.040. Ferment at 20°C *(68°F)*. Fine as soon as fermentation finishes. Prime with 85g *(3oz)* glucose chips and pour into a plastic barrel. Seal and store for three weeks.

Luncheon Ale (4 gallons) O.G. 1.036

crushed pale malt	1.35kg	*3lb*
crushed crystal malt	250g	*9oz*
flaked maize	250g	*9oz*
glucose chips	500g	*18oz*
hard water	18 litres	*4 gallons*
Golding hops	85g	*3oz*
beer yeast		
finings		

Mash at 66.5°C *(152°F)* for two hours. Boil all but a handful of hops with the wort for half an hour. Adjust O.G. to 1.036. Add the rest of the hops after the second skimming. Mature for one month.

Brown Ale 2 (16 pints) O.G. 1.030

crushed pale malt	750g	*27oz*
crushed crystal malt	125g	*4½oz*
crushed black malt	50g	*1¾oz*
dark brown sugar	125g	*4½oz*
Fuggle hops	28g	*1oz*

soft water 9 litres *2 gallons*
beer yeast

Mash at 65°C *(149°F)* for three hours. Boil hops with wort for forty-five minutes. Skim and stir well to ferment right out. Mature for three weeks.

India Pale Ale (16 pints) O.G. 1.046

crushed pale malt	1kg	*2¼lb*
crushed crystal malt	250g	*9oz*
flaked rice	125g	*4½oz*
flaked maize	125g	*4½oz*
Golding hops	50g	*1¾oz*
very hard water	9 litres	*2 gallons*
Irish moss	5ml	*1 tsp*
beer yeast		
glucose chips as required		

Mash at 66.5°C *(152°F)* for three hours. Boil all the hops with the wort and Irish moss for one hour. When cool and made up to two gallons, increase O.G. to 1.046 with glucose chips. Mature for six weeks after bottling.

Oatmeal Stout (16 pints) O.G. 1.040

crushed pale malt	1kg	*2¼lb*
crushed crystal malt	125g	*4½oz*
black malt	125g	*4½oz*
porridge oats	125g	*4½oz*
dark brown sugar	250g	*9oz*
Fuggle hops	28g	*1oz*
Northern Brewer hops	14g	*½oz*
soft water	9 litres	*2 gallons*
stout yeast		
finings		

Mash at 65°C *(149°F)* for two hours. Boil wort with Fuggles for thirty minutes, add Northern Brewers and continue to boil for a further fifteen minutes. Mature for a minimum of one month.

CHAPTER TWENTY-TWO

Problems in brewing

As with wine, problems in brewing can be prevented by good hygiene, the use of good ingredients and an understanding of the principles of brewing.

The most common problems are lack of head retention and poor condition.

Head retention

Poor ingredients, poor fermentation and poor cellarcraft are the cause of lack of head retention, although it must be said that many commercial beers also share this complaint. Heading agents can be bought to improve head retention, but good malt grains, good malt extract containing dextrin, a proper boiling followed by a steady fermentation, proper priming and adequate maturation are more effective.

Poor condition

A good beer should be bright and lively, with a foaming head. If it's not primed and sealed properly the beer will be dead and flat. If it's cloudy the cause could be poor hygiene, over-priming (so that the sediment is lifted in a gush of yeast when the bottle is opened), or simply sloppy pouring.

A dull flat beer with little life is caused by a poor beer inadequately primed, imperfectly sealed, or insufficiently matured. When you have made a good beer it must be primed with 2.5 ml (half a teaspoonful) of castor sugar or common white granulated sugar per pint, it must be perfectly sealed to prevent the escape of gas and it must be matured long enough for the priming sugar to be fully fermented. A beer in poor condition should be re-primed, sealed and matured for three weeks.

Bottles should always be thoroughly rinsed before filling to within 3 cm *(1¼ in)* of the cap, and the glasses into which the beer is poured must be free from grease or detergent. Wash glasses thoroughly in hot water and rinse them several times before draining them dry. Traces of grease and detergent can kill a head on beer and reduce condition.

Poor bouquet and flavour

This is due to poor ingredients, imperfectly brewed. You can't just throw the ingredients together! Brewing may be easy but good beers are not made without taking some trouble. Never buy cheap or poor ingredients, and brew good ingredients properly if you want a tasty satisfying beer.

Yeast gush

This is the opposite effect of poor condition. It is caused by adding too much priming sugar, bottling too soon, poor racking and the carrying over of too much sediment, and serving the beer too warm. When the seal is broken, the beer gushes out in the form of foam, lifting the sediment from the bottom of the bottle up into the beer and out with the foam. The remedy is to open each bottle in a bin, and when the foam subsides to re-bottle the beer.

Bitterness

Too much yeast, failure to remove surplus yeast by inadequate skimming and stirring during fermentation and the failure to remove the yeast ring around the bin at the liquor level cause bitterness. It can also develop in a beer fermented at too high a temperature and also in one infected by bacteria. Keep the brew well covered at all times.

Sluggish ferment

Poor yeast or a badly balanced wort with too much hop resin or too low or too high a temperature will cause a sluggish fermentation. Stir the beer vigorously and maintain a steady and adequate temperature.

Set mash

If barley grains are ground too fine, the flour will coagulate into lumps. These must be broken up and made into a smooth wort – not always easy. Crush the grains, but do not grind them into flour! Pour hot water over them slowly, stirring all the time.

CHAPTER TWENTY-THREE

Fruit and other beers

In the countryside farmers used to flavour some of their beers with fruit, herbs and vegetables when hops were not available. The best known was nettle beer, when the tops of young stinging nettles were used as a direct alternative to hops. Beetroot was the most popular of the vegetables. Yarrow, burdock, horehound and the hedgerow fruits of blackberries, sloes and elderberries were also used. Honey beer was popular in East Anglia, and spruce beer and treacle ale in Scotland. All of these beers are now somewhat alien to our more sophisticated palates.

The following recipes are but examples:

Fruit Beer

large prunes	250g	*9oz*
malt extract	500g	*18oz*
brown sugar	250g	*9oz*
water	4 litres	*7 pints*
beer yeast		

1. Wash the prunes, cut them up, pour two pints boiling water over them and leave covered overnight.

2. Bring to boil and simmer for half an hour, then leave to cool.

3. Dissolve the malt extract and sugar in two pints of water and leave to cool.

4. Strain out, press the prunes dry. Mix the malt and sugar syrup with the prune liquor, make up to 8½ pints with cold boiled water, add the yeast and ferment out, stirring the brew occasionally.

5. Move the beer to a cold place for two days, then syphon into beer bottles and prime with castor sugar at the rate of one level 5 ml spoonful per quart.

6. Seal the bottles securely and store for six weeks.

NOTES:
1. Dried apricots make a suitable alternative to the prunes.

2. 500g (*18 oz*) fresh elderberries may also be used. Clean, wash and crush them, pour on boiling water, heat to 176°F *(80°C)* for fifteen minutes, leave to cool, then strain out, press dry and discard the berries and mix the juice with the malt and sugar solution.

Nettle Beer

young nettles	1kg	*2¼lb*
malt extract	500g	*18oz*
lemon		*1*
cream of tartar	15ml	*3 tsp*
water	4 litres	*7 pints*
beer yeast		

1. Trim the nettles, discarding any tough stalks, wash them in running cold water and boil them in four pints water for fifteen minutes.

2. Thinly peel the lemon avoiding all white pith, chop up the parings and place them in a vessel with the cream of tartar.

3. Add two pints hot water, stir in the malt extract, rinse out the jar or can with another pint of warm water, and stir well until the syrup is well dispersed.

4. Strain the nettle liquor into the container, stir, cover and leave to cool.

5. Skim off any scum, stir well and add the strained lemon juice and yeast; replace the cover. When fermentation is finished in about three days, move the beer to a cold place for a day and a night while it settles.

6. Syphon into beer bottles, prime with half a level teaspoonful of castor sugar per pint, seal securely and leave for ten days. Serve the beer slightly chilled.

Treacle Ale

golden syrup	500g	*18oz*
black treacle	250g	*9oz*
lemons		*2*
ground ginger	5ml	*1 tsp*
water	4 litres	*7 pints*
beer yeast		

1. Dissolve the syrup and treacle in warm water, add the thinly pared rind and strained juice of the lemons and the ground ginger. Stir well, cover and leave to cool.

2. Add the yeast, stir the beer daily and when fermentation is finished in four or five days, move the beer to a cold place for twenty-four hours.

3. Syphon into beer bottles, prime with half a level teaspoonful of castor sugar per pint, seal securely and leave for ten days.

NOTE:
The black treacle has quite a bitter flavour.

Beetroot Beer

freshly dug beetroots	1kg	*2¼lb*
brown sugar	500g	*18oz*
home brewed stout	4 litres	*7 pints*
citric acid	2.5ml	*½ tsp*
beer yeast		

1. Scrub the beet clean and free from every trace of soil, top and tail them. Grate them into a container a few at a time, covering each layer with sugar. Sprinkle on the acid, cover the vessel and leave for twenty-four hours.

2. Stir in the home brewed stout, add the yeast, stir well and ferment in a warm place, pressing down the beet twice each day.

3. When fermentation is finished, move the beer to a cold place for twenty-four hours, then syphon into beer bottles.

4. Prime the beer with half a level teaspoonful of castor sugar per pint, seal the bottles securely and store for three months.

Honey Beer

brown honey	500g	*18oz*

lemon		*1*
hops	15g	*½oz*
water	4 litres	*7 pints*
beer yeast		

1. Boil the hops and thinly pared lemon rind in half the water for half an hour.

2. Dissolve the honey in warm water. Strain in the hop liquor, cover and leave to cool. Discard the hops.

3. Add the strained lemon juice and yeast. Cover and ferment out, skimming and stirring if any scum appears.

4. Move to a cold place for twenty-four hours, then syphon into beer bottles.

5. Prime the beer with half a level teaspoonful of castor sugar per pint, seal and store for two weeks. Serve slightly chilled.

Cock Ale

The best of these old recipes is Cock Ale, adapted by the author from an eighteenth century recipe that was very popular among farmers.

malt extract	500g	*18oz*
Golding hops	20g	*¾oz*
demerara sugar	250g	*9oz*
dry white or tawny wine	280ml	*10 fl. oz*
the carcase of a		
plainly roasted chicken		
water	3.8 litres	*6½ pints*
beer yeast		

1. Use the carcase, bones, wing tips, parson's nose, trimmings and neck of a plainly roasted chicken – no stuffing or herbs – after it has been carved for a meal, no bones being served!
Crush all these together, chopping up the bones with a stout knife. Place them in a bowl, cover with white wine and leave in the refrigerator.

2. Boil the hops in some of the water for half an hour.

3. Dissolve the malt extract and sugar in warm water.

4. Strain on the hop liquor, top up with cold water, cover and leave to cool.

5. Add the yeast, stir well and cover.

6. As soon as the beer is fermenting really well – after thirty-six to forty-eight hours – strain in the wine.

7. Place the chicken in a wide mesh nylon or muslin bag and suspend this in the brew for two days.

8. Remove the chicken, stir the beer and ferment out, keeping the beer covered at all times.

9. Move the beer to a cold place for two days, then syphon into bottles.

10. Prime with castor sugar at the rate of one 5 ml spoonful per quart; seal and store for one month.

NOTE:
This is a superb, well flavoured golden beer of good body and texture. Serve it slightly chilled.

Ginger Ale

root ginger	85g	*3oz*
malt extract	500g	*18oz*
cream of tartar	15ml	*3 tsp*
lemon		*1*
water	4 litres	*7 pints*
beer yeast		
lactose	85g	*3oz*
castor sugar	20ml	*4 tsp*

1. Bruise the ginger well, thinly pare the lemon, and boil the ginger and parings in two pints water for fifteen minutes, then leave to cool.

2. Dissolve the malt extract and cream of tartar in warm water and strain into it the ginger water.

3. Add the expressed and strained juice of the lemon and the yeast. Make up to 8½ pints with cold, boiled water, stir well and ferment out, stirring occasionally.

4. Move the vessel to a cold place for two days, then remove half a pint of beer, dissolve the lactose and castor sugar in it and distribute this evenly among the bottles to be filled.

5. Syphon in the clearing beer, seal securely and store for three weeks.

NOTE:
This ale contains approximately 3% alcohol by volume and is not suitable for young children.

CHAPTER TWENTY-FOUR

Making diabetic beers and wines

No one suffering from diabetes should drink any alcohol without prior permission from his or her doctor. Alcohol is another form of carbohydrate and contains many calories. Although wine and beer can be made with little if any residual sugar, it inevitably contains so many calories as to unbalance a prescribed diet that does not allow for it.

Furthermore, if certain diabetes tablets are taken in conjunction with alcohol they could actually worsen the complaint! It is most important that medical clearance be obtained before contemplating any alcoholic drink.

It is also true, however, that certain people suffering from diabetes, and being treated in a particular way, are allowed to drink a modest quantity of completely dry table wine and beer. Strong wines such as ports, Madeiras, sherries and vermouths or beers such as barley wine are best avoided – not only because of residual sugar, but also because of their high alcoholic content and high calorie count.

Wines

Table wines should be so dry that they register only 0.996 or lower on a hydrometer scale. The quantity of residual sugar will then be virtually nil. The calorie count in 100 ml *(3½ fl oz)* will vary from 80–90 depending on the actual strength of the wine.

Anyone suffering from diabetes who wants to make wine for

himself should bear in mind certain factors that constrain the range of suitable wines.

1. The alcohol content should not exceed 10%.

2. Accordingly the flavour should be light and delicate rather than robust.

3. It follows that certain fruits such as blackcurrants, elderberries and figs are too strong in flavour to be suitable.

4. Similarly, vegetables usually impart too much body to a wine to be compatible with lightness.

5. Flowers, herbs and leaves could be used, but these wines taste better when served sweet rather than dry. They would have to be sweetened with saccharin, not by residual sugar.

6. Suitable fruits are apples, apricots, blackberries, currants (red and white only), damsons, gooseberries, greengages, oranges, plums and rhubarb. Canned fruits and juices may also be used since the syrup is fermentable.

7. The use of a hydrometer is essential and great care should be taken to ensure that the total fermentable specific gravity does not exceed 1.070.

8. Pectic enzyme or Rohament P or both should be used to ensure the breakdown of pectin in the fruit and the early release of all constituent sugars, acids and nitrogenous matter. A period of forty-eight hours should be allowed for this instead of the customary twenty-four.

9. A sample of the wine should be removed, pressed, strained and the specific gravity checked with a hydrometer. An allowance of seven units may be made for the suspended solid particles of fruit pulp, acids, tannin, etc.

10. The quantity of additional sugar required to increase the fermentable sugar to 1.070, or just below, should be calculated as carefully as possible by reference to the tables at the end of this book. To ensure a fast and uninterrupted fermentation it would be as well always to invert the sugar used by boiling it with citric acid for twenty minutes.

11. A test should also be made with a Boots Wine Indicator Paper to ensure that the must contains sufficient acid for an uninterrupted fermentation. It is safer to err on the side of too much rather than not quite enough. Add citric acid for a good fermentation.

12. Fruit usually contains sufficient nitrogenous matter, but again, it is better to err on the side of a little too much, so always add some in the form of ammonium phosphate or sulphate or a mixture of both and of one 3 mg tablet of vitamin B_1 – a Benerva tablet.

13. The quality of the yeast is all important. Use pure wine yeast and activate it first. A strong yeast colony will ensure a complete fermentation of all the sugar.

14. In no circumstances should a fermentation be terminated with potassium sorbate or any other wine 'stabiliser'. Ferment right out and add one Campden tablet per gallon to protect the wine from oxidation and infection by other micro organisms.

Some of these recommendations should be followed by all winemakers, but they apply especially strongly in the preparation of wine for diabetics. One advantage that these wines have over many others is that they tend to mature more quickly, being light in alcohol, body and flavour. Most wines of this kind are mature enough to drink within six months of being made.

Beers

Beer too can be brewed at home with a low residual sugar content in the form of dextrin, but there will still be a high calorie count, often in the range of 80–100 units in half a pint.

Some manufacturers of beer kits have marketed hopped malt extracts so prepared as to have a very low carbohydrate content. Detailed instructions come with these kits that are produced primarily for people suffering from diabetes. Because of the low dextrin content however, a fairly high alcohol content is produced. The beer would otherwise taste too thin and watery.

The malt extract/sugar ratio in most of these kits is good – at 1500 g to 650 g *(3lb 4½oz to 1lb 6¾oz)* but because the beer can be fermented down to 0.998, the alcohol content is as high as 4.9%. The calorie count per half pint of such a beer is 83 *(78 from the alcohol and only 5 from the residual dextrin)*.

Provided allowance is made for the calorific value and blood sugar count of the dextrins a better beer can be brewed by the inclusion of slightly more dextrins to give a little extra body, aid head retention and balance the hop bitterness. The counter balance, however, is a lower alcohol content. A more 'beery' tasting beverage is the result. Start with a fairly low original gravity of around 1.030 and bottle with a little residual gravity from the dextrins when fermentation has finished at about 1.004.

For those mashing their beers from grains a higher maltose/dextrin ratio extraction can be obtained by mashing at a temperature between 55°C and 57°C *(131°F and 135°F)*. It helps if the mash is slightly more acidic and the inclusion of one level 5 ml spoonful of citric acid per five gallons is recommended. Even so, some dextrin is extracted, although less than the 20% from the usual mashing temperatures.

The diabetic patient must calculate the calorific value of his beer from its original gravity in the knowledge that his body will use the dextrins as well as the alcohol. So from an original gravity of 1.030 the total calories in half a pint of such a beer will still be 70 of which 18 are likely to come from the residual dextrin and 52 from the 3.2% alcohol. As a rule of thumb every unit of original gravity of a beer is equal to $2\frac{1}{3}$ calories. This figure will vary slightly depending on the final ratio of alcohol to dextrins. More alcohol means slightly more calories, more dextrin means slightly fewer.

An original gravity of 1.030 limits the styles of beer that can be brewed. Mostly, these are going to be mild ale, luncheon ale, lager, a light bitter and perhaps a brown ale. Export ale, best bitter and Irish stout are all too strong since they start from an original gravity in excess of 1.040 and have a fairly high final gravity of around 1.008.

When making up a beer recipe from malt extract or grains, it is better to omit sugar as far as possible. The sugar will ferment out completely and the alcohol will tend to thin the beer. By using all malt the beer will tend to have rather more body and flavour. Even so, every effort should be made to ferment it down to as low a reading as possible because the dextrin increases the blood sugar count.

With your doctor's permission try this recipe:

Diabetic Beer

malt extract	1kg	*2¼lb*
Golding hops	28g	*1oz*
citric acid	1.25ml	*¼ tsp*
water	8 litres	*14 pints*
yeast nutrient	1.25ml	*¼ tsp*
beer yeast granules		

1. Dissolve the malt extract in four pints of warm water, add the acid and hops and boil together for half an hour.

2. Strain out the hops and rinse them with one pint of hot water. Top up with cold water to two gallons, cover and leave to cool to 20°C *(68°F)*.

3. Check the specific gravity and if need be dilute with a little more water until the reading is 1.030.

4. Sprinkle on the yeast and nutrient, cover and leave to ferment out in a constant temperature. Skim and stir well on the second and third days.

5. Syphon into sterilised bottles, prime with four scant level 5 ml teaspoonsful of castor sugar dissolved in a little of the beer and distributed equally between the bottles.

6. Seal and store in a warm room for one week and a cool store for a further three weeks. Serve the beer cool.

CHAPTER TWENTY-FIVE

Making cider at home

Cider is made from a mixture of different apples that are sweet, bitter sweet, sharp and bitter sharp. About three-quarters of the apples used are sweet and bitter sweet and one quarter sharp and bitter sharp. Most of the apples are grown in the West Country especially for the purpose and are not really eating apples. They are very hard and must be mellowed for a period before they can be crushed and pressed. Only the juice is used – no water is required and the addition of sugar is necessary only in very poor years. Cider has an alcoholic strength of around 6% and so is stronger than beer but weaker than wine. It matures in three or four months, and is not difficult to make provided you can crush and press the apples properly. Few of us have access to the true cider apples, however, and must make do with eating and cooking varieties, supplemented by a few crab apples.

If you have a good supply of mixed apples and wish to make some cider, you will need a Pulp Master Apple Crusher attached to an electric drill, a strong press, at least two polythene bins and several demijohns with airlocks. Depending on the varieties and juiciness of the apples used you will need approximately 9 kg *(20 lb)* apples to make 4.5 litres *(1 gallon)* of cider. It is best made in November when the main crop apples are fully ripe and have had time to mellow.

Alternatively, different apples may be made into cider throughout the Autumn and then blended together after Christmas. This is how commercial cider is produced.

The first recipe gives a balanced cider, made from a mixture of apples.

Easily-made cider

The marketing of cans of concentrated cider juice has transformed cider making in the homes of town dwellers. A true cider can now be made as easily as a wine from concentrated grape juice. The kilogram can of juice is so concentrated that it makes two gallons of cider. As with wine, good hygiene is essential and every piece of equipment that comes into contact with the cider should be sterilised in a sulphite solution.

The second recipe shows how to make cider from concentrated juice.

Store this cider for several weeks or even a month or two before serving it slightly chilled. Remember that it is quite potent and should be drunk in moderate quantities.

If you would like to make a cider from the packs of pure apple juice sold in supermarkets buy them from different stores or choose different brand names in the hope that this will give you a greater variety of apples, for the more varieties used, the better the flavour will be. The third recipe shows how to make one gallon of cider from this non-concentrated juice.

Cider 1

Made from a mixture of apples

> 4 measures sweet eating apples
> 2 measures sharp cooking apples
> 1 measure bitter sweet crab apples or hard pears
> Campden tablets
> pectic enzyme
> Champagne yeast

1. Wash and crush the fruit, making sure that no bruised or damaged portions are included. Do not peel or core since these parts contain necessary elements.

2. One 5 ml teaspoonful of pectic enzyme and one crushed Campden tablet should be added to each 4.5 kg *(10 lb)* apples while they are being crushed.

3. Empty each batch of crushed apples into a sterilised polythene bin and keep this closely covered and in a cool place until required.

4. When all the apples are crushed, fill a coarse mesh nylon bag, place it in a press and apply pressure. Collect the juice in sterilised demijohns, seal each one as it is filled and stand it in a cool place until pressing is finished.

NOTE:
During pressing, release the pressure and stir up the pulp from time to time. This is an important process in extracting all the juice. Each bag full needs stirring up at least four times before the apple 'cake' becomes firm and dry.

5. Check the specific gravity of the apple juice and, if need be, add sufficient sugar to increase the reading to at least 1.046. Also check the acidity with a pH paper and look for a reading around 4.5. There is no simple way to check for bitterness, but if you haven't been able to include sufficient crab apples or pears add one 5 ml teaspoonful of grape tannin per gallon.

6. Since the equivalent of two crushed Campden tablets will be in each gallon of juice, leave the jars in a cold place for twenty-four hours before adding the yeast.

7. Make up a yeast starter equivalent to 5% (one twentieth) of the total volume of juice to be fermented. When this is fermenting well, empty all the juice into one bin, stir in the yeast starter until it is well dispersed, then pour the juice back into demijohns and fit an airlock to each one. If the bin has a tight-fitting lid with an airlock it is best to ferment the juice in the bin rather than in separate jars.

A slow cool ferment is preferred and it may take up to six weeks to complete.

8. When fermentation is finished, rack the cider from its sediment, add one crushed Campden tablet per gallon and leave it in a cold place to clear. If the cider is very hazy, finings may be added in accordance with the manufacturer's recommendation.

9. Syphon the clear cider into sterilised screw stoppered bottles, sweeten to taste with saccharin if desired and/or prime with castor sugar at the rate of one 5 ml teaspoonful per quart. Seal securely, store for at least six weeks, then serve nicely chilled.

NOTE:
Ciders made from mixed apples can be improved by the addition of some concentrated cider juice. One kilogram can of concentrate in a five gallon batch is adequate. No water should be added and less sugar will be needed.

The best home made cider is produced with a mixture of eating and cooking apples, supplemented with crab apples. They should be well crushed or cut into small pieces before fermentation on the pulp, then thoroughly pressed to extract all the juice. Stir up the pulp in the bag from time to time and continue pressing till the 'cake' is dry.

Cider 2

Made from concentrated juice

concentrated apple juice	1kg	2¼ lb
sugar	340g	12oz
yeast		

1. Dissolve the concentrated apple juice and white sugar in about 8 litres *(14 pints)* of water, making the total up to 16 pints.

2. Add the yeast and ferment under an airlock in a temperature between 21° and 25°C *(70° to 77°F)* for from seven to ten days.

3. When fermentation is finished move the cider to a cold place for two days to aid clarification, then syphon it into beer or cider bottles.

4. If a petillant, i.e. a slightly sparkling cider is wanted, prime each bottle with a little castor sugar at the rate of one level 5 ml spoonful per quart. If a less dry cider is required add one saccharin pellet per bottle before sealing.

Cider 3

Made from pure apple juice

apple juice	4 litres *7 pints*
grape tannin	5ml *1 tsp*
pectic enzyme	5ml *1 tsp*
sugar	
Champagne or All Purpose wine yeast	

1. Empty the apple juice into a sterilised bin, withdraw a sample to check the specific gravity with a hydrometer, then stir in enough castor or granulated sugar to increase the reading to at least 1.046 when the sugar is completely dissolved and dispersed.

2. Add the grape tannin, essential for flavour, the pectic enzyme to ensure a haze-free cider, and the yeast. Pour the must into a sterilised demijohn, fit an airlock and ferment out.

3. Move the jar to a cold place for a few days, then syphon it into sterilised screw capped bottles.

4. Sweeten with saccharin if so desired and/or prime with castor sugar at the rate of one level 5 ml teaspoonful per quart to make the cider sparkle, then seal and store for six weeks to mature. Serve the cider cold.

CHAPTER TWENTY SIX

Many kinds of mead

There is reason to believe that a fermented solution of honey was mankind's first alcoholic drink. The time of its discovery will never be known, but we do know that it has been around for some 10,000 years – long before wine.

Different flavoured honeys produce different meads and some honeys are more suitable for certain styles of mead than others.

For table meads, sparkling meads and many melomels, the creamy granulated honey is best; for dessert meads and metheglins the darker, stronger flavoured honey is more suitable.

Honey, as we buy it, consists mostly of sugar, about 77%, and water, about 17½%. The remaining 5½% consists of salts of iron, phosphorus, lime, sodium, potassium, sulphur and manganese, with traces of citric, formic, malic, succinic and amino acids, together with dextrin, pollen, oils, gums, waxes, fats, yeast enzymes, vitamins, albumen, protein and ash.

The acid and nutrient content is so negligible that it is most important to ensure that an adequate supply of both is included in the must. Failure to do so will result in poor fermentation, poor bouquet and taste, and undesirable off-flavours.

Any wine yeast will ferment a honey solution, although experience shows that the Maury yeast brings out the honey flavour best. Sauternes yeast is also very good.

Honey may be used by itself to make all the standard wine styles: aperitif, table, sparkling and dessert. It can also be mixed with fruits, fruit juices, herbs, flowers and spices to make unusual and enjoyable social style meads.

Hygiene is just as important in the production of mead as it is in the making of wine, beer and cider. The same equipment may be used and, as always, should be sterilised with a sulphite solution before use.

A honey solution can sometimes be slow to ferment out, even with sufficient acid and nutrient. The best flavours seem to be derived from a long slow fermentation at a temperature in the range 15°C to 17°C *(the low 60°s F)*. Exclude the light as much as possible to maintain a good colour.

Some meads mature very quickly – the light, delicately flavoured meads – while others take several years to reach their best, especially those made from strongly flavoured honey.

Mead is best served cool rather than cold. If it is too cold, the flavour is diminished. If it is not cool enough, the mead tastes too soft and flabby. Serve dry meads with appropriate food, notably ham, pork, Continental sausages, roast poultry, baked, grilled or poached fish, salads and vegetarian dishes. Sweet meads are best served with a sweet biscuit.

The quantities given in the following recipes have been calculated to fill a one-gallon demijohn, which should be filled to the base of the neck before fermentation starts. Any small deficiency can be made up with a drop of cold boiled water.

Table Mead (dry)

orange blossom honey	1.35kg	*3lb*
hot water	4 litres	*7 pints*
citric acid	20ml	*4 tsp*
tannin	2.5ml	*½ tsp*
nutrient	5ml	*1 tsp*
Maury yeast		
Campden tablet		

1. Dissolve the honey, acid, tannin and nutrient in the water, cover and leave to cool.

2. Add the yeast, pour the must into a fermentation jar, fit an airlock and ferment out.

3. Rack into a clean jar, add one Campden tablet, top up with another dry mead or cold boiled water, bung tight, label and store in a cold place until the mead is bright.

4. Rack again and store for one year or until the mead is mature.

Table Mead (sweet)

cream coloured honey	1.7kg	*3¾lb*
hot water	3.7 litres	*6½ pints*
citric acid	25ml	*5 tsp*
tannin	2.5ml	*½ tsp*
nutrient	5ml	*1 tsp*
Sauternes yeast		
potassium sorbate		
Campden tablet		

1. Dissolve the honey, acid, tannin and nutrient in the water, cover and leave to cool.

2. Add the yeast, pour the must into a fermentation jar, fit an airlock and ferment down to S.G. 1.016.

3. Rack into a jar containing 1 g potassium sorbate and one Campden tablet, top up, bung tight, label and store in a cold place until the mead is bright.

4. Rack again and store for one year or until the mead is mature.

Dessert Mead (sweet)

clover or heather honey	1.8kg	*4lb*
hot water	3.4 litres	*6 pints*
citric acid	30ml	*6 tsp*
tannin	5ml	*1 tsp*
nutrient	5ml	*1 tsp*
Tokay yeast		
light brown sugar	250g	*9oz*

1. Dissolve 3 lb honey, the acid, tannin and nutrient in the water, cover and leave to cool.

2. Add the yeast, pour the must into a fermentation jar, leaving room for the rest of the honey and the sugar. Fit an airlock and leave the jar in a suitable place.

3. After ten days, remove one-third of the must, dissolve half the remaining honey in it and return it to the jar.

4. Repeat this process one week later with the last of the honey and one week later still with the sugar.

5. When fermentation is finished and the mead is clearing, syphon it into a clean jar, bung tight, label and store in a cold place until it is bright.

6. Rack again and store for one year or longer until this strong, sweet mead is mature.

Cyser (dry)

This is a mixture of apple juice and honey. It may be made by replacing some or all of the sugar with honey in the first of the apple wine recipes on page 96, or by adding apple juice to a table mead.

cream coloured honey	1kg	*2¼lb*
apple juice	2 litres	*3½ pints*
hot water	2 litres	*3½ pints*
citric acid	10ml	*2 tsp*
tannin	2.5ml	*½ tsp*
pectic enzyme	5ml	*1 tsp*
nutrient	2.5ml	*½ tsp*
Maury or champagne yeast		
Campden tablet		

1. Dissolve the honey, acid, tannin and nutrient in the hot water, cover and leave to cool.

2. Dissolve the pectic enzyme in the two cartons of apple juice.

3. Mix the honey solution and apple juice, add the yeast, pour the must into a fermentation jar, fit an airlock and ferment out.

4. Rack the cyser into a clean jar, add one Campden tablet, top up, bung tight, label and store in a cold place until bright.

5. Rack again and store for one year.

NOTE:
A sweet cyser can be made either by sweetening a dry cyser with saccharin or by dissolving honey in a bottle of dry cyser when poured into a decanter immediately before serving.

Pyment (dry)

This is a mixture of grape juice and honey. It may be made by adding honey instead of sugar to the recipes for English wine grapes. Alternatively a concentrated grape juice may be added to a table mead.

cream coloured honey	1.1kg	*2¼lb*
concentrated white grape juice	*approx.* 250g	*9oz*
hot water	3.7 litres	*6¼ pints*
citric acid	15ml	*3 tsp*

tannin	2.5ml	$\frac{1}{2}$ *tsp*
nutrient	2.5ml	$\frac{1}{2}$ *tsp*
Maury yeast		
Campden tablet		

1. Dissolve the honey, acid, tannin and nutrient in water, cover and leave to cool.

2. Stir in the concentrated grape juice and yeast, pour the must into a fermentation jar, fit an airlock and ferment out.

3. Rack into a clean jar, add one Campden tablet, top up, bung tight, label and store in a cool place until the pyment is bright.

4. Rack again and store for one year.

NOTES:
1. A sweet pyment can be made either by sweetening a dry pyment with saccharin or by dissolving honey in a bottle of dry pyment when poured into a decanter immediately before serving.

2. Other pyments may be made by replacing with honey the sugar required to be added to a can of concentrated grape juice when being made up into wine. Remember that only three-quarters of the weight of honey consists of sugar, so that 25% more honey than sugar will be needed e.g. 227 g *(8 oz)* honey instead of 170 g *(6 oz)* sugar.

Melomel (sweet)

This is a mixture of any or several kinds of fruits or flower infusions with honey. All of the fruit and flower recipes in the wine section may be turned into melomels by the substitution of honey in place of some of the sugar. The following recipe is also good.

cream coloured honey	1.7kg	$3\frac{3}{4}$ *lb*
orange juice	2 litres	$3\frac{1}{2}$ *pints*
hot water	1.7 litres	*3 pints*
tartaric acid	10ml	*2 tsp*
tannin	2.5ml	$\frac{1}{2}$ *tsp*
nutrient	5ml	*1 tsp*
Sauternes yeast		
potassium sorbate		
Campden tablet		

1. Dissolve the honey, acid, tannin and nutrient in the water, cover and leave to cool.

2. Add the two cartons of orange juice and the yeast, pour the must into a fermentation jar, fit an airlock and ferment down to S.G. 1.016.

3. Rack the melomel into a jar containing 1 g potassium sorbate and one Campden tablet. Top up, bung tight, label and store in a cold place until bright.

4. Rack again and store for one year or until the melomel is mature.

Metheglin (sweet)

This is a mead fermented in the presence of herbs or spices. It is something of an acquired taste and is best when made sweet rather than dry. It is at its most pleasant when served mulled.

brown honey	1.6kg	*3½lb*
hot water	3.4 litres	*6 pints*
lemon	1	
tartaric acid	10ml	*2 tsp*
malic acid	10ml	*2 tsp*
bruised root ginger	28g	*1oz*
whole cloves	24	
cinnamon	1 stick	
brown sugar	200g	*7oz*
nutrient	5ml	*1 tsp*
Sauternes yeast		
potassium sorbate		
Campden tablet		

1. Thinly pare the lemon avoiding all white pith. Place the parings in a bin with the acids, ginger, cloves and cinnamon. Pour on hot water and stir in the honey. Cover and leave to cool.

2. Add the yeast, pour the must and spices into a fermentation jar, fit an airlock and leave it in a warm place for three days.

3. Strain out and discard the solids, stir in the sugar, pour the must back into the jar, re-fit the airlock and ferment down to S.G. 1.016.

4. Rack the metheglin into a clean jar containing 1 g potassium sorbate and one Campden tablet, top up, bung tight, label and store in a cold place until bright.

5. Rack again and and store for one year or until the metheglin is mature.

NOTE:
A bouquet garni of herbs may be used instead of the ginger, cloves and cinnamon.

CHAPTER TWENTY-SEVEN

Fortified wines and liqueurs

It is increasingly becoming the practice among winemakers to serve their own liqueurs after a meal. These very strong, and usually sweet, beverages can be made in the home by marinading fruits, herbs, beans or spices in a spirit. The French are masters at this craft and are able to buy a colourless spirit called *'eau de vie pour les fruits'* for the purpose. In the United Kingdom we mostly use vodka, but also gin for sloes and oranges, and white rum for coffee.

The fruit used should be the very best obtainable, fully ripe and free from blemishes. Small fruits should be pricked with a bodkin or fork so that the juice and flavour can be leached out by the spirit. The quantity of sugar used depends on the sweetness of the fruit but may also vary to suit your palate. It is best to start off with, say, 170 g *(6 oz)* sugar per bottle and to increase this by small additions until you are satisfied with the result. You can always add more sugar; but it is difficult to reduce excessive sweetness. Castor or some other finely ground white sugar should be used since this dissolves more readily than granulated sugar.

The method is the same for most fruits so only a few examples will be given.

Brightly coloured liqueurs
make a satisfying finish to a meal.

Bullace Vodka

bullaces	450g	*1 lb*
castor sugar	170–225g	*6–8oz*
vodka	75cl	*26⅔fl oz*
glycerine	15ml	*3 tsp*

1. Stalk, wash and prick the bullaces and put them in a wide mouth glass jar.

2. Dissolve the sugar in the vodka, add the glycerine and pour it over the fruit.

3. Seal the jar and leave it in a handy place where it can be shaken each day for one month to extract the juice and flavour. Leave it for a further two months, in a cool dark place.

4. Strain out, drain and keep the bullaces, they are delicious to eat. Taste the vodka, sweeten it further if required, then bottle and keep it for a further three months before drinking it.

Sloe Gin

sloes	450g	*1 lb*
castor sugar	225g	*8oz*
gin	75cl	*26⅔fl oz*
glycerine	15ml	*3 tsp*

1. Stalk, wash and prick the sloes, then put them in a wide mouth glass jar.

2. Dissolve the sugar in the gin, add the glycerine and pour it over the fruit.

3. Seal the jar and leave it in a handy place where it can be shaken each day for one month to extract the juice and flavour. Leave it for a further two months in a cool dark place.

4. Strain out, drain and discard the sloes (or add them to a wine must). Taste the gin, sweeten it further if required, then bottle and keep it for a further six to nine months before drinking it.

NOTES:

1. Damsons may be used instead of sloes and when strained out these may be used to make an excellent fruit tart.

2. The thinly pared rinds, excluding all white pith, of one orange, one lemon and one mandarin, may be chopped up and used instead of the sloes. Leave them in the gin for only one week, shaking the jar each day, then strain them out, bottle the gin and store it for six to nine months.

Prune Brandy

Agen prunes	450g *1lb*
castor sugar	100g *3½oz*
eau de vie	75cl *26⅔fl oz*

1. Wash and prick the prunes and put them in a wide mouth glass jar.

2. Dissolve the sugar in the eau de vie and pour it over the fruit.

3. Seal the jar and leave it in a handy place where it can be shaken each day for one month. Leave it for a further two months in a cool dark place.

4. Strain out, drain and eat the delicious prunes. Taste the brandy, sweeten it further if required, then bottle and keep it for a further three months.

NOTE:
Large dried apricots are equally successful but only half the quantity is needed. Wash them first and prick them.

Cherry 'Brandy'

fresh or frozen morello cherries	450g *1lb*
light brown sugar	450g *1lb*
strong ale	2 litres *3½ pints*

1. Stalk, wash and prick the cherries and place them in a wide mouth sweet jar or similar vessel.

2. Dissolve the sugar in the beer and pour it over the fruit.

3. Loosely cover the jar or fit an airlock and leave it in a warm place 21°C *(70°F)* for one month for further fermentation.

4. Strain out and drain the cherries and use them to make a superb tart.

5. Leave the *'brandy'* in a cool place for a few days to clear, then bottle and store it for three months before drinking it.

NOTES:
1. This is a strong beverage with a fine flavour akin to the Kent cherry brandy. A strong home brewed beer that has just finished fermenting is ideal for the base. The 'brandy' is still when poured and has no head or need of condition.
2. Damsons may be used instead of the morello cherries.

Very simple liqueurs, that are nevertheless most pleasant, can be made from a liqueur essence, some strong wine, vodka, sugar, glycerine and capsicum tincture. The liqueur takes only a few minutes to make and may be drunk at once.

T. Noirot liqueur essence*	15ml	*3 tsp*
strong white wine	370ml	*13fl oz*
vodka	250ml	*9fl oz*
castor sugar	170g	*6oz*
glycerine	15ml	*3 tsp*
capsicum tincture		*12 drops*

Dissolve the sugar in the vodka and wine, stir in the liqueur essence, glycerine and capsicum tincture and taste the liqueur. If necessary, add a few drops more essence and/or a little more sugar to suit your taste. The liqueur is now ready for drinking although it improves if kept for one week to homogenise.

The wine should be bland and strong. A concentrated grape juice wine fermented on with extra sugar is ideal. If a very sweet wine is used, less sugar may be needed. The glycerine makes the liqueur taste very smooth, while the capsicum tincture imparts a warm glow to the liqueur, giving the impression of a high alcohol content.

This recipe makes a full standard bottle (26 fl oz) of a liqueur that has an alcohol content around 22%. There is a very wide choice of essences from which to choose.

Alcohol fortification

There are two ways of fortifying wine. The most common is to fortify its strength by adding more alcohol. The second way is to fortify its flavour by adding an essence or a commercial wine.

If the methods advocated for making dessert wines are followed carefully there is little need for further increasing their alcohol content. Given sufficient acid, nutrient and a steady temperature, a Tokay or Madeira yeast can often ferment a must on to 16% or 17% alcohol. Dry sherry or vermouths are usually about 17% alcohol and Madeiras, sweet sherries and port wines are around 20%. If it is felt necessary or desirable to fortify a wine with additional alcohol, the best spirit to use is vodka, because it is colourless, odourless and tasteless. Other spirits like gin, whisky,

* A red wine should be used with the cherry brandy essence.

brandy and rum have specific flavours which alter the flavour of a wine when added to it. As a rule of thumb one bottle of vodka containing 40% alcohol will increase the alcohol content of five bottles of strong wine by about 4%. A more precise calculation can be made with the aid of a formula known as Pearson's Square:

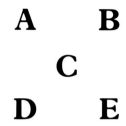

In the corner marked A write the alcohol content of the spirit to be used, say 40%.

In the corner marked B write the alcohol content of the wine to be fortified, say 14%.

In the centre marked C write the alcohol content required in the fortified wine, say 18%.

In the corner marked D write the difference between C and B i.e. 18% – 14% = 4%.

In the corner marked E write the difference between A and C 40% – 18% = 22%.

The ratio between D and E is the proportion of spirit needed to fortify the wine, i.e. 4 parts of spirit to 22 parts of wine, or one bottle of spirit to five and a half bottles of wine.

Flavour fortification

The flavour of a wine can often be enhanced by the addition of a small bottle of essence. These are available in a variety of flavours. The most effective appears to be a sherry essence and a few experiments along these lines are well worth while. Alternatively, a bottle of suitable wine added to a gallon of an appropriate fruit wine at the bottling stage can also be very effective. For example – a bottle of dry sherry added to a dry sherry style wine and left for some months to mature will impart some of its flavour and characteristics to the home made wine. A bottle of ruby port or a Boal or Malmsey Madeira also enhances compatible wines. It is important to allow a minimum of six months for this kind of fortification to be effective. These commercial wines are not inexpensive so it is important only to add them to fine examples of your craft to improve them still more. You then have seven bottles of quite outstanding wine for the price of one and the actual costs of your own wine.

CHAPTER TWENTY-EIGHT

Winter mulls and Summer cups

Mulls

In the days before central heating and wall to wall carpeting, mulls were a very popular drink on the cold winter days. With the wide range of alcoholic liquors now available in the home, interest has re-awakened in this old fashioned way of drinking beer, cider, mead and wine. All of these beverages may be made into a mull and there is but one factor to observe – the temperature.

Alcohol boils at a much lower temperature than water and is driven off in vapour if the mull is allowed to boil. It is important, then, to use a thermometer all the time while you are heating a mull. The critical temperature is 60°C *(140°F)*. Below this temperature the mull does not taste hot enough, above it the mull loses its alcohol. At 60°C the mull both tastes hot and retains its alcohol.

The spices normally used to flavour a mull are bruised root ginger, whole cloves, cinnamon and nutmeg, together with the thinly pared rind of a lemon and its juice – although it is not necessary to use them all at the same time. Brown or white sugar may be used for sweetening, also honey or golden syrup.

A mulled wine is an ideal nightcap on a cold night. Keep it in a vacuum flask at the correct temperature of 60°C (140°F) and serve it in warmed glasses.

There are a great many variations and recipes. One includes baking an orange in which cloves have been stuck and then adding the orange segments to the mull. Another includes a baked apple, the flesh of which is mashed and added to the mull. A sound basic recipe is given on page 242.

Red Wine Mull

One bottle strong sweet red wine*
One lemon
A large piece of bruised ginger root
12 whole cloves
Sugar as necessary

1. Thinly pare the lemon and place the parings in a saucepan, add the piece of well bruised ginger root, the cloves and one or two tablespoonsful of brown or white sugar.

2. Pour in the wine, place the pan on a low heat and stir gently but steadily to dissolve the sugar and distribute the flavours.

3. Check the temperature constantly and when 60°C *(140°F)* is reached, turn off the heat. Stir in the lemon juice, strain out the solids and return the pan to the heat.

4. When the temperature again reaches 60°C *(140°F)* pour the mull at once into pre-heated glasses. Serve with hot mince pies or sausage rolls.

Cups

A cup is to summer what a mull is to winter, although beer is seldom used for this purpose. Light wines and ciders, especially those that are petillant or sparkling are particularly suitable, but a light and fragrant mead could also be used. Sometimes a small quantity of a liqueur, sherry or gin is added, sometimes a lively mineral water or lemonade. Ginger beer can be added to increase the quantity available or to reduce the alcohol content in a long drink.

Fruits of all kinds are used for flavouring and enhancing the appearance of the cup. They should be cut into manageable pieces with a very sharp knife so that they do not look crushed. Raspberries can be cut in half, large strawberries into quarters, grapes and orange segments cut in half and the pips removed. A peach should be stoned, peeled and cut into segments and then halved.

Sometimes the leaves of mint are washed and chopped then used for flavouring with thinly sliced cucumber or thin slices of lemon. Whatever is used should look elegant.

Small ice cubes or spheres, or crushed ice is always added and it

* Beer, cider or mead may be used instead of wine.

helps if the base liquid ingredients are also chilled beforehand. Some of the fruit may be served in the glasses, hence the need for small pieces.

Sugar is nearly always needed since the cup is meant to be served very cold. Finely ground or castor sugar is best, but a tablespoonful of honey or golden syrup may also be used. Indeed, cups and mulls may be made to suit your ideas and tastes from the ingredients available to you. It is not necessary to follow precise instructions. However, the following recipe will show you the way.

Orange & Gin Cup

One bottle of orange wine		
One sweet orange		
castor sugar (or sugar lumps)	60g	*2oz*
gin	85ml	*3fl oz*
small ice cubes		12
tonic water	280ml	*10fl oz*

1. Thinly pare the orange or, preferably, rub off the zest with lumps of sugar. Peel and clean the orange from all white pith, cut it into thin slices which then quarter. Place the parings or zested sugar lumps in a large glass jug or suitable bowl, together with the orange pieces, sprinkled with castor sugar if used.

2. Pour in the gin and stir gently to dissolve the sugar and marinade the orange in the gin.

3. Add the small ice cubes, pour on the orange wine, cover and leave for five minutes.

4. Add the tonic water and serve at once in six tall glasses or tumblers. Each glass should include some ice and fruit.

CHAPTER TWENTY-NINE

Drinks for children

Ginger Beer

dried root ginger	56g	2oz
lemon		1
cream of tartar	15ml	3 tsp
white sugar	170g	6oz
boiling water	4.5 litres	1 gallon
beer yeast		
saccharin to taste		

1. Thinly pare the lemon rind avoiding all white pith, chop it finely and add to it the well bruised ginger roots, the cream of tartar and the sugar.

2. Pour on the boiling water and stir until the sugar is dissolved. Cover and leave to cool.

3. Add the strained lemon juice and yeast and ferment in a warm room for thirty-six hours, removing any scum that may arise.

4. Strain through fine mesh nylon and a funnel into screw stoppered mineral water bottles, sweeten with saccharin, seal securely and leave for one week to finish fermenting.

5. Chill the bottles before serving.

NOTE:
Very little alcohol is formed and no priming sugar is necessary. The beer should not gush when opened but pour with a lively effervescence.

Lemonade

fresh lemons		4
cream of tartar	15ml	3 tsp
glycerine	15ml	3 tsp
white sugar	170g	6oz
boiling water	4.5 litres	1 gallon
beer yeast		
saccharin to taste		

1. Thinly pare the lemon rinds avoiding all white pith, chop them finely, add the cream of tartar and the sugar, pour on the boiling water, stir well, cover and leave to cool.

2. Add the strained lemon juice and yeast and ferment in a warm room for thirty-six hours removing any scum that may arise.

3. Stir in the glycerine, strain through a fine mesh nylon and a funnel into screw stoppered mineral water bottles, sweeten with saccharin, seal securely and leave for one week to finish fermenting.

4. Chill the bottles before serving.

NOTE:
Four sweet oranges may be used instead of the lemons or two of each. A medium sized pineapple (topped, tailed, washed and well crushed) is a third alternative.

Raspberryade

fresh or frozen raspberries	680g	1½lb
cream of tartar	15ml	3 tsp
glycerine	15ml	3 tsp
white sugar	170g	6oz
cold water	4.5 litres	1 gallon
pectic enzyme	5ml	1 tsp
beer yeast		
saccharin to taste		

1. Stalk, wash and crush the raspberries, add the pectic enzyme, pour on the cold water, stir well, cover and leave for twenty-four hours.

2. Stir in the cream of tartar, sugar and yeast and ferment in a warm room for thirty-six hours, keeping the raspberries submerged and the vessel well covered.

3. Add the glycerine then strain through fine mesh nylon and a funnel into screw stoppered mineral water bottles. Sweeten with saccharin, seal securely and leave one week to finish fermenting.

4. Chill the bottles before serving.

Syrup Flavourings

Almost any fruit may be used to make a syrup flavouring that can be diluted with ice cold water or, better still, chilled effervescent soda water. The method is the same for all fruits.

1. Stalk, wash, stone and crush or liquidise the fruit.

2. Add one level 5 ml spoonful of pectolytic enzyme or Rohament P for each 2.5 kg (*5½lb*) fruit, cover closely and leave in a warm room for twenty-four hours.

3. Strain out the pulp through a fine nylon sieve or bag, rolling the pulp around and around to remove as much juice as possible without carrying forward too much fine pulp.

4. To each 560 ml *(1 pint)* of juice add from 340 g to 450 g (*¾ to 1 lb*) of white sugar depending on the acidity of the fruit. Stir steadily until all the sugar is dissolved. This task is easier with castor or finely ground sugar.

5. Pour the syrup into sterilised bottles leaving an air space of 3 cm *(1¼ in)*. Lay on sterilised screw stoppers or loosely insert sterilised corks.

6. Stand the bottles on a grid, cloth or slats of wood in a fish kettle, preserving pan or large stew pan and fill the pan with water to the syrup level.

7. Place the pan on a stove, bring the water to the boil and simmer it steadily for twenty-minutes.

8. Fasten the stoppers tightly or push home the corks to their limit and leave the bottles to cool.

9. Remove the bottles, dry and label them, then store them in a cool dark place until required. Use them within one year since the colour and flavour slowly deteriorates.

NOTE:
The 280 ml (*10 fl oz*) screw capped mineral water bottles are ideal containers for fruit syrups.
Fruits that are low in acid should have citric acid added with the pectic enzyme. Use one level 5 ml spoonful per 450 g (*1 lb*). Fruits that are low in juice may have a small quantity of cold boiled water added when they are liquidised or crushed. Use 100 ml (*3½ fl oz*) per 450 g (*1 lb*).

CHAPTER THIRTY

Making vinegar

Beer, cider, mead and wine can all be turned into vinegar without much trouble, but keep them well away from other fermenting beverages or you will end up with far more vinegar than you wanted.

The base ingredient – beer, cider, mead or wine – should have an alcohol content of between 4% and 7%, but one of 5% or 6% produces the best home made vinegars. A strong beer that is not too heavily hopped or a cider may be used as they are. Mead and wine have to be diluted with an equal quantity of cold boiled water to reduce their alcohol content.

Five measures of the beer, cider, mead or wine must then be mixed with one measure of malt vinegar. This mixture should be poured into a sterilised container capable of holding at least twice as much, e.g. half a gallon of mixture into a one gallon container. A demijohn may be used but a one gallon plastic container is even better. Some holes can easily be bored or burned into the walls of the container just above the mixture level to encourage the flow of air across the surface. The area of this surface can be increased by laying the container on its side. It should be supported near its mouth with a small wedge to stop the mixture running out.

Cover the container with a fine mesh nylon net to keep out flies, wasps and similar insects and place it in as warm a situation as you can find. A fairly constant temperature around 25°C

(77°F) is ideal, but a well ventilated position is equally important.

Leave the container for some three months while the alcohol is converted into acetic acid. At first the mixture will become hazy, then a skin may develop on the surface, eventually the vinegar will fall bright and be ready for pasteurisation.

Syphon it into screw capped mineral water bottles holding 280 ml *(10 fl oz)*, or some similar sauce or vinegar bottles that have been washed clean and sterilised. When the bottles are full, stand them on a board or cloth in a fish kettle, preserving pan or large stew pan, fill the pan with cold water to the level of the top of the vinegar in the bottles. Make sure that the screw caps are only laid on and are quite loose. If they are fastened too tightly the bottles may burst. Place the pan on a stove, bring the water to the boil and simmer it steadily for twenty minutes.

Screw down the caps tightly and leave the bottles in the water until they are cool enough to handle. Remove and dry them, then label and store in a cool place for a few months to mature. Pasteurisation of the vinegar is essential, otherwise the acetic acid will be further reduced to water and carbon dioxide by other bacteria.

Reference tables

HYDROMETER TABLES

Specific gravity	Sugar per litre	Sugar per gallon	Probable Alcohol content
1.010	30g	4¾oz	0.4%
1.015	44g	7oz	1.2%
1.020	57g	9oz	2.0%
1.025	70g	11oz	2.8%
1.030	83g	13¼oz	3.6%
1.035	97g	15½oz	4.3%
1.040	110g	17½oz	5.1%
1.045	123g	19½oz	5.8%
1.050	136g	21½oz	6.5%
1.055	149g	23¾oz	7.2%
1.060	162g	25¾oz	7.9%
1.065	175g	27¾oz	8.6%
1.070	189g	30oz	9.3%
1.075	202g	32oz	10.0%
1.080	215g	34½oz	10.6%
1.085	228g	36½oz	11.3%
1.090	241g	38½oz	12.0%
1.095	255g	40¾oz	12.7%
1.100	268g	42¾oz	13.4%
1.105	281g	44¾oz	14.2%
1.110	295g	47oz	14.9%
1.115	308g	49oz	15.6%
1.120	321g	51¼oz	16.3%
1.125	335g	53¼oz	17.1%
1.130	348g	55½oz	17.8%
1.135	361g	57½oz	18.5%
1.140	375g	59¾oz	19.3%

Note

1. The probable alcohol content is percentage by volume and assumes adequate acid, nutrient and fermentation temperature to convert 47.5% of the sugar to alcohol.

2. There is usually some obscurity in the figures at the upper and lower end of hydrometer readings. The upper range readings often include minute particles of fruit pulp, proteins, tannin, acids, etc. and a reduction of 5 units should be allowed for these. At the lower end of the scale the water can be diluted by the alcohol because alcohol is lighter than water.

3. 2lb of sugar increases the volume of a liquid by 1 pint. 1kg of sugar increases the volume of a liquid by 0.62 litre.

4. The temperature of a must or wort affects the specific gravity. Hydrometers are sometimes graduated at 15°C *(59°F)*. If the temperature of the test sample varies from this norm, then an appropriate allowance must be made to the last figure of the specific gravity reading.

Temperature		*Correction*
10°C	50°F	Subtract 0.6
15°C	59°F	No correction
20°C	68°F	Add 0.9 to last figure
25°C	77°F	Add 2.0 to last figure
30°C	86°F	Add 3.4 to last figure
35°C	95°F	Add 5.0 to last figure
40°C	104°F	Add 6.8 to last figure

METRIC CONVERSIONS

Liquid Measurements		
1 fl oz	=	28 ml
2 fl oz	=	57 ml
3 fl oz	=	85 ml
4 fl oz	=	113 ml
5 fl oz	=	142 ml
6 fl oz	=	170 ml
7 fl oz	=	198 ml
8 fl oz	=	227 ml
9 fl oz	=	255 ml
10 fl oz	=	283 ml
1 pint	=	566 ml
2 pints	=	1.136 litres
3 pints	=	1.704 litres
4 pints	=	2.273 litres
5 pints	=	2.841 litres
6 pints	=	3.409 litres
7 pints	=	3.977 litres
8 pints	=	4.546 litres

Solid Measurements		
$\frac{1}{4}$oz	=	7g
$\frac{1}{2}$oz	=	14g
$\frac{3}{4}$oz	=	21g
1oz	=	28g
2oz	=	57g
3oz	=	85g
4oz	=	113g
5oz	=	142g
6oz	=	170g
7oz	=	198g
8oz	=	227g
1 lb	=	454g
2 lb	=	908g
3 lb	=	1.36 kg
4 lb	=	1.81 kg
5 lb	=	2.27 kg
6 lb	=	2.72 kg
7 lb	=	3.18 kg
8 lb	=	3.63 kg
9 lb	=	4.08 kg
10 lb	=	4.54 kg

1 litre	=	$1\frac{3}{4}$ pints
750 ml	=	$1\frac{1}{3}$ pints
500 ml	=	$17\frac{1}{2}$ fl oz
250 ml	=	$8\frac{3}{4}$ fl oz
10 ml	=	$\frac{1}{3}$ fl oz
5 ml	=	$\frac{1}{6}$ fl oz (1 tsp)

1 kg	=	2 lb 3 oz
750g	=	1 lb $10\frac{1}{4}$ oz
500g	=	1 lb $1\frac{1}{2}$ oz
250g	=	$8\frac{3}{4}$ oz
100g	=	$3\frac{1}{2}$ oz
50g	=	$1\frac{3}{4}$ oz

COMPARATIVE TEMPERATURES

0°C = 32°F	35°C = 95°F	70°C = 158°F
5°C = 41°F	40°C = 104°F	75°C = 167°F
10°C = 50°F	45°C = 113°F	80°C = 176°F
15°C = 59°F	50°C = 122°F	85°C = 185°F
20°C = 68°F	55°C = 131°F	90°C = 194°F
25°C = 77°F	60°C = 140°F	95°C = 203°F
30°C = 86°F	65°C = 149°F	100°C = 212°F

IMPORTANT TEMPERATURES

10°C *(50°F)* for serving white, rosé and sparkling wines, also for fermenting lager beers.

20°C *(68°F)* for serving dessert and red table wines, also for fermenting wines and beers.

60°C *(140°F)* for serving mulled wines.

65°C to 70°C *(149°F to 158°F)* for mashing grain beers.

DRIED AND FRESH FRUIT COMPARISON TABLES

Dried Fruit	Sugar content	Acid content	Tannin content	Fresh fruit equivalent *(Multiply weight of dried fruit by)*	Water content fresh fruit	Carbohydrate content
Currants ⎫ Raisins ⎬ Sultanas ⎭	66.5%	M	A	4	81.5%	17.3%
Apples	54%	M	L	6	84.8%	14.1%
Apricots	46.5%	M	L	5½	85.3%	12.8%
Bananas	65%	L	L	3	75.7%	22.2%
Bilberries	18.5%	L	A	4½	83.2%	15.3%
Dates	60%	VL	L	2	25%	60%
Elderberries	15%	VL	H	4	79.8%	16.4%
Figs	56.5%	VL	L	3½	77.5%	20.3%
Peaches	43.4%	L	A	5½	89.1%	9.7%
Pears	39.5%	L	L	3	83.2%	15.3%
Prunes	44%	L	L	4	82.1%	16.6%

As an example: 1 lb of dried currants equals 4 lb of fresh.
1 lb of dried apricots equals 5½ lb of fresh.

NOTE: Since the quality of fruit varies so much from variety to variety, from place to place and from year to year, the above figures are averages. They nevertheless give a valuable guide to the relative contents of popular dried and fresh fruits.

Acid/Tannin content   VL – very low   L – low   M – moderate
A – adequate   H – high

Poisonous plants

The following list of fairly well known plants are best avoided when making wine. They are known to contain some toxic element. Whilst one glass of such a brew is unlikely to kill you, larger quantities might at least make you ill. When there are so many splendid fruits available in such a wide variety of forms, it makes no sense to experiment with any of the following plants:

Acacia, aconite, alder, anemone, aquilegia, azalea.

Baneberry, belladonna, berberis, bitter almond, bay tree leaves, beech nuts, box tree leaves, black nightshade, bindweed, bluebell, bryony, broom, buckthorn, buddleia, buttercup.

Campion, celandine, charlock, cineraria, clematis, clover, coton-easter, columbine, cow-bane, crocus, crowfoot, chrysanthemum, cuckoo-pint, cyclamen.

Daffodil, dahlia, deadly nightshade, delphinium, dwarf elder.

Fool's parsley, figwort, foxglove, fungi of all kinds.

Geranium, gladiolus, goosefoot, green potatoes.

All members of the helebore family, hemlock, henbane, holly, honeysuckle *(both flowers and berries)*, horse chestnut flowers and conkers, hydrangea, hyacinth.

Iris, ivy.

Jasmine, jonquil.

Laburnum, laurel, lilac, lilies of the valley, lilies of all kinds, lobelia, lucerne, lupins.

Marsh marigolds, meadow rue, mezereon, mistletoe, monkshood.

Narcissus.

Orchids.

Pheasant's eye, peony, poppy, privet.

Ragwort, rhododendron, rhubarb leaves.

Snowdrop, spearwort, spindleberries, spurge, sweet pea.

Thorn apple, tobacco plant, tomato stems and leaves, traveller's joy, tulip.

Wood anemone, woody nightshade.

Yew.

Index

256